FROM JERUSALEM TO JACKSONVILLE

Seniors Reflecting on the Meaning and Significance of Biblical Texts

A Work of Fiction (?)

Henry L. Ruf

Dedication

To:

Reverend Ray Kiely who released a 13 year old boy's religious imagination.

and

Mason Ellison who showed what Christian kindness was all about

TABLE OF CONTENTS

Forward		4
Chapter One	Getting Acquainted in Jacksonville	7
Chapter Two	Religious Inheritance of Jerusalem's Writers	32
Chapter Three	Jacksonville Responds	57
Chapter Four	Jerusalem Writes the Great Hebrew Epic	64
Chapter Five	Jacksonville Responds	93
Chapter Six	Jerusalem to Babylon to Jerusalem	103
Chapter Seven	Jacksonville Responds	150
Chapter Eight	Jerusalem's Quarrel with Rome	169
Chapter Nine	Jacksonville's Final Response	239

FORWARD

Amateurs Inc.

There are professionals. Professional scholars on religion. Professional Biblical scholars. Professional philosophers. Professionals who know Hebrew and Greek, German and French. Professionals who write books for other professionals. Professionals who write books read by amateurs.

Then there are full time amateurs. Professional amateurs who don't pretend they are professionals. Professional amateurs who try to read the books written by professional scholars for professional scholars.

This book is written by a professional amateur who is not pretending to be a professional scholar and is not pretending to be a would-be professional scholar.

This book is written by a professional amateur who has read professional scholars for years and has been wrestling with the topics on which professional scholars write.

This book is written by a professional amateur for amateur readers struggling with the same problems as the writer of this book.

This book is a work of fiction. The scholars who speak do not exist. The would-be scholars who speak do not exist. The listeners do not exist.

This book is not a work of fiction. The names of the fictional scholars, would-be scholars, and listeners are constructed out of first and last names of scholars, would-be scholars, and listeners who do exist.

This book is not a work of fiction. The ancient religions did exist. The Biblical writers did exist. The artifacts and texts mentioned did and do exist. Many of the people and events mentioned in the texts did exist.

This book is a work of fiction. The myths written about in the book are not reports by on-the-spot observers, but are creative products refined by many creative producers over many years. The epics and narratives, the short stories and songs, written about in this book are not reports by on-the-spot observers but are texts written by authors with their purposes for writing determining what gets written and how these materials get organized.

This book is not a work of fiction. There are truths expressed by the myths, epics, narratives, short stories, and songs written about in this book. These are truths about the significance of things, the significance of human life, the demands of justice, the character of love and compassion, the attitudes towards the world and oneself that are needed for a workable way of life.

This book is a work where fiction/non-fiction are so intertwined that its author often does not know and does not care which are which.

This book is a work of fiction/non-fiction which requires the reader to think critically when reading it.

This book is a work of fiction/non-fiction such that, after the reader has critically read it and reflected on what was read, the reader also will end up not knowing what is fiction and what is non-fiction.

This book is a work of fiction/non-fiction written to show that both the fiction and the non-fiction in this book can have a positive impact on its readers, no matter what the reader ends up affirming as fictional or non-fictional, true or false.

Chapter One

Getting Acquainted in Jacksonville

O.K. I'll begin. My name is Yoshiko Yamaguchi, but people call me "Yochan." I was born in the United States but moved to Japan after World War II when I was nine years old. I lived there for sixty years until I returned to the States. Before the war, my father was a businessman working for a Japanese company here in the States. In 1938, he was transferred to work for his company in China. He remained there until 1944 when his company called him back to Japan to help keep the company alive despite the American bombings that had become relentless. After the war he worked in Nagoya, but my mother and I lived in Ise Ken, near his relatives who for hundreds of years had served as priests at the Ise Shrine. My mother had come from a long line of samurai.

After moving to Japan, I went to Japanese schools. Even though both of my parents were native Japanese citizens, my classmates always treated me as a foreigner. When speaking Japanese, there always remained a noticeable accent. In my English classes it was obvious that I was a native speaker. My father's status always protected me from physical harm, but my classmates made sure that I knew that I never really was one of them. The same was true of the relatives of my parents.

Every Sunday, back in the States, I went to a Christian Sunday School. We sang "Jesus loves me; this I know." In Japan, I was taken to Shinto shrines, washed and clapped my hands even though they had no meaning to me. My parents and relatives recognized that I always would be very different.

One evening in July 1945, one month before the end of the war, an American B-29, returning from a raid on Nagoya, decided to get rid of its last remaining phosphorus bombs before landing back on Guam. A safety precaution for him but living hell for my grandparents on the ground. When they first heard the bombs explode they ran from their house, scared to death, past a field of burning phosphorus to the bomb shelter they had built. Although the wooden door to the shelter burned to charcoal, they survived the heat and smoke. The next day my grandmother discovered that my grandfather had hung himself, leaving a note saying that his world had been destroyed and he was too old to learn to live in some future world. Later, when I was fifteen, I learned what had happened to my grandparents. I remembered the Sunday school songs I sang. I remember feeling that it just does not make sense to sing about knowing that God loves me. The Shinto world in which I now lived didn't fill the emptiness I felt in my heart. I felt that washing hands and clapping hands could not remove the stain of the excruciating suffering Japanese and American warriors had caused.

Even at fifteen I knew that I would have to live in this new world. The war ended one month after my grandparent's home was bombed. It ended after atomic hell burnt out Hiroshima and Nagasaki. It is impossible for anyone not there to realize how horrible it was for the people, living and dead, who experienced these atomic blasts.

My father put the war behind him, picked up the pieces, went back into business and earned more and more money, providing the services Americans needed during the Korean war. After studying English literature at a Presbyterian mission college in Nagoya, I made use of my skills in English and Japanese by working in the library established in Hiroshima. From then, until my retirement and return here to the States, I helped collect and preserve the stories of the people who experienced the nightmares of atomic war.

For over half a century, Professor Kennedy, I have asked myself. "Why me?", "Why them?" "What's the use?" "Am I doing something worthwhile in preserving these stories?"

When I read that the university here was sponsoring this class to discuss what the writers of the Bible were trying to say, I decided that perhaps here, by hearing their stories, I would get some better understanding of my own stories and the stories entrusted to me. I hope that maybe, just maybe, those old Sunday School songs were saying something important.

Yoshiko - "Yochan" - Yours is a powerful story, as are the stories you preserved in the Hiroshima library. All of us in this class have stories to tell. Yours, of course, is unique and always will remain unique. Your stories always will color how you hear the stories told by the many writers of the Biblical stores. Your stories will enrich the way all the rest of us in this class deal with what we hear the Biblical writers are saying. Perhaps I should say a little bit about myself and why I am teaching this class.

My name, as you already know, is Raymond Kennedy. I am not really a professor, but the university lets me teach as if I were one. I have been a Methodist pastor for over 40 years, serving churches in Ohio, New Jersey, Upstate New York. Michigan and Wisconsin. Now, retired here in Florida, I stay engaged by talking with elderly people who have many stories to tell. When teaching "Life-Long-Learning" classes here at the university to people just like you, I do not pretend that I can tell you the truth contained in the Biblical texts. I am not an expert Biblical scholar, although I have studied the Bible for over five decades. Also, I am not here to preach to you how these texts can help you deal with the issues troubling your spirit. Many of your questions are ones I have wrestled with all my life, ever since I first studied the Old Testament and New Testament back in seminary at Drew University.

I teach this course because I and my previous students have found the writers of the Biblical texts saying things that we, each in our own way, have found important to us. By focusing on these writers, and the social and cultural worlds that have made them and their worlds what they are, we have found that we can personally relate to their stories. Given the differences that are present here among you, we will never understand perfectly each other. No one perfectly understands even themselves. There is so much we don't know. The same is true of our knowledge about these writers and what they wrote. In listening to their stories, my hope is that by thinking about what inspired them to write, you personally, in your own way, will find something inspiring in what they say.

Mr. Kennedy, how should we call you. Pastor? Teacher? Mr. Kennedy? Raymond?

Just call me "Ray." That's what all my friends call me.

O.K. Ray. My name is Mark Shapiro. I am a retired lawyer. I specialize in Medical law and ethics. For years I have served on hospital medical ethics boards. I decided to come to this class because I want to try to get a better understanding of the things that the Jewish Rabbis and Christian priests and ministers serving with me on these boards have to say, especially when considering the decisions that need to be made in end-of-life cases and abortion cases.

I am not a Christion. I think you could call me a "cultural Jew." I don't attend services regularly in some temple or synagogue. I had my son circumcised and arranged his bar mitzva. I wanted him to know the 3,000 year history of the Hebrews and Jews. I especially wanted him to feel that we were inseparably tied to the holocaust in which many of our relatives were murdered by the Nazis.

As I said, I am a lawyer specializing in medical care issues. For over three decades now I have served on hospital medical review boards along with other lawyers, doctors, priests, ministers, and psychologists. I understand how believing in a God and life after death can provide comfort to people facing medical crises. What I have been unable to understand is why many Christian priests and ministers want to use the legal power given to medical review boards to prevent people, who do not share such beliefs, from exercising freedom to make their own decisions about their medical care in these controversial areas.

Some patients want to be permitted and enabled to end their suffering or their loss of conscious control of their existence. Many women want to terminate their pregnancies, not sharing the belief that some God placed some soul in the embryo or fetus that they want to terminate. In my debates with the priests and ministers on our board, I have tried to show that there are no justifying reasons that can be given to such women who do not share their beliefs about being bound to some God who supposedly gives life and takes it away. Whenever I try to argue for not taking away the freedom of dying patients and distressed women, I am always met with claims about some supernatural, metaphysical God.

I keep pointing out that we can justify our claims to people who do not agree with us only by providing observable evidence to support those claims. For people, who find no reason to believe in life after death, death means death. They want to decide for themselves how to live through their final days of life

When it comes to the issue of abortion, the Christian ministers and priests claim that they that they have the best possible reason to require woman not to kill the unborn child. No one, they claim, not even these women, are morally free to commit murder. This would be a trump care to play in this debate, if it were obvious that abortion was in fact murder and that one should call an unwanted fetus 'an unborn child' in the sense that it was a person with a moral right to live.

Scientifically we can describe the journey of life from parents to embryos and fetuses, but science cannot tell us how to evaluate the moral significance of these human embryos and fetuses. As I understand ethics and the law, socially and legally adults are given rights because they can demand them and justify their demand not to be forced to do anything unless there is a good reason to do so. Women seeking an abortion do not find beliefs about souls being such a reason. Nor do they think they are committing murder or killing an unborn child who has a right to live. I agree with them for several reasons.

I believe that the paradigm case of a human being having rights is the case of adults who also have duties. These are the humans we call persons. Being a human is a biological description but being a person is a moral and legal ascription. There is no doubt that terminating the life of a fetus or an embryo is a matter of killing something human. That, however, does not show that it is murder in the moral and legal sense of the word. Every one of our cells and organs is human but we are not committing murder when we surgically terminate the life of an appendix, or cancerous cells, or a heart to replace it with a new, healthy one. Talking about the beginning and end of biological life does not settle the question about where the boundaries around personhood should be located.

For many reasons, societies have found moral reasons for expanding the domain of individuals with rights beyond the domain of people with duties. Comatose patients do not lose their rights because they no longer are assigned duties. From infancy on, children are protected with rights even before they gradually are assigned more and more duties as they become more and more able to do things for which they can be held responsible. Newly born infants have no duties, but societies morally condemn infanticide and they give infants protective rights because this gives more moral protection to the rights of adults. Neither nature nor something supernatural determines the boundaries of personhood. People set those boundaries, and this is done morally when they have good moral reasons for setting the boundaries of personhood as they do. In the judgement of many people, including the American Supreme Court, pushing those boundaries back into the first or second trimester of pregnancy shows greater disrespect for women than it strengthens respect for any human persons.

I'm sorry for burdening you with all this legal talk and moral theorizing. At least I hope you understood enough to see why I decided to join this class. I am not opposed to people being religious, but I can't buy the kind of supernatural and metaphysical beliefs that many religious people use to justify their restrictions on other people's freedom. I especially am opposed to the legalistic way these people apply the legal talk in the Bible to current cases. I enrolled in this course to try and hear why the Biblical writers wrote as they did. For a long time, I have been convinced that the laws stated in Leviticus could not be applied automatically to cases in our world. There may or may not have been good reasons to establish such laws then, but that doesn't mean that it makes sense to blindly apply them today. Rules governing temple rituals are irrelevant for Jews no long worshipping in temples. There may have been good health reasons for instituting dietary regulations, but those health concerns are not relevant today. Ecclesiastical rules are like civil case laws. They should not be ignored but one must consider the point and purpose of the law to judge its applicability today. Blind legalism often hurts people and almost never does anyone any good.

I have great respect for the covenants, constitutions, and mandates that have given the Hebrew and Jewish people an identity for so many years. I have great respect for the Biblical rejection of that kind of hubris that makes people worship themselves and their political, economic and social practices. I have great respect for the prophets who condemned absolutizing existing laws and practices that had become more important than the people they were meant to serve. I hope in this class to learn how to listen to Biblical cries for justice when thinking about how to deal with current concrete situations. As a lawyer, I always must deal with questions concerning the evidence that can be presented to defend a legal indictment or to show its lack of evidentiary support. In reading the Bible and hearing people talk about God, I keep reminding myself that the use of the word "God" is governed by human, social, linguistic norms and that laws specified in the Bible are laws set forth by humans, no matter how inspired these law-givers were. I am hoping that I can learn, from you and what we hear, how to listen in a way that lets me hear something that helps me live my Jewish life in my home and at the hospitals where I work.

Mark, don't worry, many of us are in the same boat as you. We also want to learn from what you hear so that now we can better listen to Biblical voices. My name is Dorothy Rilling. I am a retired math teacher who now teaches new recruits at H & R Block how to help people file their Federal Income Tax Returns. Some people would say that I am a cultural Christian. Since childhood I have regularly attended church, but I do not believe in any supernatural beings. I never have felt any need to have any such beliefs.

I cherish the sense of awe I get every Sunday when I enter my church's sanctuary and listen to our great pipe organ. I find our Christmas and Easter services very inspiring even though I don't take literally any of the talk about wise men and angels or a resuscitated body of Jesus. I take communion and feel a sense of being part of a community of people trying to live a Christian way of life, whatever that is. I don't take literally Biblical talk about Adam and Eve and the parting of the Reed Sea. The God I worship does not live out there, above the clouds, in some supernatural world. My God lives in my heart. I can't put into words exactly what it is that these Biblical stories do mean to me, but they do give me a sense of living in world that is more than my everyday world of teaching, doing taxes, buying and cooking food, changing lightbulbs, writing checks, and being involved in political causes. I enrolled in this course hoping, that by hearing the stories the Biblical writers wrote, I would find words to express better my religious way of life.

Mark, I can appreciate your difficulty in finding sensible what some Christians say they believe when they talk about supernatural gods and souls and when they treat their interpretations of Biblical laws as being eternal and binding on all people. I am a mathematician and the only timeless and universally applicable laws that I know are mathematical norms. My God and my soul is nothing like the real number 2 or the imaginary number, the square root -2. In mathematics, we deal with proofs and for 40 years I graded student's mathematical proofs as valid or invalid. I always have been fascinated with the supposed proofs philosophers have given for the existence of God. I have found all such proofs to be unsound either because of the invalid reasoning used in them or because of the falsity or unjustified premises from which their reasoning began. I have noticed that often the unsoundness of the proofs is due to people's confusion about how words like "existence" or "explain" work.

It seems to me that, in the case of today's creationists, they simply attach to astronomical, big bang theories or biological evolutionary theories the tag line "that's how God does things." As I understand it, many of the Biblical writers wrote their stories before Greek philosophers like Plato and Aristotle started the metaphysical project of giving "proofs" for the existence of a god that transcends the natural world. I have been told that other Biblical writers, such as Paul and the poet, Job, rejected Greek metaphysical reasoning in favor of the wisdom present in Hebrew or Christian ways of life. They didn't need any philosophical proofs and neither do I. I know that I do not believe in religious supernaturalism. Now in this class, by hearing what Hebrew and Christian writers had to say about living faithfully in a Biblical way of life, I hope that I, a rational mathematician, can deepen my religious faithfulness.

Woh! Mark and Dorothy. Much of what you have told us about your thinking and questioning goes over my head. Too abstract for me. My name is Anita Harris and I am nothing but a church going farmer's wife. For forty years we lived in upstate New York farming 75 dairy cows. I attended regularly our little Presbyterian Church and served as one of the elders in the church. We did not debate theological issues but worried about paying for the roof that needed fixing and arranging for the summer Bible school that we sponsored. When our son became old enough to run the farm, we turned it over to him. I always had loved to read and, with him taking charge of the farm, I now had the time to follow my passion. At first, I read a great deal of biography and historical fiction. Then, I am not sure why, I started to read books on economic theory. I was fascinated by what I learned. I was drawn to the attempts by economists to provide an overall picture of our economic practices and their influence on almost every aspect of how we live. My family and I voted Republican for as long as I can remember, but now I found most enlightening the things Marx wrote about how economic practices influenced the political, social, and cultural aspects of who we are and how we live.

Five years after we turned things over to our son, my husband died. He left me enough of an inheritance to be able to move here to Florida. What a shock I experienced when I went to the Presbyterian Church down here. It was so radically different from what I had known back home in upstate New York. Even in our little church back there we cherished the sense of awe we experienced in our house of God as we focused on what the Bible said about what God had and was doing. Down here the accent was all on Jesus. "Jesus can save you." "Accept Jesus as your savior and trust him. Then all your problems in life will be solved." "Walk by faith with Jesus as your friend now and you will walk with him and all your loved ones after you shed your earthly body." People, they said, who believe that Jesus is God don't die; they pass on to a better life. I was amazed that, in the obituaries of their Christian brothers and sisters, they didn't even mention when they were born, and they always talked about again meeting their loved ones who had gone on to heaven before them.

I was amazed at how they interpreted the Bible. They focused on the stories the Biblical writers were telling and not on the religious faith of the writers who were telling the stories or on why they were writing them. They told me that they read the Biblical stories literally, as If CNN TV cameras could have filmed what was happening. The Biblical writers, they said, were nothing but the faithful writers serving as God's tools in writing his book. Reading the Bible this way, they said, would let us hear the laws God has set down to govern the lives and thoughts of all people in all places. This, they said, is the only way to understand what they called "the literal meaning" of what the Bible said. God's universal and lasting Truth, they claimed, is expressed in the Bible when read "literally."

Mark and Dorothy, I may not understand your legal and moral arguments or your logical treatment of arguments about God's existence, but I can appreciate your rejection of their extreme and dangerous legalism. I too sense that they don't understand the literal meaning of what the Biblical writers wrote because they don't consider what these writers and their readers were like, in what sort of situation they wrote, what was the literary form of what they wrote, what was the point and purpose of their writing. The economists I was reading kept pointing out that specific economic events could be understood only if located in the historically changing social contexts in which they occurred. As I see it, it is because people live a certain kind of economic life that corporations, monetary exchanges, and government regulatory agencies are very real to them, even though they don't exist tangibly like milk and cows. I think that something similar is true of God. For worshippers, God is very real. I don't need to prove God's existence. God is real for me because he lives in my heart. If God didn't live in the hearts of people worshipping God, then I don't know in what sense one could say that God exists at all.

Biblical writers, it seems to me, were writers who were inspired by their own religious ways of living, but they were the actual writers, and not some handcuffed, brain dead robot being used by some otherworldly god. In their religious way of life, they refused to make a god out of themselves but instead lived grateful for their world and their own lives, recognizing their unfaithfulness to the good God they worshipped in attitude and action. I have concluded that, just as money is real to people living in a monetary way of life, even though millions of dollars can move ten thousand miles by the push of a computer key, so for people living a religious way of life their God is just as real for them, present for worship, prayer, comfort, challenge and inspiration no matter where they are. I know I did not create this God, but I recognize that God became real to me as I joined my friends in worshipping God. I have no idea why this happened. I just know that it did and that, thank heaven, it made me the servant of God that I think I am.

I decided to enroll in this course because I wanted to hear and understand what the Biblical writers wrote and meant. I disagree with Marx on many things, but he has convinced me that only by locating writers in their unique social world can we understand the meaning of what they wrote. I hope to learn here about the historical and social religious context in which they wrote and it which they were read. I hope to learn how their God lived in their hearts, inspiring them to write as they did and to act as they did.

Anita, what you experienced, by leaving your New York church and beginning to try to worship in a church in the "Bible Belt," is something I have had to live with all my life. My name is Scott Washington and I am a retired Tech Sergeant in the United States Air Force. During my time in the military I have attended services in Air Force chapels conducted by many different Christian chaplains. Some conducted services of the kind Anita cherished in upstate New York and some, now more and more, offered only "Bible Belt," fundamentalist, evangelical services. Over the years I learned to tune out what was being said in these services unless it dealt with what I took to be the fundamental in Christianity, the ability to speak to the horrors of the three wars I lived through. As Yoshiko was speaking, images flashed through my mind of what I experienced during the wars in which I was involved.

I joined the air force in the summer of 1950, two weeks after the beginning of the Korean War. I didn't feel like staying at home in Alabama. I wanted to be where the action was. The Air Force trained me in tele-communications. At first, that meant that I was a telephone linesman. They sent me to Nagoya, Japan. From time to time I went on temporary assignment to Korea. When I first arrived in Nagoya, I couldn't believe my eyes. Phosphorus bombs had burnt out half of the city. Yoshiko, when you described your grandparent's house being burnt down, I found myself imagining the horror that people in Nagoya experienced when block after block of their homes went up in flames and dozens of their neighbors were burnt to death.

Back in Alabama I had gone to church with my parents on almost every Sunday and then on Wednesdays to Bible classes. Occasionally, we went to revival meetings. I accepted Jesus as my savior when I was eleven. I loved singing the hymns and old spirituals, clapping our hands and crying out "Amen! Amen." Walking around burnt our Nagoya, and then seeing what war had done to Korea, I couldn't help asking myself what my "old time religion" could possibly say about this much carnage and suffering that was caused by bombs and bullets.

In Japan, I often got into long arguments and discussions with the guy bunking next to me. He worked as a chaplain's assistant at the Air Force hospital in Nagoya. He worked with many pilots suffering horrible burns when their planes were shot down in Korea. He was asking the same questions I was. He was white from a small city in northern Wisconsin. I think I was the first Black person that he ever got to know personally. He said that there were no black families living in his home town. The Air Force had just desegregated a few years before the Korean war. There was still a lot of racism among the people with whom we worked. He kept asking me questions about what it is like to be a Black teenager in Alabama. He had no idea what our lives were like. He said that he also couldn't comprehend what was going on in the minds of racists to cause them to hate so much and to be so violent.

We never became buddy-buddy friends, but we spent hours trying to make sense of the cruelties of the world in which we lived. I think he became a bit less naïve about the lives of Black people and, little by little, I think he helped me understand better what I had been taught about Christian forgiveness and that returning hate for hate never helps anyone. We both came to see that we would be dishonoring those who had suffered and died if we pretended that their suffering really wasn't horrible because it was part of some big plan that made everything all right. He had read somewhere that it is morally wrong to treat people as only a means to achieve some end. Neither of us could believe that a loving God would approve burning to death a young child to get the Japanese generals to surrender.

I stayed in the military for thirty years, but he got out and went back to college. I think he became a minister or a professor. His job in the Nagoya hospital left him with lots of time to read about religion, philosophy and psychology. That is why I loved to talk with him. I knew, however, that my brain was in my hands and not in philosophy books. I spent my life working with machines. For years after our talks, I would remember ideas he shared with me and I used them in my effort to better understand suffering and my religious faith.

After the end of the Korean war, I went back to the States and got training in handling the new electronic equipment the Air Force was using. I eventually was assigned to duty in Viet Nam and experienced again the horror of war. I was especially appalled at the Air Force's dehumanization of the Vietnamese people and the cavalier way that my fellow airmen talked about collateral damage. I kept thinking that in the Twentieth Century some devastating war always was going on. I was never convinced that any of them really were necessary. The Americans could have prevented the French from imperialistically going back into Viet Nam after World War II was over.

After returning to the States I served out my thirty years teaching telecommunications to young Air Force recruits. After retirement, I have been doing the same at a community college here in North Florida. When one of my students was killed in Iraq, all my old questions about religion and justice poured back into my mind and they gave me no peace. I couldn't stop thinking about how the death of my student is tied to the fact that we murdered the president of Iran, supported Iraq in its war with Iran, and supported Afghanistan warlords in their resistance to the Russian occupation of their country. I couldn't stop thinking about our dehumanization of Japanese, Germans, North Koreans, Vietnamese, Iranians, Taliban fighters, and Palestinians.

War and racism never seem to cease. The Middle East War never ends. The racism never ends, now more and more blatantly in the U.S. What do my spirituals say about this? What would my friend in the bunk next to mine in Japan say about all this? What does the Bible have to say about this? I am not sure that any of them have any answers that I would find satisfying. Still, I enrolled in this course hoping that the writers of the Bible will have something to say that will help me deal with these cruel realities that challenge so deeply my desire to be a Christian.

Horror and injustice. I can hear you, Mr. Washington. Like you, I have a story to tell about horror and injustice. I too find myself living with memories that just won't go away. To make matters worse, I now can't see anything as simply just or unjust. Life is so complicated. What's a good end and what's an acceptable means to reach that end. Individuals, groups, and nations often are seeking honorable ends, but are there lily-white means that can enable them to achieve their goals. So often, out of ignorance or ineptitude or hidden perverse motives, we produce horrible unintended consequences in our pursuit of what we think are good ends.

My name is Zhang Binyan. I moved here to Florida after my husband died and my daughter moved to San Francisco to work in the accounting office of a Chinese Plumbing Co. My husband and I married after I had been in the United states for fifteen years. I was born and raised in Szechuan Province in China. Like most Chinese women, I kept my Chinese name and did not take my husband's family name and become Mrs. Reinhardt. My husband had been in the candy business for decades.

I remember very clearly the Cultural Revolution in China, even though I was one of the lucky ones. My father was an officer in the Chinese army. I saw horrible things being done by the Red Guards to my neighbors. These "Guards" were high school and college age students who followed without question Chairman Mao's call for them to go after all people still holding anti-revolutionary, capitalist ideas. It was a time of sheer chaos. No one could trust anyone. I was relieved when the Chinese army and my father stepped in to end the chaos. I knew that the chaos had to end, but I never could convince myself that so much suffering and death was necessary to achieve Mao' stated goals.

I believed Chairman Mao when he said that the cultural revolution was necessary to re-establish the revolutionary spirit that had saved China from

Western imperialism, the Japanese invasion, and the attempt by the rich Kuomintang to oppress the poor. I never was convinced, however, that Mao had chosen the right method this time. I remember that previously Mao had chosen horrible means to achieve good goals. Trying to industrialize China, Mao advocated the "Great Leap Forward" in which peasants melted down metal pots and plows in back-yard furnaces. This resulted in a huge reduction in food production causing millions to starve to death. I never have figured out how to compare the cost of the suffering of the people I meet face to face against the benefits of policies aiming at national benefits.

At the end of the cultural revolution, I joined the first class of students going back to college. One of my closest college classmates had suffered greatly during the cultural revolution. Her father, a geologist, had been sent to prison for a poem he had written. He had been blinded by guards beating him. My friend had been sent to a re-education peasant farm where her best friend had been raped by the local party leader. After college in China, both of us found ways to come to the United States to study. She studied English and I studied American Studies.

I was not prepared to read about the anti-Chinese hatred and discrimination that Chinese had experienced in the United States. In my graduate studies I learned about the terrible treatment experienced by the Chinese workers recruited to build the American railroads through the Rocky Mountains. I learned about the anti-Chinese immigrations laws passed that said that only Nordic people were real Americans. That history of discrimination has left scars on the attitudes of many Americans today. Often, I was treated as someone who didn't really belong here. After marrying a white American man who ran a successful candy business, I often felt that the people I met at social events were whispering to each other, "He could have been really successful if he hadn't married a Chinese." Our son told us that often he was called a "Chink" by his classmates.

My husband was a regular church goer and I went with him. I never became a Christian. I looked at how these Christian church goers always saw me as something foreign and at how they gave only token aid to poor people, veterans in homes for the elderly, blacks, and migrant workers. I saw that they believed that America's past treatment of slaves and native Americans had nothing to do with them. They could not understand a word I was saying when I suggested they were partly responsible for the current Palestinian-Israeli confrontations that were influencing everything happening in the Middle-East. I tried to tell them that Western interests in oil after World War I led The French and British to create the Middle-Eastern, Islamic countries now involved in civil and regional wars. I tried to point out that America's refusal to admit European Jews during and after World War II is partly responsible for the Palestinian-Israel confrontations during the past seventy years. What I had to say usually fell on deaf ears. They gave money to support missionary work around the world, but they lived their own lives in very small provincial bubbles.

A few of my friends and I loved to sing, and we decided to go to a nearby veteran's hospital to lead the men in sing-a-longs of their old favorites, like "Let me call you sweetheart." We never got any members of my husband's church to join with us. They all had "something they just had to do." They all said that the God they worshipped was a God who loved them so much that he died for them. They kept talking about being like Christ. I never saw them sacrificing anything except a few dollars they did not really need.

Two years ago, my husband died. I don't know what he was thinking in the weeks leading up to his death. At his funeral, church members kept telling me that now his suffering was over, and he is rejoicing with his heavenly father. I am glad that his suffering came to an end, but I can't make any sense of this talk about heaven. I only know that now that his suffering is ended so are all the wonderful days we spent together. I keep thinking about my own death. Probably all of you do. There is not that much sand left in any of our hourglasses. It is so difficult to think of my own death. Sometimes I think that after my life is over everything will be just a blank nothing for me, but then I remember that there won't be any me or any blank nothing for me. I remember my husband and sometimes he seems very alive to me, but I know he is dead and it is only my memories of him that live, memories that also will be gone sooner than I want.

Christians keep talking about life after death. I just don't know what they are talking about. The Bible says that Jesus Christ rose from the dead, but I just can't figure out what they possibly could mean by that.

When I learned that I would hear in this class what the writers of the Bible are saying, I said to myself, "this is something I want to hear." Perhaps they are saying something which will help me deal with my dilemmas. Perhaps they are saying something that makes sense when talking about a death that is not really being dead.

Zhang Binyan, let me apologize to you for the way that American Church goers have treated you. Please know that not all Americans are like that. I have known many who were as you describe, but I have found many others who cherish people who are different from them, racially, economically, sexually. The Christians I work with spend many days a week at food pantries and soup kitchens for the homeless. They sponsor and participate in Jewish-Christian, Buddhist-Christian, and Islamic Christian dialogues. They actively defend people who are discriminated against. Sometimes that discrimination is by some of our own members who harass us because of our liberal understanding of the Bible. Many of us liberal Christians also share your dismay when many Christians talk so flippantly about heaven and life after death.

My name is Christopher Phillips. Until retirement I was a high school music teacher. Since retirement I have enrolled in many of these "Life-long Learning Lecture" seminars. In them I learned about the dark side of American history and its lingering effects on contemporary American attitudes and actions. I am now a worshipper in an Episcopal Church. I was raised in a very conservative, evangelical church. Over the years I have moved beyond that. I couldn't buy its talk about a supernatural god, its use of selected Bible passages to legitimate its dogmatic and often prejudicial moral commandments, its use of our political and legal system to punish those who reject in word and action their commandments. Part of my reason for joining the Anglican, Episcopal Church is that many of its Bishops have rejected taking the Bible's talk about God and resurrection as talk about a supernatural being or a supernatural, miraculous event. I may reject a great deal of

"Old Fashioned Religion" but, sitting in my church and listening to our beautiful organ, I feel that our finite bodily and workaday world really points to something not captured by our words and concepts. When I participate with my fellow Christians in celebrating the Eucharist I feel a union with them, in a community that is different from every other community. In that communion I sense that we are the living body and blood of the resurrected Christ.

My father was a Methodist minister in Arkansas. I grew up in the Bible Belt and revival meeting part of our country, similar in many ways to the world described by Scott. In the 1960s our world seemed to fall apart because of the sexual revolution, the rise of feminism, the open use of drugs, the civil rights clashes, the Vietnam War protests, the Cuban crisis, the assassinations of the Kennedys and Martin Luther King. My father and the people in his church turned to their old-fashioned religion to give them an anchor in the turbulent seas sweeping over them. Religiously they tuned in to radio and television preachers calling for a fourth "Great awakening" and calling for them to reject intellectual elitists talking about "Death of God Theologies" and religious and moral relativism.

My dad bought into all of this, but while I was in college I began to doubt all this evangelical fundamentalism. I found many good aspects to all these "Great Awakenings," but overall they seemed to be proud of their ignorance and to be preaching hatred and not love." In a course on Christianity in America, I found truth in the charges leveled by frontier preachers in the first "Great Awakening" that Churches along the Atlantic Sea coast were offering only empty, stuffy, and pretentious rituals. Also, their preaching was too sophisticated and intellectual for ordinary people to understand. For frontier people, Christianity had to be a matter of personal decisions, feeling, and commitments. They wanted their preachers to stir their hearts with sermons about joyful salvation in heaven. I found very disturbing, however, their willingness to send sinners to the horrors of hell and their anti-intellectual conviction that the Bible had a single message and that one could understand what was written in the Bible without doing the hard work of studying it as a literary text. For them the literal meaning of the Bible was what it meant to them as they read it on their own and not what its writers meant in writing it or what it meant to different readers at different times in history. That is one of the reasons why I was very interested in taking this course and learning what the writers in the Bible were trying to say.

It was when I learned in college about the second and third "Great Awakenings" that I concluded that evangelical fundamentalism was not only intellectually shallow and misinformed, but it also was motivated by very un-Christian and unjust interests. It had become legalistic in a petty way. It had become racist and in collusion with the rich and powerful against the poor and oppressed. Every time I went back home to Arkansas my father and I got into argument after argument. What I saw as wonderful differences and enlightened calls for justice, he saw as dangerous threats to Christianity. I argued that he was paying too high a price to defend his little bigoted tribe of "Christians". He argued that I had become a relativist who had thrown away "The Truth" and that I had become brainwashed by my Communist college professors.

The second Awakening in the early parts of the 19th century was aimed at halting the damage being done to families by drunkenness, something I saw all around me in our little town in Arkansas. As a teenager, however, I was never persuaded that it's "all or nothing" approach made sense. To me it seemed to make puritanical legalism, enforced by social branding and legal prohibitions, an essential demand on all Christians. I didn't object to Christians saying we don't want to drink, but it just didn't seem right for them to pass laws warning people that the police would arrest them if they sold any one any liquor.

The policies advocated as Christian by Third Awakening evangelists at the turn of the 20th Century is what made me realize that I couldn't be both a Christian and an evangelical fundamentalist. They started attacking what they called the invasion of un-Christian tendencies that came into America with the immigration during those years of millions of Jews and Irish and Mediterranean Roman Catholics. The Jews, my father argued, had murdered Jesus Christ, the Son of God. The preachers at the revival meetings attacked Catholics for following the word of the Pope rather than the Word of God's holy Bible. As I saw it, white fundamentalists, who already were racist towards former slaves and their children, now made Jews and Catholics new people to hate. In college I met Jews and Catholics who seemed much kinder than many of the preachers in the Third Awakening. I hated it when my father used the ideas of Dwight Moody who hatefully had attacked Jews and Catholics. Today, for fundamentalists, the targets of this hatred are Muslims and homosexuals.

My eyes really were opened when I learned that Moody and his Bible institute were funded by rich oilmen. The evangelist, Billy Sunday, and Charles Fuller's radio show, "The Old Fashioned Revival Hour, were funded by big business men such as Rockefeller, Carnegie, Morgan, McCormack, Armor and Swift. It was in England and Europe that protests began against the terrible exploitation of workers and the collusion of big business with government. Their protests rang true to me, especially after I read the books written by "muckrakers," such as Sinclair Lewis and Upton Sinclair. Lewis attacked both wealthy capitalists and huckster evangelists. Sinclair described the terrible conditions in the meat packing industry. I understood why Armor and Swift supported Sunday in his claims that the social gospel is godless social service nonsense and that capitalism is godliness.

Bringing concerns about social justice into mainstream Christianity caused my father great anguish. On the one hand, he tended to agree with those who claimed that when the churches came under the influence of the social gospel they forgot about the need to preach a gospel that led to individuals accepting Christ as their savior. On the other hand, he knew first-hand the good that Roosevelt's New Deal was having on the poor in his parish. He had read Sheldon's book, "What Would Jesus Do?" He knew that Jesus had condemned the mistreatment of the poor by the rich. Still, until his dying days he condemned liberalism, identifying it with Communism and identifying that with Stalin's dictatorship. He was a pastor concerned with individual people. He never knew about people who saw socialism as a movement aimed at creating economic democracy as well as political democracy.

I am here today because I want a chance to see if the Biblical writers themselves could deal successfully with the dilemmas causing my father such anguish. For me, religion must be a very personal thing, but it also must be concerned about big, real life economic and political practices.

Chris – I hope you don't mind me calling you 'Chris', "Christopher is such a mouthful. My name is Hannah Smith. I can understand your desire to be personally religious and socially engaged, trying as a sort of social engineer to construct a more just society. I am not sure, however, that the engineering part can ever be carried out successfully. I have been pretty much convinced that a part of living religiously is learning how to find spiritual peace when one's efforts to love other people and build a just world fail.

I guess you can call me an unreconstructed "flower child." I was at Woodstock. I was a member of the Hari Krishna movement for several years. For the past forty years I have practiced Zen meditation. I don't think I am a dogmatic Buddhist, however. In my experience, most Buddhists are very tolerant people. The tribal warfare going on in what used to be called Burma is a Buddhist aberration. Buddhism does not need a government calling itself Buddhist carrying out a policy of ethically cleansing the country of Muslims. In my many year practicing Zen meditation, I never have sensed any craving need to tear down other religions.

I think that Christianity is a very important way of life. That's why I have chosen to join this class and hear what the Biblical writers are saying. When I heard about this class I said to myself, "For years you have been studying and practicing Asian religions. It's about time that you took another look at what the Biblical writers actually have to say". After all, Jews, Christians, and Muslims all trace their religion back to the early Biblical writers.

What first attracted me to Hinduism was its claim that we can find a workable way of life that can give us inner peace and contentment, but only if our goal in life is something greater than physical pleasure, power over others, or social propriety. One must get beyond mere animal or social life, beyond treating things and people in terms of the way we verbally classify and identify them. I admired the fact that in Hinduism it was recognized that different kinds of people had to work with different ways (yoga) to gain liberation from unworkable ways of life. Even when it came to the Bhakti religious way of life, it was acknowledged that different kinds of people needed to worship different kinds of gods to gain spiritual liberation. As I see it, the current conflict between Hindus and Muslims in South Asia, is another example of tribal aberrations of Hindu and Muslim ways of life. That's also my take on the decades long battle between Palestinian Muslims and Israeli Jews.

I tried to practice the Hindu yoga aimed at achieving a mystical experience of consciousness not bound by sensory and conceptual control, but it didn't work for me. Maybe I didn't stay with it long enough. Eventually I realized that it was my craving for spiritual liberation that prevented me from gaining it. That is when I understood why the Buddha abandoned his Hindu pilgrimage in search of spiritual liberation. He experienced enlightenment and began to teach his four simple truths. For years in a Zen manner I have tried to live these truths. I recognized that it was because of my cravings that I was making myself miserable and at times suicidal. I craved to stay in charge of everything and even save myself from myself. The Buddha taught me to give up my craving to be the master of my fate. This craving was just one manifestation of a much more all-inclusive craving. I craved to be better than everything else. I craved to be better than other people, wealthier, prettier, smarter, more envied and honored. I craved to be more powerful than everything: nature, other people, the past, the future.

The Buddha taught me to give up craving liberation and thereby simply let liberated life be what it would be for anyone who would get out of its way. Through Zen mediation I try to let things be in their suchness, as they are before people classify and try to control them, so they can satisfy their cravings. I try to let the past be and thus escape the deadly feelings of guilt and shame and the fear of embarrassment, pain and death. I try to let the future be whatever it will be, and thus free myself from fear of what might happen, free even of fear of death.

I try, but, as is obvious to all who know me, I often do not succeed in my efforts. I am hoping that in this class I can learn something from the Biblical writers that will help me in my Buddhist journey. I still am getting in the way of my own liberation. Old cravings keep reappearing. It is so hard not to be furious at what many people are doing today. New cravings keep sneaking into my life. Like Chris, I keep hoping that our economic and political life will become more just. I want to learn how to passionately pursue justice without falling into despair because the world will not become what I passionately, cravingly, want it to be. I am hoping that the Biblical writers can teach me how to do that. Facing disaster and moving on seems to be a hallmark of Jews, Christians, and Muslims.

Ray, do you think there is any hope for me?

Hannah. A strange question coming from you. You have done so much in your life to rid yourself of false hopes. That you have decided to come join this class shows that you still are focused on further spiritual growth. You have equipped yourself well to listen to these Biblical writers. Only as you listen will you be able to judge whether they are saying something to you that you can blend into your life. By listening to all of you today tell your stories, I know that in me hope has risen.

Lydia, we haven't heard from you. Do you want to tell us a little about yourself? You are the final one to introduce yourself. We don't want you to feel left out.

I am not sure that I belong here. My son suggested that I come. He was afraid that I have been spending too much time by myself. I moved here three months ago. My husband died a year ago and I had no one left in North Dakota. My son keeps business books for people. He lives now in Savannah. He paid for the nursing home where I am staying. I've never been to anything like this. I'm not much for words. I read the newspaper, but I don't read books. It seems like all of you are big shots in this book reading business. So, if it is O.K. with you, I'll just sit and listen.

At least, let me tell you my name. I am Lydia Reinhart. I have worked all my life as a cook in an all-night café. From 8:00 at night until 4:00 in the morning. I have two boys and a daughter. She died four years ago. A mother never should have to bury her child. My youngest son is in the navy. I hope that someday soon the navy will send him here. I go to church every Sunday. I used to go to a Lutheran church when as a child I lived on a small farm. After I got married and moved to a small city south of my parent's farm, I started going to a Presbyterian church.

I never have had time or energy to think about these religious ideas you are talking about. I always was so tired when I got home in the morning. In the afternoon, I had to cook and bake and sew for my children and husband who often was out of work. I got one day off a week and then I baked bread for the week and canned fruit and vegetables that we can eat in the winter. We grew them in a little garden next to our house. I worked on Saturday nights. I got up on early Sunday to go to church. Then I went home, cooked, read the Sunday paper and got ready to go to work again. I just go to church, listen to the beautiful music, listen to the minister pray and preach. The people are very nice. They don't know me, but they always are polite and say "hello." When my kids were young, we gave a blessing before eating supper. I taught my children to say a prayer before going to sleep. They sort of stopped when they got to junior high. They went to Sunday school until high school. They all were baptized. My daughter became a catholic when she got married to this very good Polish guy who worked in the paper plant. She worked at an insurance company. They had six kids. When she was dying, her priest said to her "Your heavenly father is waiting for you." The last thing she said was, " I'm not ready."

Like I said, we never talked about church and religion. We just tried to be good people. I am kind-a glad to be in this class. Maybe I can learn something about what I have been doing. I never read very much in the Bible, but I know it is a good book. I think I am sort-of looking forward to hearing what the teachers here says it has to say.

Lydia, thank you very much for telling us about yourself. You don't have to talk if you don't want to. Having served as a pastor, I always felt that it is in people like you, worshipping in practical ways, that the heart of religion lives. As we shall hear, in Biblical times people worshipped in a shrine or a temple, by hearing words they heard many times before and by singing songs that were old and familiar to them. They did so without debating in their minds about theoretical issues. The words they recited or sang let them express their gratitude for simply being alive. Like you, they came to the shrines tired from days of hard work and found themselves being refreshed and filled with the hope needed to face the next day. Lydia, just sit back and listen. I think you will discover that your way of worshipping is very close to the way many people in Biblical times worshipped.

I think that this is enough for today. Let's break and get to know each other better. There is coffee and tea available in the lounge. Beginning next week, we will have the very good luck to view and hear dramatic presentations of what the people who are responsible for the Biblical texts had to say and write. These presentations will be given by students in this university's religion and speech and drama departments. There are two professors, in particular, who should be thanked for creating these presentations: Professor Heinrich Hamann from the Religion Department and Professor Arthur Marquardt from the Speech and Drama Department. After each presentation, we will have plenty of time to talk to each other about what we have seen and heard.

Chapter Two

The Religious Inheritance of the Biblical Writers

Good afternoon. My name is Heinrich Hamann. I teach religion at this university. I am sorry that I could not be here last week. Rev. Kennedy told me that you introduced yourselves to each other and explained why you chose to join in this study of the Bible. I would have loved to hear them. Through your discussions of what will be presented here, I hope that I too can get to know you.

Today's presentations are aimed at giving you some familiarity with the religious life and writings that existed in the Eastern Mediterranean Area prior to the time that the Biblical writers wrote their texts. As you will learn, this pre-history of the Biblical world had great influence on what was written by Biblical writers. These writers were inspired to write as they did by their own religious practices, attitudes and beliefs. This whole religious way of life of theirs, however, did not arise out of nothing. Conditions and events in which they were involved at the time they wrote led them to use in very creative and original ways the cultural and literary world that they had inherited. That pre-Biblical religious world had existed for 100,000 years before the writers of the Bible lived. It is that world that we now will try to make come alive for you. Students in our drama department will try to do that for you. Let the curtain rise.

Dan, give me a hand.

What's the matter, Chuck?

I can't get out; I've got a beastly cramp in my leg. I've been sitting in the back of this truck for hours, squeezed in along with all these supplies.

Drink some water. You probably got dehydrated. In this southeast corner of Turkey, you can't drink too much water. This hot weather, Chuck, is not impressed by all the muscles you built up by all that weight lifting.

That's not it. It's that ten-mile ride from Urfa on the worst roads I have ever bounced over. You were lucky, Dan, riding up in the cab. Anyway, we are here and that's all that matters. Ever since Grad School I have been waiting to visit the site of "The Temple of Eden." As you know, this is earliest temple ever constructed, buried right here by people 12, 500 years ago on the top of the tallest peak in the Gobeki Tepe mountain range where we are now standing.

Well then, Chuck, let's get going up to the Museum. That is where Professor Klenk said he would meet us. You were lucky to study in grad school under him, the famous Hans Klenk. He worked here with the archeologist, Klaus Schmidt, who first gave this temple its name "The Temple of Eden." Schmidt died a few years ago, but Professor Klenk can tell us all about the temple. Luckily there is a model of the temple in the museum.

There he is, Dan, just outside the door. Hello, Professor Klenk. We just got here. This is Dan Zyburski. He is originally from the States, but he has been studying in Paris with Jacques Foucault for several years now. We have been texting back and forth for the past two years.

Glad to meet you, Dan. Professor Foucault is here with us. The museum is very fortunate to have him and Father Joseph Reimer to speak to our conference tomorrow. There will be twenty scholars here at the conference eager to hear what Professor Foucault will say about the religious life of the ancient hunters and gatherers, who built the Temple of Eden. They also are waiting to hear Father Reimer follow that up with his analysis of the religious world of the agricultural people who replaced them. Professor Foucault believes that the door to an agricultural form of life was opened by this temple.

I am so happy to meet you, Dr. Klenk. Ever since Chuck told me about this chance to be here with you the day before your conference begins, I have thought about little else. Chuck and I are two of the luckiest students in the world to have this private tutorial with you and Professors Foucault and Reamer. It was so good of you to agree to Chuck's request to have me join him. Excuse me for blabbering on. I just think that there is so much we can learn from the three of you.

We are the lucky ones, having two students like you who are so passionate in trying to understand the religious life of people who lived so long ago. Let's go inside and start with an examination of the model of the Temple of Eden. By understanding it we will be gaining an understanding of the tens of thousands of years of religious life that culminated in its construction and use.

There it is, Dan. What do you think?

It's awesome, Professor Klenk.

Yes, it is, Dan. To really appreciate how awesome it is, it is necessary to let your imagination soar. This model represents a structure that was over three football fields wide and long. It was built over 14,000 years ago, just after the end of the ice age. It is over 7,000 years older than the pyramids in Egypt. It was built by hundreds or thousands of people who were living as hunters and gatherers before the age of agriculture had begun. Most likely, after it was built, people from many different tribes traveled hundreds of miles to worship here.

It is not just its size that is so amazing. Dan, look at its structure, a gateway leading to a series of circular and oval walls. Look at the giant pillars located at the center of the rings. If we estimate the size of the pillars, given the diameter of the circles surrounding them, they are huge, at least 15 feet tall and weighing around ten tons. It is an architectural marvel.

This is probably old stuff to you Chuck, given your past studies with Professor Klenk, but to me it is overwhelming news.

It is never old, Dan. The model does what descriptions and pictures never could do. Whoever made the model did a fantastic job. Look at how they captured the engravings on the pillars. I can see now what Professor Klenk pointed out in class. The engravings symbolize the world in which the temple worshippers lived. There are images of the animals that were a constant threat to them: lions and leopards, scorpions and snakes, and vultures. The pillars themselves are representations of people, with arms carved into the sides of the rectangular pillars and small blocks standing on top of the pillars symbolizing human heads.

A good description, Chuck. We don't know what the worship practices were like of the people who came to this temple. After years of studying and thinking about this temple, however, I have come to see it as an expression of the religious attitudes of the people who were living as hunters and gatherers. On the one hand, they lived as animals in ways very similar to the animals they hunted. On the other hand, they sensed that there was something different about themselves. For 500,000 years our ancestors buried their dead, but other animals didn't. We have discovered burial sites that go back that far. None of our earliest ancestors could imagine what it could be like to be dead, any more than we can. They were aware that human bodies rot away when dead, but the people they had been living with seemed still close to them even after they died. In addition, they lived with people and animals being born and dying, with life coming into the newborn and life passing out when death occurred. Although they experienced life only in themselves and animals and plants, I think that it is very likely that for them life itself always was present and that into and out of it living creatures moved. I think that here at the Temple of Eden people worshipped that life spirit on which all living things depend. That the pillars themselves are human is a recognition that people are different from animals, while the engravings on the pillars symbolize the dynamics within the singular world in which all living things are bound together.

This helps me understand what Professor Foucault was teaching us when he claimed that hunters and gatherers personalized everything in their world.

Your right, Dan, but I don't like that word 'personalized'.

Professor Foucault, I didn't know you were here.

I just came over here by the model a few minutes ago. Hans, I am sorry to interrupt what you were saying.

No need to apologize, Jacques. You came at the perfect time. I think that what I was saying about the temple would make more sense if you could share with us some additional background on the religious life of hunters and gatherers. You already know Dan. This is Charles Hill, but we all call him "Chuck." He is one of my graduate students and I invited him and Dan to come visit this museum and spend some time with us.

Good to meet you, Chuck.

O.K. Let me begin my pointing out why I think it is misleading to say that people living prior to the origin of agriculture 'personalized' everything in their world. When we talk about people personalizing things we are talking about people taking what really are non-personal things and then treating them as if they were persons. These people did not do that. For them, nothing was a non-personal thing. In their world everything was treated personally – other animals, mountains, rivers, the sky, the soil. What does it mean to say that someone treats something personally? At least two things. First, they attribute agency to them. Persons do things. The sky rains down life-giving rain and life-destroying tornados. The rivers provide fish and devastating flooding. Second, to treat something personally is to show respect to it. For these ancestors, nothing is a mere thing just there for people to use in any way that they desire. There is no sharp division between humans and animals, living things and inanimate things. The world of our early hunting and gathering ancestors was personal and nothing but personal. They probably had no concept of a mere thing and thus could not experience anything as a mere thing.

For most of the history of mankind, our ancestors lived in such a personal world. They were hunters and gatherers, not theoreticians. They lived with the persons surrounding them; they did not play the explaining business, explaining why any of these people existed as they did. They lived out their attitudes of respect for other persons, even though in their respectful treatment of them they differentiated in practice between humans, other animals, mountains, rivers and the sky. A remnant of that world lives on in the Japanese Shinto notion of 'kami'. Kami is present in every mountain, river, and flower. There is something sacred and deserving of respect in all of them. Ask the tree for permission before cutting it down; ask the flower for permission before cutting it and placing it in a flower arrangement.

They lived with an attitude of respect for their whole personal, living world, as individual humans and animals came in and out of it. In their differentiating practices they did treat humans differently from most non-human persons, as shown by their burial practices. They showed in the way they lived with birth and death that life flows into and out of humans, but they also showed in their burial practices that their human companions live on in their lives even after life has gone out of them. They showed in the way they lived out their attitudes that they differentiated the earthly realm in which they lived from the domed sky above them and the lower realms beneath them. They treated their dreams and the altered states of shaman as encounters with the upper realm and they crawled through caves deep into the earth to draw paintings to encounter symbolically the underworld. Shaman and caves, with animals painted on their walls, dating back before the rise of agricultural life, have been found all over Europe and Asia.

The Volpe Caves in the Pyrenes on the border of France and Spain were discovered in 1912 and first studied by my teacher and friend, Henri Breuil. They date back to more than 18,000 years ago. They contain an excellent artistic expression of the attitudes of humans at that time towards the personal world in which they lived. One cave tells us a great deal about the religious life of these humans, whose men hunted and fished and whose women gathered nuts, berries and edible plants. It is 500 feet long, composed of different chambers, one with animal bones carpeting its floor, some with walls covered either with patterns of red and black dots or handprints or pictures and sculpted reliefs of animals that were not to be found anywhere near the cave. Engraved in the ceiling, and painted over and over for thousands of years, is an amazing figure. It has the legs and feet of a human, the eyes of an owl, the ears and antlers of a deer, a beard stretching from its chin to its waist, the paws of a bear, the torso and thighs of an antelope.

This complex of caves might well have been used to initiate young humans into full standing with the adults. The youngsters would have had to crawl through the tight passageways and crawl carefully along the narrow ledges they needed to creep along to be able to see the final symbolization of the holistic personal world in which they lived. Maturing into this world required possessing, in one's style of living and in one's attitudes towards life, an understanding of the meaning of this world, an understanding that did not require any verbal theorizing.

Chuck, Dan has heard me talk about these things many times, but I wanted both of you to keep this in mind when thinking about what the "Temple of Eden" meant to the humans living here in this region thousands of years after humans had lived around the Volpe caves. Look again at the model of the temple. As difficult as it is, imaginatively locate yourself in this holistic, totally personal world. See the concentric circles and appreciate your location in this world, not as the separate grains of sand that our modern accent on individualism has led to our way of living, but as functional creatures in one interdependent world, similar to the way that our hearts and lungs are what they are only by functioning in our living bodies. Over thousands of years. the realistic characterization of animals unified in one creature in the caves was changed into massive pillars abstractly symbolizing the unity of humans and animals in one personalized world. Only by appreciating what this temple is giving expression to, can we appreciate the radical change in human history that this temple caused. The person to tell us that story is Father Joseph who, I see, has just joined our little group.

Father, let me introduce you to Chuck Hill and Dan Zymanski, two of our graduate students.

Hi, Chuck, Dan.

Father Reimer is an expert on the religious life of people after the agriculture era began. He studied for years at Harvard University with the late Frank Cross who was one of the world's experts on the religious life of the Canaanites and its influence on Biblical writers. The floor is all yours, Father Reimer.

Thank you Professor Klenk. Let me begin with a bit of information about the Temple of Eden. It probably took thousands of builders, working over many years, to construct this temple. These had been hunters but now they were construction workers, craftsmen and artists. They needed housing and someone to supply them with food and water. The city of Urla was established ten miles away. The people supplying their food could not follow animal herds as they did as hunters. They became farmers and they domesticated animals to help supply meat and eggs to the workers pulling the stones and pillars used in building the temple.

For an uncountable number of reasons, a hunting and gathering way of life was replaced throughout most of the world with an agricultural way of life. Basic changes took place in the attitudes that people had towards creatures in their environment and towards their whole world. People became different kinds of people with different senses of who and what they were. The old holistic, personal world in which they saw themselves as functionally alive, now became a world in much of the inanimate items surrounding them became mere stuff, things, raw materials they could control and use to meet the needs of their tribe and themselves. The dirt was something to be dug up and used to crow crops. Other animals became meat and beasts of burden.

Many archeologists and historians have hypothesized that life in an agricultural world was a much harder form of life than the way of life enjoyed by hunters and gatherers. Farmers had to bend to the demands of time: planting time, harvesting time, winter waiting time. They now lived in fear of droughts and floods, and of new physical threats of starvation caused by no longer running with animals. We know they lost on average six inches in height due to diminished protein intake. Their whole new life of trying to control things led to tragic miscalculations of their own power over nature and other people and to a tragic sense of being superior to everything else.

Humans in the Age of Agriculture no longer lived as people within a personalized world. Farmers did not treat everything as an agent doing something. Every raining cloud was not a person acting. Every growing plant was not a person acting. Still, the old presumption, that everything happening is caused by someone, lived on.

Agricultural people were concerned about the origin of the whole "natural world" and about the changing course of human actions. Agricultural worlds all around the earth show a concern about origins of everything in their world, including themselves, and a concern about the proper ways of responding to these concerns. In ceremonial rituals and in oral and written stories, creation narratives appeared as did historical narratives of their tribal lives. These rituals and stories were used in socializing and enculturating new generations with a sense of tribal identity. A common pattern appeared in these stories and rituals. In the beginning was the hunter's and gatherer's paradise (Garden of Eden) which humans lost because of their desire to be the masters of everything, even the social rules now needed to give order to their lives and actions. Now they lived in troubled times. However, just as their current age began in paradise, so someday, they believed, somehow life in paradise would be regained as the hubris causing the fall out of paradise is eliminated from the lives of actors.

With the development of the agricultural way of life a new way of life emerged, one outside of paradise and ruled by hubris. The respect for the personal character of the hunter's and gatherer's world, and everything in it, was replaced by concerns about control, by efforts to maximize human control over as much as possible, even over what they could not directly control: the kind of weather needed by their crops, the diseases that could decimate their animals and their fellow humans. As I already mentioned, there was a carryover from the world of the hunter and gatherer. In the understanding embodied in an agricultural way of life, nothing just happens. Someone is causing crops to grow or wither. Someone is causing floods, hurricanes, volcanic explosions, invasions of locusts and human plagues. In this new world, humans treated the agents causing such things to happen in the only way available to them, as beings with very human-like qualities, only now raised to the superhuman level needed to cause such life sustaining and life-threatening phenomena. The new farmers and herders lived in a world controlled by a pantheon of Gods, whom they had to try as best they could to pacify with rituals of praise and sacrifice.

The religious life of hunters and gatherers focused on a "Lord of Beasts" who was a master over animals and a guardian of the forests, whose guidance they prayed for in finding prey and whose good side they sought to stay on by making offerings. Evidence of such worship has been found all over the earth. There is the engraving in the Volpe caves, the pillars found here in the Garden of Eden, and the stone and ivory carvings on knives found throughout Mesopotamia and Egypt. This all changed with the inauguration of the agricultural age. Now it was a mother goddess that they worshipped, a goddess who received the seed planted by farmers and upon whose care of these seeds their livelihood depended. Now their gods died and came back to life from the underworld just like the crops in their fields. Now revered even more were their ancestors buried in the earth whom they sensed could intercede with the gods who would bring forth crops every spring and nurture them until harvested in the fall. In 1953 a British archaeologist, Kathleen Kenyon, discovered human skulls that were placed on top of clay heads, buried under hundreds of farming homes, and over 8,000 years old. These functioned as family shrines through which humans maintained the life of their ancestors and expressed their continued respect for them while at the same depending on them to communicate with the gods upon whom they depended.

There were many different gods in the new pantheon of gods, but they were all very human, superhuman, and they interacted with each other in very human ways. For the humans, who constituted the gods in this pantheon, they were the ones originating life and causing it to behave as it does. There were three main gods: An or Anu – the sky god, Enki – the wise god, and Enlil – the controller of fate. For the people living with these gods it meant living with a certain attitude towards their whole agricultural world. They acknowledge that they are not lords of their world. They inescapably live under the sky dome which is An. They live on the earth governed by Enlil's fated lawfulness of the cycles of birth and death. They do not curse this way of life but rather treat their lives as governed by the wisdom of Enki.

This religious expression of their living understanding of who they were and what their world fundamentally was like, however, was troubled by what this understanding left out. Although, for almost all humans living then, this concern was not put into words, still, some sort of attitude towards what was left out was required. What about the roaring seas surrounding our tilled land? How did our ordered land arise given the chaos of the seas? Why was our land fated to be as it was? What was the point and purpose of Enki's wise planned ordering of our land? Why did these gods exist at all? How did they originate?

Over time, the pantheon of only three gods changed due to internal pressure and the local character of the environment in which these humans lived. Among Indo-Europeans living in southern Europe and Iran, the sky god, An, remained under the name Dyeus , but now the sun was focused on as the key heavenly god. In addition, fire, with all its uncontrollable but fascinating disorder, was deified. A god of a primordial water, not yet divided into raging seas and ordered land, was introduced. In Egypt, the sun god remained first among equals in the assembly of gods. Among the sea-faring Myceneans, Dyeus became Zeus and Poseidon became the god of the raging seas, now distinguished from the earth and its goddess, Gaia. As the political arrangements among humans changed, so did their treatment of their gods. In the era of small villages, Mother Earth was the ruler of the fertility gods. In the era of city states, warring against each other or organized into confederations, warrior gods appeared acting under the control of heavenly assemblies. Once Sargon established the Akkadian Empire 4,500 years ago, one major god appeared with the power and authority to overrule decisions by the assembly of gods.

These gods lived in the consciousness of people through the stories that were orally transmitted from generation to generation. The stories not only maintained the attitudes needed for these gods to be real to their worshippers, but they were exiting to hear, and to create. We know about these ancient gods only because the oral stories were turned into written texts. The early Sumerian/Babylonian creation myth, *Enuma Elish*, was written around 4,000 years ago. Written a little later was the *Epic of Atrahasis,* the fore-runner of the Babylonian *Epic of Gilgamesh* (1,200 BCE) that was the fore-runner of the Biblical story of Noah and his Arc (550 BCE).

Excuse me, Father Reimer. I am sorry to interrupt but Mr. Hill is writing his thesis on these three documents. I thought it would be good for him to tell us his take on these texts. Dan probably would like to learn what Chuck has been learning.

Fine, Professor Klenk. I have been talking too long anyway. Mr. Hill, the floor is all yours.

These are three great stories. I am amazed that Marvel Comics hasn't already brought them out as adventure, other-worldly movies. The problem is that readers can get so caught up in characters and action that they forget that they are myths which convey deeper religious truths. The humans who first wrote the myths, along with their early readers, probably also got deeply involved in the stories about gods battling each other. Even for them, however, these myths gave expression to the attitudes that gave significance to what they were doing and who and what they were.

On the surface the Babylonian Myth of Creation, *Enumma Elish*, is the story of a male and a female god, their children and grandchildren. It is a tale about the disorderly behavior of their children leading to an attempt to murder them by their father. It is a story about the revenge of the mother against the gods who just stood around while the father attempted to carry out his plan and against the one god who did prevent the murder by murdering the father. It is a story about the murder and dismembering of the mother by a powerful warrior selected by the assembly of gods, a warrior who was offered kingship over the gods if he carried out the murder of the mother, a warrior who created the sky, the earth, and all the people on the earth who were as savage as he was. A captivating story. It would make a great movie.

The religious significance of the myth becomes apparent when one learns who these gods symbolized to those who heard or read this story. Apsu is the father and Miamet is the mother. They are the gods of the primordial water (fresh and salt) that existed before there was any differentiation and individuation between living things, earth and sky, the gods. In the primordial waters, salt water and fresh water lived harmoniously. In modern language one might compare this primordial world of water to the world of matter and energy that field theory in physics describes. In the Babylonian myth of origins, the primordial ocean without finite boundaries was not dead and inert. It was dynamic and alive. Just as the sexual activity of humans creates human children, so the activity in the primordial waters by Apsu and Miamet created all the heavenly gods and that over which they were gods. Through the activity of these gods, humans were created. The infinite world of primordial water, existing peacefully and harmoniously, is the origin of everything finite. It is the actions of finite gods and humans that causes all the problems and conflicts in life.

Apsu and Miamet gave birth to twins, a son, Lahmu, and a daughter, Lahamu. Lahmu is totally loyal to Apsu and serves as his protector. No conflict between father and son here. The origin of the finite is not the source of any of the problems humans will come to have. Lahmu will continue the creative work of Apsu and Miamet by giving birth to Anshar (the whole heaven) and Kishar (the whole earth). So far, so good. The spirit of the primordial waters permeates the whole earth and heaven. If people could live in peace with heaven and earth they could live in peace with the primordial origin of everything. Things do not remain this peaceful, however.

Lahmu, Lahamum, and Lahamu's children are not just fully controlled extensions of Apsu and Miamet. They are not just docile offspring of their parents, but they are brother and sister to each other. They are independent gods capable of acting on their own. Furthermore, Lahamu has given birth to Anshar and Kishar, the heavens and the earth, who also are independent actors. Heaven became the father of Anu, the god who was equal to Apsu, the actor who was to be revered equally with the primordial water, the actor who did not acknowledge himself as inferior to anything, even the primordial waters, the actor who was the spirit of life itself. Thus, for the Babylonians, an independent historical actor, bowing down to no one, was treated as equal to the primordial water out of which everything originated. It was not the creator of historical actors that was to become their object of ultimate concern. Their religious attitudes and cultic practices were focused on the God who was mightiest among the Gods who caused all those things to happen that humans could not control. Anu's son was Nudmonud, who was the god of wisdom and knowledge, mightier in strength than any other god, mightier even than his grandfather, Anshar, the god of heaven itself, mightier even than his father Anu, who chose to stay out of the spotlight. Freed from concern about his primordial origins, able to knowingly control everything in heaven and on earth, Nudmonud for a while completed the insurgency of history against the primordial spirit of al life.

Anu and Nudmonud might revolt and try to install themselves in the place of Apsu and Tiamet, but the latter two would not give up their seat of authority without a counterattack. All this rebellious activity disturbed Apsu and Tiamet greatly. Apsu wanted to destroy all the historical offspring to whom they had given birth. Tiamet was upset about the revolt but wanted to keep alive the offspring whom she had originated. No matter how much the rebels turned against the primordial water from which they originated, they could not drive out the spirit that makes their existence possible.

Apsu was not willing, as Tiamet was, to wait for the rebelling gods to come to their senses and recognize and acknowledge the spirit of life on which they are inescapably dependent. Apsu wanted to destroy the whole lot of their offspring and begin again. Tiamet seemed to realize that starting again would simply mean creating the problem again. The living dynamics in the primordial waters meant the inevitable creation of finite beings and thus once again the emergence of ungrateful, rebellious offspring. The Babylonian worshippers located in their creation myth an understanding of the need for both attitudes of gratefulness to their primordial origins and attitudes of respect for the gods controlling what they could not control, as well as a need for strategically and tactically devised cultic practices aimed at influencing such powerful gods.

Urged on by his son, Mimmu, a brother to the twins, Apsu devised a plan to kill off all his children and grandchildren, and all the gods he created. EA, the wise old god of the skies sees through Apsu's plan. He informs the council of gods under the leadership of his son, Nudmonud, what Absu plans to do, but they do nothing to stop Apsu. Historical actors, even heavenly ones, are not yet strong enough to directly confront the god of the primordial fresh water. Ea acts on his own, incapacitates Apsu, and builds an irrigation system to control the needed fresh water. He eventually has enough water in the reservoirs that he can kill off Apsu. He knows that this is not enough. There is still Tiamet with whom he must deal. The Babylonian myth makers show that controlling fresh water is not enough to guarantee the independence of historical actors from their primordial origins.

Tiamet is furious when she finds out what happens. The heavenly council of gods, her offspring, were not strong and faithful enough to stop Apsu's plan and they went along with Ea's actions, controlling Apsu and then killing him and eliminating him from the picture, thus guaranteeing that the primordial waters would give birth to no more gods. She declares war against the assembly of gods. She sends against the gods and their world all the sea monsters not controlled by the gods. She elicits Kingu to be the head of her army attacking the assembly of gods. In many ways the weak gods are warring with themselves, with the primordial spirit without which they cannot live.

Unable to save themselves from Tiamet's fury, they search for a savior. Ea, the wise god of the sky, and his consort, Damkina, the goddess of fertility, have a son, Marduck, a powerful and feirceless god of storms. He appears before the assembly of gods, and volunteers to destroy Tiamet and the threat she poses to their very existence. Murduck is the paradigm of a historical actor willing to revolt against the primordial. He demands one thing in payment for his services. Upon victory he is to be made supreme god in the assembly of gods. To the myth maker, this only makes sense. The assembly of gods can be an independent assembly only if they are liberated from their primordial roots. They are too weak to do this on their own. Murduck is able and willing to be the ultimate rebel. Only by making him king over them, and acknowledging him as king, can they live free from the primordial spirit within them still demanding recognition.

Murduck kills Tiamet. He cuts her body up and uses half of it to make the sky bowl above them and the other half to make the earth below the sky. He crushes Tiamet's skull and legs and the bones of Kingu, and as the playful artist he is, he uses them to create savage humans whom he demands live primarily to serve him and the gods he controls. These savages, however, are not any more robots controllable by Murduck than the gods were robots controllable by Apsu and Tiamet. The bones and blood of Tiamet, the spirit of Tiamet, lives within them even as that spirit lives in the sky and earth made from her body.

The creation myth, Emuma Elish, gives expression to the living understanding in the Babylonians of what they are, what their life-defining attitudes are to be, and what they are to do. As one might expect, what the myth expresses as their nature is as complex as they know themselves to be. They are savages, created by a rebellion against the very spirit of life, a rebellion that stains who they are. The staining, however, is not so severe that it prevents them sensing that the spirit of life resides within them and everything else in the sky and on earth. Given their understanding of their origin they do not live in despair but with a hope that the peace and harmony present in their primordial origin might again be theirs in their daily lives. Given who they are, and that much of the uncontrollable forces of nature are not governed by a concern for them, life here and now is not going to be without tragic conflicts, but this is no reason to act without hope. They recognize the need to trust in the primordial, harmonious, goodness of life, and to do the best they can to deal with the challenges of living in a world not fully controllable by humans or structured to protect humans from suffering and death.

There are two other texts written during the Mesopotamia era that show their writers wrestling with the issues of the origin, character, and destiny of human life. The Sumerian half of this era stretched from 3,500 BCE to 2350 BCE and the Babylonian era was the period from 2,350 BCE to 612 BCE when Babylonia was conquered by Persia. The first text, *Atra-Hasis*, named for the protagonist in the myth, written during the Sumerian era, includes a creation myth, explaining why humans are to serve the gods who created them for that very purpose. It also includes an epic about the gods trying to destroy with a flood all humans except those the God of the primordial water saved by forewarning them about the impending flood. The second text, *Epic of Gilgamesh*, named after the king of Uruk in the kingdom of Ur, gives expression to human concern about the significance of the civilized life of humans, given the threat that death poses to all living things. Written around 2,100 BCE, the epic includes a conversation between Gilgamesh and the one survivor of the great flood, Utnapishtim, now portrayed as having survived both the threat of the flood and the threat of death itself. He had gained immortality.

In the creation myth, *Atra-Hasis*, Sumerians once again encounter new exploits by the early Sumerian gods: Anu -god of the sky, Enlil – god of earth and wind, and Enki – god of fresh water. In the myth, Enlil requires lesser gods to care for his earth, to maintain the rivers and canals. The lesser gods protest over the hard labor required of them. Enki, wise advisor to the gods, suggests that humans be created to do all the hard labor required. The mother goddess, Mami, molds clay figurines out of the dust of the earth and the flesh and blood of the slain god of intelligence. The clay figures are kept in a specially made womb for 10 months until it opens, and humans are born.

Humans, however, overpopulate the earth, and even though the ruler of earth, Enlil, does everything he can to control population growth through causing famines and droughts, it is not enough. Therefore, Enlil decides to destroy all humans with a flood, and gets the whole assembly of gods to say nothing about this plan to the humans. Enki, however, to make sure that life continues, through an oracle warns Atrahasis about the flood that is coming. He is told to build a boat and bring his family and animals on board. The boat is to have a roof "like Apsu" and a subterranean fresh water source provided by Enki. After seven days the flood ends, and in thanksgiving Atrahasis offers thanksgiving sacrifices.

The Sumerians have packed so much meaning in this myth/epic. The text lived not only in a written form but in the stories told orally in the home and during festivals. It provided them with answers to so many of their concerns about who and what they are and why things are as they are. Their lives involve so much hard labor because fate is written right into who they are and why they exist at all. The famines and droughts which threaten the existence of all living things have meaning; they are caused by their own unwise and uncontrolled behavior, such as giving birth to too many humans. Eventually, their destructive behavior will threaten the very existence of life itself. Thankfully, humans are not only too weak to control their own destructive tendencies, but they also are too weak to destroy life itself. Life continues no matter what people do. It cannot be controlled totally by people. Also, even when a flood of disasters appears, enough intelligence is part of their created nature that they will act to save at least some humans and some animals. Gratitude for what they have been created to be, hard laborers and intelligent controllers of their destiny, is what is needed to live on in the world into which they have been thrown, a world in which, the gods be thanked, life surges on.

Gilgamesh is not satisfied with new generations still being alive after the death of individual humans. It is his own immortality that he seeks. In the *Epic of Gilgamesh*, it is the significance of individual humans that is at issue, given that each of them is mortal, born into life for a little while and then torn out of life when they die. What significance does the life of any individual have if death totally obliterates its existence?

The main characters in this epic are six: **Gilgamesh** is the cruel and degenerate king of Utruk who seeks to control all his subjects by minimizing the strength of the men in his kingdom and by forcibly stealing on their wedding night the virginity of all new brides.

Enkidu is a wild and uncivilized human, living in the wild protecting his fellow animals by setting off all the traps of a "civilized trapper." He is chosen by the gods to stop Gilgamesh's oppression of his people and he is initiated into civilized life by a sun goddess temple prostitute. As a newly civilized wild animal he is not strong enough to defeat Gilgamesh. Eventually he becomes his friend, aiding Gilgamesh to pursue his passion for fame and glory.

Shamash is the sun goddess who sustains all living things, acts as the agent of the gods in their efforts to restrain Gilgamesh by recruiting Enkiku and protecting Enkiku from the deadly threat posed by the fierce guardian of the sacred Cedar forest that Gilgamesh wants to possess to gain fame and fortune. This guardian controls mud slides, powerful wild animals, fire blowing dragons. She accuses Enkiku of betraying his original nature for the sake of seeking civilized fame and fortune with Gilgamesh. She seeks but fails to console a dying Enkiku that he will gain fame and honor in the great funeral Gilgamesh will give him.

Utnapishtim is the survivor of the great flood, who, although being the father of all later generations, alone was granted immortality. The father of all generations is Life itself and it does not die. He tries to show Gilgamesh, distraught over the death of Enkiku and now trying to live as Enkiku did, as a wild animal, while searching for a pathway to immortality, that all humans are mortal. He succeeds in so far as Gilgamesh focuses on the structures built by him and his workers in Uruk, which will live on even after Gilgamesh's death.

Gilgamesh's time with Utnapishtime deserves special attention. The story of the flood contained in this epic bears striking resemblances to the story of the flood contained in in the Summerian *Myth/Epic of Atra-Hasis.* The Biblical story of Noah and his Ark is linked back in many ways to these two stories of the flood. Utnapishtime tells Gilgamesh the story of the flood and how the god Enlil, the controller of the fate of life on earth, with the approval of the assembly of gods, acted to destroy all human life with a great flood. He says that the god Ea (Enki), the god of wisdom, tells Enlil that it is wrong to attempt to destroy life. Utnapishtime says that Ea told him to build a boat and put on it his family, the craftsmen who helped build it, and all the animals of the field. When the storm ends after six days and the boat lands on a mountain top, he sends out three birds (a dove, a swallow, and a raven) to see if they are near dry land. When only the raven does not return, he knows that dry land is not in their immediate place but still not too far away. When the waters recede. everyone gets out of the boat and offers thanksgiving offerings to the gods who now, inspired by the lament of the goddess Ishtar, the goddess of love, sex, and fertility, are very happy that the life they created was not destroyed. Ishtar even was able to convince Enlil that it was a mistake to attempt to destroy life. A repentant Enlil, according to Utnapishtime, blesses him and his wife by giving them immortality. He also tells Gilgamesh, however, that all their offspring, including Enkiku and Gilgamesh, will only make themselves miserable if they vainly try to escape the certainty of death. Mortality and not immortality is imprinted in the very nature of individual living things.

Expressed in the *Epic of Gilgamesh* is much of the understanding expressed in earlier Summerian/Babylonian myths and epics. First, humans, out of nostology for the free days of life in an age before their current hard working agricultural age, are expressing a lament, like Enkiku, over having left the good old days forever behind them, days they have no power to recover again no matter how much they might wish for it to happen.

Second, the Babylonians are expressing their understanding that, even though now they have the power to control many things, life itself faces the threat of total extinction. Furthermore, they understand that they themselves may be contributing to this very threat, as some people use the power they have gained in their "civilized" world to treat other humans in uncivilized ways as mere tools to be used for their own pleasure and sense of power, for their pursuit of the goals of personal fame and power. As they see all around them the horrible consequences of such cruel selfishness, they understand that even the most powerful humans will not find satisfaction in such self-centered behavior. It stands in opposition to the behavior necessary for all humans to prosper. This is a necessity built right into the very nature of human life, as if stamped there by wise gods creating them that way and ordering their world that way. The mighty and powerful will not find satisfaction in their way of living because they are warring against who they inescapably are. The attitudes and actions of these power-hungry humans, who see themselves as absolute monarchs over all other people, live by a hubris that prevents them from possessing a reverent gratitude for the timeless and inescapable wise moral ordering of the historical world of human action, an attitude that requires therefore respecting the sacred worth of each and every human being.

Third, these texts express the insuppressible hope that humans continue to have, even in the face of horrendous domination and oppression. The very factors that make humans what they are exhibit the wise orderliness of human existence if they would not mess it up by not respecting the requirements of harmonious human living, by not respecting each other. The hard struggles demanded of all humans acting in the world cannot be avoided, but this is no reason for despair. Even the worst misuse of human power is never the last word. Life itself, especially human life, has too much supporting its significance and value to be overwhelmed by powerful despots. Even death does not get the last word. Without denying the death that faces every human, the epic expresses the faith that the significance of what humans produce lives on after they are dead.

Please don't misunderstanding what I have just said. I am not suggesting that the three sets of reflections I have just made were anything that the Babylonians back then were thinking to themselves. They were not doing what I have been doing, interpreting talk about the gods in their pantheon as expressions of attitudes towards the point and purpose of human existence. Probably, almost all of them never doubted the existence of their gods doing what their myths and epics said they were doing. They thanked their gods. They feared their gods. They offered sacrifices to their gods hoping the gods would render assistance. They paid serious attention to what the myths and epics said, and they told and retold them. They lived not only as actors in an agricultural world but also in a world in which their gods were battling with each other and acting upon them in hostile and benevolent ways. The interpretations I have given constitute my interpretation of what I think was going on, even if that was not what they would have said if they even had talked about their attitudes and their world.

Dan, that is what I am trying to get across in my thesis. What do you think? What I am presenting, of course, is just my interpretive reading of these three texts. Other readers have given different interpretations. I am not interested in comparing or evaluating these other interpretations. My purpose in developing my interpretation is to show that these myths and epics have so much to say to contemporary readers. That many different interpretations are possible only shows how rich are the insights expressed in them.

Chuck, I was fascinated by what you were saying. It is going to take me some time to begin to digest what these texts can say to me. I knew about them before in a cursory way, but I now have so many new ideas to think about. I sense that the attitudes expressed in these myths and epics are similar in some ways to attitudes expressed by people in a pre-agricultural era when they painted and engraved the human-animal hybrid on the ceiling in the Volpe caves and when they built the Temple of Eden, whose model we have before us right now in this museum. As one might expect, given that these artifacts were created by humans living in very different social and cultural worlds, there are significant differences between them. Yet, there are enough similarities to show that they are produced by families of artists and writers and that they bear important family resemblances between them.

That's all I have to say now. Let me turn the floor over to Professor Klenk.

Thanks, Chuck. I can't wait to read the final thesis. Before we break up, there are three other movements that I think we should look at again. I would like to have Father Reimer tell us about the Canaanite Mythic Cycle of Ba'l and Anat, since he is aware of Frank Cross's brilliant reconstruction and interpretation of it. After all, Father, you have been his student. After Father Reimer is finished, I would like to say something about Amenhotep's effort in Egypt and Arathustra's attempt in Persia to replace the pantheon of Gods in the heavenly assembly with a monotheistic god. Father Reimer.

Thank you. First, a word or two about the Canaanites. They are not a single tribe of people but consist of farmers, sheep herders, and sea-faring people (Hittites, Amorites, Hurrians, Phoenicians, Philistines). They lived along the Eastern Mediterranean shore from Turkey to Egypt, from 3,200 BCE until conquered by Alexander the Great in 332 BCE. For much of this time, Canaan was a vassal state of Egypt. There was a brief period from 1720 BCE to 1550 BCE when they invaded and conquered Egypt. The Egyptians called them "rulers of foreign countries", Hyksos.

It was during the 14th Century BCE that the cycle of myths of Ba'l and Anat were produced. 'Ba'l' means 'Lord' and in these myths it is Haddu, the god of storms and fertility, who is Lord in the assembly of gods. Anat is Haddu's concert and the goddess of war. It is she who fights to protect Haddu's rule as Lord when threatened by his two major enemies, Yamm (the sea) and Mot (death). El, the father of all the gods, speaking for the assembly of gods who are scared to death by the threats of Yamm, agrees to Yamm's demand that Haddu be enslaved and that he, Yamm, be made lord over all the gods. Haddu for a time is enslaved but then Kotar, the wise craftsman of the gods who builds the sacred implements used by humans in their temple worship of the gods, builds two clubs with which Haddu defeats Yamm and again for a while is accepted as Lord (Ba'l).

Haddu's reign as the god guaranteeing fertile life faces a second deadly challenge. Aware of the threat that he posed to life, Haddu went to battle with Mot (death), another one of El's sons. He is enslaved again and loses his station as the Lord of the gods and the world of living things they have created. This time it is Haddu's consort, Anat, the goddess of war, who frees him by slicing Mot up and winnowing him through a sieve, burning him with fire, grinding him with millstones, and scattering him in the fields as fertilizer for new life. These activities of Anat were simulated for years in Canaanite fertility rites. As a result, Haddu is acknowledge as the Lord of heaven and earth, a kingship backed up by the warring power of Anat.

To make sure that everyone in heaven and on earth knows that Haddu is Ba'l, Haddu and Anat slay the seven-headed dragon of the sea, Lotan, the beloved offspring of El. In these myths, the Cananites declare that, just as Haddu rules the heveans, so the dynastic kings of Canaan rule on earth. El gives instructions to Kotar to build a temple-palace for Haddu, their king, their Ba'l, their Lord, and to build the implements needed by humans in their cultic worship of Ba'l.

This cycle of myths expresses very clearly the attitudes that informed the Canaanite agricultural and religious activities. The chaos that surrounds ordered life, represented by Yamm and Lotan, and the mortality of all living things, represented by Mot, are inescapable factors in life, represented by El's having fathered them. Chaos and death, however, do not have the final word in the agricultural world in which they live. The cyclical pattern of planting and harvesting, of life and death, will provide enough order to make possible decent life, if humans will respect and honor such natural order. All living things are mortal, and death will drag them all to the underworld, but out of the decaying remnants of one cycle of life another cycle will be born.

These myths do not address the concerns of individual mortal people about the significance of their short period of life, but the Epic of Gilgamesh did that and there will be many more texts that will address this issue which seems to have haunted humans for thousands of years. Already around 1750 BCE, in the text *Dispute over Suicide*, the Egyptians expressed their concern about the threat that death posed to meaningful human existence. Similarly, the Acadeian/Babylonian poems, *I Will Praise the Love of Wisdom, were* written in the same time frame as the myths of Ba'l and Anat. They dealt with the human concern about death making life meaningless. These, of course, are the issues wrestled with by the Biblical writers of Ecclesiastes and Job a thousand years later.

Prof. Klenk, I believe you said you had some additional material to share with us.

I do Father Reamer. You and Chuck have done a marvelous job of reminding us of the myths and epics that have been written. Let me make a couple of general remarks about the religious life of people in these places and during these times. For almost all of them, there were many gods to be worshipped. At first these gods represented forces in nature and then later, as we get closer to the Greek pantheon of gods, they represented abstractions such as beauty, love, rationality, wisdom. Sometimes, there was one god seen as the supreme king of the assembly. Sometime, one specific god was singled out as the patron god of a specific city or state, with religious worship centered in cultic practices in one specific temple or shrine.

There were two times, however, when an attempt was made to establish religious monotheism, worship of one god seen as the only god. In Egypt, in 1353 BCE, when he became emperor of Egypt, this emperor was worshipping the sun god, Amun, as the supreme head of Egypt's pantheon of gods. His name at that time was Amenhotep (Amun was pleased). He modified the understanding of Amun, by viewing him as Aten, the sun disk god who shed his rays on all people. He made him the official god of his royal family. Amenhotep reported that he had a personal, intimate experience with Aten, and came away convinced that Aten was the only god that existed. He changed his name to Akhenatum (beneficial to Aten), destroyed the old polytheistic temples, built a new temple to Aten in a new city (today's Amara), and declared worship of any other god illegal. His efforts, however, failed to preserve monotheism. With his death, Egyptians went back to worshipping Amun as the head of the pantheon of gods.

Two hundred years later, in Persia (Iran), a man, trained as one of the priests aiding Persians to worship gods in the Persian assembly of gods, abandoned the priesthood and started wandering in search of a satisfying understanding of the gods. His name was Zarathustra (Zoroaster). He had an experience with what he took to be the sole god and lord of the universe, *Ahura Mazda*. This name was only a name of his god; it was not a description. He claimed that one could not say it was a storm god, a war god, or a fertility god. He was one without any second, one who could not be distinguished from other gods because, Zarathustra said, it is impossible even to think of another god. One can only name God as Ahura Mazda and then gratefully appreciate what Ahura Mazda had done: make the heavens and the earth, separate night from day and light from darkness, make the moon wax and wean. One could only accept the universal and eternally unchanging nature of wisdom, truth, power, love, unity, and immortality, guaranteed by Ahura Mazda. Ahura Mazda also judged beliefs as true or false and actions and intentions as good or bad, and issued rewards in heaven to good people and punishments in hell to bad people. Zarathustra turned the old gods into angels and demons. He saw himself only as the vehicle of Ahura Mazda's voice, a prophet who wrote down what he understood his God to be saying, writings now contained in Persia's hold book, the *Gathos.*

Zaruthustra's monotheism also did not last once he died. His reflections lay dormant until they were revised in a radially dualistic form during the reign of Cyrus the Great in the 6th Century B.C. Ahura Mazda's activities became the activities of six different gods. His two children became good and evil gods battling for domination in the soul of individual humans. The good god was given the name of Ahura Mazda and the evil god was given the name *Ahriman*. Monotheism did not appear again in the region until Hebrew priests, captives in Babylon, edited the final version of the great Hebrew epic just before Cyrus defeated the Babylonians and allowed the Hebrews to return to their homes in and around Jerusalem.

Enough. Our thanks to the drama students who did such an excellent job in presenting this material to us. Now, let's all get something to eat and drink. Ask any questions you have after we sit down.

Chapter 3

Jacksonville Responds

Did everyone get what they wanted? Coffee is over on the right; tea is just left of the door. Cookies are under the big window through which you can see "Old Main." That's the oldest building on campus. I love its old red brick structure, but it is completely modernized inside. The "Life Learning Building," in which we now are, was made possible by gifts from many previous students who say they remained intellectually alive because of the lectures and discussions they had here. The lounge in which we are sitting was furnished by a gift from one the historians, now deceased, who gave many lectures here.

So, who would like to share your thoughts after listening to these presentations? Didn't the students do a great job? We should also thank Professor Hamann for writing the scripts. You can tell that he drew upon decades of research and reflection on these materials.

Let me begin, Rev. Kennedy.

All right. Anita. Go to it.

Well, I was fascinated by what was said about the religious attitudes of people living before and after the development of an agricultural way of life. I felt kinship with them. The artists who created the human-animal engraving in the Volpe cave and the Temple of Eden found a way to celebrate our kinship with all living things. I have always felt that all living things are tied together in our ecosystem. When you are a farmer, it is hard not to be an environmentalist. Unfortunately, there are fewer and fewer farmers and more and more people who live only in the concrete and asphalt worlds they have made for themselves. I can't remember who said it, but I read somewhere about some philosopher who lived in a forest in Germany who said that feeling a kinship with other living things is an attitude almost totally absent in our modern, Western, commercial and technological way of life in which everything (inanimate, botanical, animal, and human) is treated as just stuff, raw materials to be used by humans who individually and collectively try to control everything). Among hunters and gatherers, apparently, there was none of this imperialism that we humans now exercise over all other living species.

I was also intrigued by the way people in the age of agriculture sought to walk a thin line between acting, in their farming, fishing, and domestication of animals, and respecting the limits and the requirements that our ecosystem places on what we do. As I have learned many time, nature always resists if we attempt to be the absolute master over it. I kept thinking about this brute fact facing all farmers when I read about this French philosopher who said that all humans resist if other humans attempt to exercise dominating power over them. So many of current problems, it seems to me, stem from humans trying to be an all-powerful god dominating nature and other people, rather than trying to act in harmony with nature.

There is one last comment I want to make. When you live on a farm, you live constantly with death. I often killed a chicken for Sunday dinner. Every year my husband killed one of our pigs for Christmas when all our relatives came over. That pig gave us pork to eat for months afterwards. On my farm I couldn't help but think of death. My husband's father lived with us. He was very old. Each morning we never knew if he would die that day. Each day, as he tried to take a short walk outside, he had to carry his bag with him, his bladder and bowels no longer working. He hardly could talk anymore. He was ready to die. We were ready to say, "good bye." He had lived with us for a long time. When he did die, we took it as just a fact of life. As someone once said, "No one gets out of life alive." I am glad that at his funeral our minister focused on his good days when he was alive and on us who were still alive benefitting from the fact that he had lived. I don't want my memories of him distorted or diminished by imagining seeing him again after I die. Life is life. Death is death. For me, never the twain shall meet.

Thank you, Anita. I am so glad to hear what you just said. I don't know if you remember my name. I'm Hannah. I'm the "Flower Child." Let me add some examples of my own to further emphasize what you said. These might explain why I am proud when people call me a "Flower Child." As I see it, we live in a mobile world. People move from one region of the earth to another. At times they bring with them plant and animal species from one local ecosystem into another different eco-system. Sometimes this is praiseworthy since it brings new beauty and vitality into places that did not have it. Sometimes, however, it consists of a destructive invasion of life forms into a local ecosystem that wars with the demands of that system. Sometimes people do this accidentally, but often it is done through negligent ignorance or selfish, total disrespect for ecosystems and the requirements of life forms within them.

Pythons are brought in as pets and they end up destructively multiplying in the Florida everglades. Sometimes, industrial corporations do it deliberately to meet certain cravings of people. I know a woman who lived as a child and young adult on a potato farm using chemical fertilizers. She ended up having one miscarriage after another. I was told of a young child who lived on a dairy farm that gave hormones to pregnant cows to abort their fetuses while they continued to give milk. At age five, this child began menstruating and developed breasts and pubic hair. Scientists report that artificial food products containing ground up animal parts are fed to cattle and they come down with mad-cow's disease. For years, men in West Virginia lived by mining coal. Now, blinding themselves to the effect of burning coal on climate change and our ecosystem and other people, they use their political power to maintain their old way of earning money. They say that they need to feed their own families and they don't have the privilege of worrying about coal's effect on other people. Our government, instead of assisting them to find new honorable ways to feed their families, encourages coal companies to dig more coal and electric companies to burn more coal.

What I hear these ancient religions saying to me is a warning about the need to be very careful going from the hunter-gatherer Garden of Eden into the world in which one tries to control the growth of crops and the use of animals and then into an industrial world in which people rape the earth. It was so reassuring to hear that people thousands of years ago were saying what I and my friends are saying now. People must not worship their ability to exercise power over plants, animals, and minerals. They must not lose sight of their limited power over nature and their need to continue to respect nature.

I recognize that, given the billions of humans now existing on Planet Earth, we can't all go back to being hunters and gatherers. We can control, however, the number of humans we reproduce. We can recognize that it is counterproductive, even for humans, to imperialistically seek total domination over other life forms. I am not a tree-hugger. I am opposed to having individuals use violence to stop the destroyers of our environment. I do believe that governments, however, have the right and duty to enforce regulations protecting our environment.

I am not at all persuaded that the attitudes and actions that people need to avoid our own ecologically disaster are consistent with the attitudes that monotheists (Jews, Christians, Muslims) possess. So many of them act on the conviction that the god they worship, who is master over everything, has made them in this god's image, and that their god has given them the right to have dominion over everything else. I realize that some Jews, Christians, and Muslims interpret such talk about dominion in an environmentalist way. People are to be good stewards of the earth and care for it as a loving God would do. That, however, seems to be such a minority voice. Repeatedly, we flower children have had to deal with the scorn and disdain showered on us by "good" Christians and Jews. Perhaps, if these enemies of the earth learned about these ancient myths, they could become friends of the earth.

Well, Anita and Hannah, what you just said is something that we will have to think about as we examine what Biblical writers have to say about your concerns.

Hannah, you mentioned that many monotheists say that people are not to dominate nature but are to be good stewards of this gift given to humans. I assume that this will not satisfy you because it still expresses a disrespectful attitude towards nature. Nature is seen as something a god could possess and something humans could receive as a gift to be used prudentially for the welfare primarily of people. Perhaps these ancient texts challenge us to rethink the whole idea of agents controlling things. As one contemporary writer puts it, monotheists must start thinking about God being much less powerful than he traditionally has been thought to be. It may be God's weakness when it comes to nature that is God's strength when it comes to rebellious humans.

I think you are right, Rev. Kennedy. I think we may have to rethink a great deal of what the "Biblical Word of God" has to say about God and about ourselves. This is the kind of great awakening that I think we really need. Just so you know, I'm Chris. This is what some of the bishops in my Anglican Church have been saying for quite some time now. I know that in the weeks to come, as we listen to Biblical writers, we will have to think again and again about our relationship to the natural world, because we never can escape our home in nature no matter how much we also create social and cultural worlds in which to live.

I know that many times, in listening to others, we hear what we want to hear. As I listened today to these interpretations of these ancient myths and artifacts, I heard what I have been trying to tell others for years. You can understand a text only if you locate it in its historical and literary context. This is what I heard the presenters say today repeatedly. The Volpe engraving and the Temple of Eden can be understood only if located in one context and the epics and the creation myths need to be located in a different context. You can't just look at the engraving or temple and know what they are expressing. You can't take the myths and epics, produced after the age of agriculture began, as events that a CNN TV camera could have recorded. I have been saying the same thing about what Biblical texts say. The work of Biblical historians and literary experts may be dull and difficult to read. One might wish to avoid being educated by scholars and one might try to act on the hope that one can just pick up the Bible and read it straight through, from the first word in Genesis to the last word in Revelation. To me, however, that is just another instance of hubris, thinking you have the power to do something that you do not have. The Biblical writers, telling the story of Noah and his arc, certainly were aware of the Sumerian and Babylonian flood stories, even if they gave them a distinctively Hebrew twist. That they wrote with that knowledge in the back of their minds is something we must consider when interpreting the Bible's story about Noah. The big truths expressed through the story gets lost if we treat the story as a journalistic account of flood victims.

You're right, Christopher. The presentations that professors and their students will be presenting in weeks to come should inspire us to rethink much of what people now believe about what the Bible is and what it is saying.

Does anyone else have anything they want to say before we adjourn? Anyone? Lydia, I have been watching you and I keep sensing that you have something you want to contribute.

I don't know, Rev. Kennedy. I have never thought very much about nature and I have never listened to any of these Bible preachers on radio or the TV. We had our garden and I canned a lot of the vegetables. We could not afford to buy much meat at the store. That was why my husband raised rabbits. We ate a lot of rabbit meat, and we did sell their furs. On my family's little farm, as a child I used to sell eggs and some milk to get a little money to buy things. I used the money from the rabbit furs to buy milk, flour and lard. We never used any special chemicals in our garden. I am not sure what was in the pellets we fed our rabbits. We never got sick from eating rabbit meat. We never had a car. Neither my husband nor I ever knew how to drive. We walked two miles to get downtown and our children walked a mile and a half to school. It never hurt us, but it did mean dressing very warmly when the temperature went below zero in the winter.

It was nice to hear how these people long ago worshipped together even though they didn't think or talk very much about their gods. They just told stories. That seemed to be enough to get their kids to continue what they were doing. I wasn't very good in telling stories, but I sent my kids to Sunday School and they told them stories. In a couple of cases, it worked. Eventually, they went to different kinds of churches and told different stories. That's O.K. with me. My daughter became a

Catholic when she married, and they do things very differently from what we do in our church. I suppose they may be worshipping a different God from me, but I am not sure I even know what that means. I always try to let people do whatever they want to do in their religion, but I don't like it when some of them tell me that I am wrong in doing what I am doing. I have been going to church in the same way ever since I was a child.

It was very nice hearing all these different stories. I am glad I came. I'll be back next week.

Thank you, Lydia. You too have given us a great deal to think about. So, finish your coffee. The lounge stays open for another hour. Plenty of time for more conversation, if you choose to do so.

Next week, the focus of the lectures and presentations will be the old epic of the Hebrew people which since ancient times they told to remember and celebrate who they are as a religious community.

Chapter Four

Jerusalem Writes the Great Hebrew Epic

Good morning. Leave your umbrellas and wet rain coats in the back of the lecture hall. I congratulate you on working through the pouring rain outside. I promise you that we will get you out of here in plenty of time to get back home and to finish up preparing for the hurricane. This is only the early fringes and the weather man tells us that the heavy rain and winds won't come until late tomorrow afternoon.

Let me introduce again Professor Heinrich Hamann of our religion department. He will explain what is going to happen today. Professor Hamann.

Thank your Rev. Kennedy. Today we are going to try to help you understand what is written in the first four books of the Bible: Genesis, Exodus, Leviticus, and Numbers. Preserved there is the final version of the ancient epic that circulated for generations at the oral level among the ancient Hebrew people. It is an epic that tells a religiously inspired story of the origins of the Hebrews as a people defining themselves as a unique religious community. I said "origins" because the epic deals with two different sets of founding events. One set of events deals with Abraham and his descendants up to the time that Joseph welcomes them into Egypt. The other set deals with Moses, who leads the Hebrews out of captivity in Egypt and reconstitutes them as a religious community.

An epic is not what we would call a history book. Epics are created by story tellers. What is unique about this epic is that this story is being told by people as a way of participating in religious rituals in which they are retelling the story of their origin as a religious people and then pledging to be a faithful, religious people in the manner their ancestors were. In this epic we have a religious story. Most of the people who heard this story being told, and who often recited part of it, did not know how to read or write. The priests leading the people in the retelling of the epic may or may not have known how to write, but they were not doing what we call historical checking to see if what the epic says happened really happened. They were interested in larger religious truths and not in taking what the epic narrates as claims about family quarrels that really did or did not occur. For generations the epic was told and retold. The ones telling this story did not create this epic out of their imagination the way that J.K. Rowling created the legendary epic of Harry Potter. No one knows when people started telling this story and how it changed over time. Historians recently have provided some well evidenced judgements about the origins of the epic and the events talked about in the epic. Knowing these historical theories, and the evidence and arguments backing them up, will help in understanding the literary character of the epic and the historical situations which fed data into the epic, but it will not tell us how to think about the big religious truths being expressed in the epic.

Today we would like to do three things to help you think through the epic's big religious "truths." First, I have asked Arthur Hill, professor of ancient Middle-Eastern history here at the university, to describe the historical context in which the two earliest versions of the epic were written. Then, Ms. Beverly Sayer, a speech major, will present a shortened version of Harold Bloom's book, *The Book of J*, in which he has put in Modern English the earliest written version of the Epic. Dr. Bloom is a professor at Yale University and has written dozens of books as a literary critic and poet. Following Ms. Sayer's presentation of the epic, one of my graduate students, Archebold Rilling, will present his interpretation of the historical context in which the final edited version of the epic was written and the influence of that context on the editing of earlier versions of the epic. He also will give his evaluation of the significance of what the editors added as a prologue to the epic.

Please welcome Professor Hill.

Thank you, Professor Hamann.

I understand that in this lecture series, your focus is on the Hebrews and then on the Christians. Neither can be understood unless we know at least a little about what the much more powerful non-Hebrew people were doing just before and during the time when the ancient Hebrews were alive. I understand that last week you learned about the religious icons and texts of ancient people in the Middle-East. Today, let me tell you something about the political dynamics of tribes and empires in and around the region that is called "The Fertile Crescent", a region stretching from the southern mouth of the Tigris-Eupraxies Rivers north to their source, then over to the Mediterranean Sea and down to Egypt.

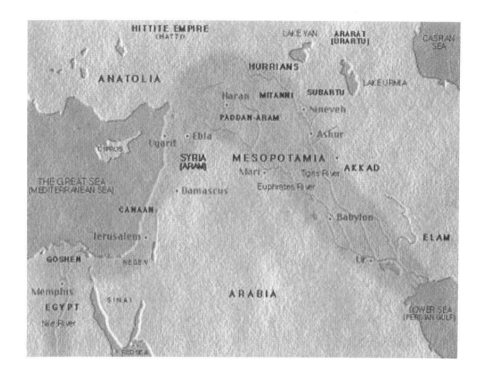

Focus on the map I have just put up. Thank god for power-point. Before the Hebrews began to function as a unified tribe, there were many other powerful empires striving to take possession of the fertile crescent because of its lucrative location for growing crops and rising sheep and goats. The movement of the Hebrew people into one small section of this area is a small factor in the geo-political activities of these other empires.

Just below the southwest end of the fertile crescent stands Egypt, whose people, since the adoption of an agricultural way of life around 5,500 BCE, began developing into a powerful nation. This development reached its maturity around 3,600 BCE. With one short exception, it maintained its national independence until the Greeks and Romans came along over 3, 000 years later. At the other end of the fertile crescent, in the southern portion of the Mesopotamian Valley of the Tigress-

Euphrates rivers, the mighty Sumerian Kingdom with its remarkable civilization existed from 2,850 BCE to 2360 BCE. It was replaced by the Akkadians, who lived up the valley just north of Sumer, when their leader, Sargon I, built an empire that lasted for two hundred years. When invading barbarians from the Zagros mountains to the East swept down and destroyed the Akkadian empire in 2060 BCE, the Sumerians returned to power for a mere sixty years. During that brief period, however, with their power centered in the city of Ur, they built an impressive tiered tower in honor of their king, and they set forth the Ur-Nammu code of law. Sumerian rule was ended when another group of mountainous invaders (Elamites) from the East (modern Iran) swept down into the rich Mesopotamian valley.

The Elamites had sufficient power to end Sumerian rule but not enough to build a new kingdom in the valley because beginning in 2000 BCE massive migrations of semi-nomadic Semitic people out of Arabia (the Amorites) spread throughout the fertile crescent. In addition, around the same time, the non-Semitic Hurrians came south from the Caucasian Mountains (modern Armenia) and the Hittites invaded from the home base of their empire in the Northwest (modern day Turkey). The fertile crescent was like a magnet drawing people from everywhere around it.

The Amorites had their capital at Mari on the northern edge of the Tigress-Euphrates valley and then moved it south to Babylon when Hammurabi conquered Mari and established what is known as the 1st Babylonian Empire. Soon Amorites dominated in all regions in the Fertile Crescent. Hammurabi's law code became the model throughout the region. Many proper names used by Amorites were used to name many of the first Hebrews. Ur and Haran are cities mentioned in the Hebrew epic as the home cities of early Hebrew leaders. The Amorites had their own creation, lost paradise, and flood myths and epics.

The Hurrians had been infiltrating northern Mesopotamia since 2,000 BCE and by the 15th Century were the majority population around Mari and Haran. Politically they were known as the Mitanni. They migrated into Canaan, the southwest region of the Fertile Crescent. Excellent warriors, they often clashed with Egyptian armies. The Egyptians called them the *Hurru*. The Hittites had established a kingdom in present day Turkey before 2,000 BCE. From time to time they left their mountain homes and moved down into Canaan and clashed with Egyptian armies. In 1720 BCE, a group called by the Egyptians, 'Rulers of foreign countries" (Hyksos), invaded and conquered Egypt because of a new military weapon they had invented – the chariot. The Hyksos were a mixture of Hurrians, Hittites, and Amorites.   Not until 1550 were the Egyptians able to drive them out.

In addition to these people who built powerful empires, there were two other groups of people seeking entrance into the Fertile Crescent. First, there were sea faring people such as the Philistines, who sailed down from the Aegean Sea around 1200 BCE, and the Phoenicians, whose ships carried trade around the whole Mediterranean Sea and who built colonies in Canaan around 1,000 BCE. Second, there were nomadic wanderers who were not citizens in any of empires. These rootless people were called the *Apiru*.

The earliest Hebrews seem to have been such wanderers who entered the Mesopotamian Valley with the Semitic Amorites around 2,000 BCE. After wandering around the Fertile Crescent until they entered Canaan, they tagged along with the Hyksos when they invaded Egypt. According to the great Hebrew epic, when the Hyksos were thrown out, the Egyptians enslaved the remaining Hebrews for three hundred years until Moses led their exodus from Egypt. After exiting Egypt and infiltrating back into Canaan, they eventually banded together into twelve tribes and formed a confederation of the tribes (resembling the confederation of colonies that existed in America before they were united into the United States of America). Around 1,000 BCE Saul, David, and Solomon united the twelve tribes into a single Hebrew empire. The unification project fell apart after Solomon died. The ten northern tribes formed the Nation of Israel with its capital at Samaria. The two remaining southern tribes formed the nation of Judah with its capital remaining in Jerusalem. Israel was conquered by the Assyrians in 720 BCE and Judah was conquered by the Babylonians in 570 BCE.

To summarize, the early settlers of the Fertile Crescent were the Sumerians and Akkadians, who had lived along the banks of the Tigress and Euphrates since 3,000 BCE. Then Semitic Amorites migrated in from Arabia in the south and non-Semitic

Elamites, Hurrians and Hittites migrated west and south from Iran, Turkey and the Caucasian Mountains in Armenia. Finally, sea-faring people (the Philistines and Phoenicians) established colonies in Canaan. As part of the Amorite migration, the nomadic, wandering Hebrews moved up the Mesopotamian Valley and then traveled along with the Hurrians as they moved down into Canaan and then Egypt. All This time Egypt stood just south of Canaan trying to keep Canaan as a vassal colony but often having to war with eastern empires and invading northerners. The great Hebrew epic centers on the exit of the Hebrews from Egypt, with prologues being added narrating the origin of the Hebrew community and the origin of the natural world and human life.

Before describing the history of the creation of the epic, let me say something about the empires of Assyria and Babylonia that conquered and destroyed Israel and Judah. The Assyrians lived as a pastoral and trading people for centuries under the rule of the Babylonians, Hurrians, and Hittites. By 1,300 BCE, however, they had become a military power and gained victories over the Hittites and Babylonians. From 900 BCE to 612 BCE they were the dominant empire in the Fertile Crescent. In 612 a coalition of armies from peoples who had been under Assyrian rule revolted and destroyed Nineveh, the capital of Assyria. This included the Medes of Northern Persia and the Babylonians in the lower Mesopotamian valley. Just seven years later, in 605, at the battle of Carchemish, the Babylonian army defeated the army of Egypt allied with the remnants of the Assyrian army. Babylonia's reappearance as an empire, however, was short lived. In 549 BCE, Cyrus, who had defeated the Medes and unified Persia, conquered Babylonia.

The final written version of the epic was not completed until around 550 BCE by priests who had been forced to live in Babylon after Jerusalem was conquered and destroyed by the Babylonians. As we shall see, these priests edited and merged the two written versions of the epic they had brought with them from Jerusalem. They also added material borrowed from Babylonian creation myths and they gave a Hebrew take on the presence of towers celebrating military victories by Babylonian kings. The two earlier versions of the epic basically tell the same story with slight, but important variations. The earliest written version of the epic appeared during Solomon's reign as king. It seems to be aimed at achieving two purposes. First, it praises and legitimates the reigns of David and Solomon by telling a story about everything in Hebrew history pointing to the establishment of their empire as the final product of their worship of their god, Yahweh. Second, it is a reminder to David, Solomon, their royal entourage, and temple priests that they are not to think of this achievement as something for which they can take credit. It is not David, Solomon, Jerusalem, and the temple that should be worshipped but rather their god, Yahweh.

The second written version of the epic was composed over a hundred years later after Solomon's empire was divided into Israel and Judah. It was written in Israel whose ten tribes never wanted to be a part of a unified nation with a capital and central temple in Jerusalem. It is written by local priests who did not look fondly on the effort of Jerusalem temple priests to delegitimize all priests outside their circle. It does not treat Moses as a mighty leader, a forerunner of a king like David or Solomon. It treats Moses more as a priest than a king. It includes the story of Jacob being willing to sacrifice his son if it was necessary to be a loyal worshiper of Yahweh. This is not found in the other written version. In this second version of the epic, it is emphasized that nothing other than Yahweh is sacred, not David's throne nor the Jerusalem temple and its temple priests.

German scholars in the 19th Century discovered the need to conclude that there were these two written versions of the epic. They named the Jerusalem version 'J' because God in this version was always addressed as Yahweh (in German, 'Jehovah'). They named the northern, Israeli version 'E' because the common noun used to refer to a god 'Elohim' was used to name their God. These scholars found that many persons and locations bore different names in the two versions: Abram vs. Abraham, Sarai vs Sarah, Horeb vs. Sinai. They concluded that hundreds of years after the writing of these two versions of the epic, the priests exiled to Babylon by the Babylonians added stories claiming that one set of names had been changed from an earlier set.

Let we turn the podium back to Professor Hamann. I hope this historical background will help you understand the big religious truths that this piece of epic literature has to say and show.

Thank you, Professor Hill. Now Ms. Steinbeck is going to tell us a short version of the story found in the J version of the epic, as put into modern English by Harold Bloom.

Thank you, Professor Hamann.

Before I tell you J's version of the epic, let me raise a warning flag. You can't just open your Bible and find J there. After Assyria destroyed Israel, the E version was brought to Jerusalem. Priests there combined them together without changing much in them. After the Babylonians destroyed Jerusalem and forced the Hebrews into exile in the city of Babylon, priestly editors there edited the J/E document they brought with them from Jerusalem. They provided stories about how names appearing in J changed to the names appearing in E. They added new materials. Professor Bloom drew upon decades of research by Biblical scholars to pull out of P's final version of the epic the version called J. I am going to follow his outline of the epic, but I will put things in my own words and give an abbreviated version of the epic. I trust that these are words that will help you understand the great truths being expressed in this Biblical epic.

At a time when there were not yet any living things or any earth on which things could grow, Yahweh made the heavens and the earth. A mist rose from under the earth, moistened the land, and it became a garden filled with fruit bearing trees. Yahweh then took a lump of moistened dirt, shaped it into a flesh and blood man, gave it life, and placed it in the garden where he could live by gathering the fruit from the trees. Yahweh saw that man was lonely, living all by himself, and so Yahweh again took wettened soil and surrounded man with a world of animals and birds. Living with animals and gathering fruit was still not enough for man, and so Yahweh, thinking that the problem was man's loneliness, took a rib from the man and made a woman. From then on, for the Hebrews, it became a tradition that men and women leave their parents and become one flesh in marriage.

Yahweh told Adam and Adam told Eve that they must not try to become Gods by eating from the tree of knowledge of good and evil and by thinking that in this way they could be the final authority on how they should live with nature, with other animals, and with other people. Instead of gratefully accepting everything as a gift for which they should be thankful, Adam ate from the forbidden fruit, thereby rejecting any Lordship over him by anything other than himself and his personally chosen laws. The results were disastrous. Adam and Hava (Eve) lost their free and happy existence in a world of animals and nutritious fruit. Eve, no longer giving birth like most animals did without noticeable pain, now you will have to go through painful hours of labor. Adam could no longer live simply by gathering fruit. He must become a farmer working hard and long hours, slaves to cycles of planting and harvesting and to floods and droughts. Eve, giving birth to new life just as the plants and animals did, once had a close relationship to animals. This was lost as some of them (snakes) became threats to her and others became creatures threatened by her as she domesticated them. Furthermore, leaving animal life in the garden of Eden, the paradise they could have had is lost forever. Now they must live in a world of people, who, like the two of them, make rules governing human behavior. Animals feel no need to wear clothes governing their nakedness, but now they will be forced to deal with feelings of shame when they know that others know they have violated their customs and rules. Even worse, rather than living like the other animals who do not worry about returning to dust upon death, eating from the tree of knowledge of good and evil forces them to know about the immortality that is the fruit on the tree of life and also to know that immortality is reserved for the gods and it never will be humanity's possession no matter how much people painfully desire it. The bottom line big truth is that people rebel against Yahweh and disaster follows.

The epic continues. Yahweh was almost ready to give up on humans. Perhaps life itself should not have been created. Yahweh decided, however, to try one more time. It is as if God concluded that if there is even one innocent person who does not crave to be God, but is willing to gratefully let God be God, then all of life will be significant. For that one person, life itself is accepted as a gift to be cherished and not something to be used by people making themselves the center of all significance. If life in all its forms is not cherished, then it is as good is dead. If even one person accepts humanity's place, then life remans significant. Yahweh found Noah innocent of the sin of hubris, self-worship. Life went on.

Noah accepted the assignment to save every form of life from annihilation in insignificance by building a life-preserving ark that would not be destroyed by the flood that rebellious people have caused Yahweh to rain upon the earth. His family and seven pairs of every living thing, all respected and cherished by Noah, were brought into the arc. All the forms of life, that were treated as mere materials to be used to satisfy the desires of worshippers of themselves, would die under the flood of judgement caused by Yahweh. After sending out a dove three times so that Noah could learn whether dry land was near, it did not come back the third time. Noah disembarked and built an alter thanking Yahweh for permitting the experiment of life to begin again. This time, Noah heard the promise from Yahweh that never again would life itself be drowned in meaninglessness or insignificance. Even if most humans rebel again, their treatment of life as insignificant will not cause life to lose its significance, even if it is the hard life of farmers. Noah heard Yahweh make this promise and the rainbow sealed the promise.

The epic then leaps from the primordial time of Adam and Noah to the historical time of Abram. Abram was the leader of a tribe of wanderers, people who were not residents in any city. They treated the area around the City of Ur near the mouth of the Tigress-Euphrates rivers as their home base. Abram and his tribe found a unique identity as a people by becoming a Yahweh worshipping group of people. Abram made a contract (covenant) with the God they worshipped (Yahweh). They promised to worship only Yahweh and they heard their God promise that they would become a mighty nation ruling everything from the Tigress-Euphrates to the Nile.

Under the leadership of Abram and his nephew, Lot, these wanderers left Ur, traveled north to Haran, west to the coastline, and then south to Shechem and Beth El where they made alters to worship Yahweh. Their trip was inspired by Abram's hearing Yahweh's instruction to leave Ur and travel through the lands that had been promised to him. Abram tried to continue down into Egypt, but the Pharaoh chased them out when he found out that Abram had foolishly tried to protect himself and his wife by deceiving the Pharaoh by saying that Abram's wife, Sarai, whom the Pharaoh had taken into his palace, was his sister.

Abram returned to Beth El and he and Lot began living as shepherds. They began quarreling with each other over grazing rights, thus weakening their ability to fend off the threats of the Canaanites also living in that area. They decided to separate. Lot chose to move north into the lush Jordan valley while Abram moved into the hill country and settled at Hebron.

Abram was unhappy that he and his wife, Sarai, had no children of their own and thus he would have no heir to inherit Yahweh's promise that his tribe would become a great nation. Sarai agreed to let Abram have a child by her maid, the Egyptian Hagar. When Hagar started treating Sarai as her inferior, Sarai chased her out. Hagar eventually gave birth to a son, Ishmael, who had many offspring, as stubborn as he was, who ended up in conflict with each other.

One day Abram escorted down the road a group of strangers who had visited their house and predicted that Sarai would give birth to a child even though she was very old. The strangers were going to Sodom where Lot had settled. Abram was going to show them the way. While walking, Abram felt the presence of Yahweh within himself. He was pleased to hear again that, as a worshiper of Yahweh, his household would desire to worship Yahweh and would be committed to tolerance and justice. Abram grew anxious as they approached Sodom and Gomorrah, because he knew that the people of Sodom held in contempt the worship of Yahweh. He had heard compassionate Yahweh's reassuring word to his household, but he was unsure whether Yahweh, the just God with knowledge of good and evil, would show tolerance to the contemptuous people of Sodom and Gomorrah or instead would punish them as people in Noah's age were punished. In his inner debate with Yahweh, Abram appealed to Yahweh's spirit of tolerance and his compassion for the innocents living in the two cities. Abram heard Yahweh saying that he would spare the cities if there were 50, 45, 40, 30, 20, or even 10 innocent people living there. With Noah, it had taken only one. Satisfied that Yahweh truly was a God of justice, Abram turned around and started to go back home.

Lot, living near Sodom, saw the two visitors who had traveled with Abram as Angels of Yahweh. He urged them to stay with him. When the townspeople demanded to see these visitors so that they could show their contempt for Yahweh worshippers, Lot tried to buy the villagers off by offering to them his two daughters. They were insistent, however, on getting to the visitors whom they thought wanted to push the law of the god Yahweh on them even though they did not want to worship that god. The townspeople failed in their effort to force their way into Lot's home, He and his family escaped to the mountains, even though the people there also had contempt for Yahweh. Lot chose to live in a cave near a small village. He thought that these villagers would never bother him, even though they also were haters of Yahweh. His wife, however, lamented losing the good life she had enjoyed in the luscious Jordon Valley, even though the people there were contemptuous of Yahweh worship. She wanted to go back. Her desire made it impossible for her to be a worshipper of Yahweh. She became crystallized, as if she now were a salt statue. A volcano erupted and buried Sodom and Gomorrah. Abram wondered whether God were punishing the two cities, given that not even one person there worshipped Yahweh.

The effects of having lived in the Jordon valley continued to contaminate Lot's family. Lot's daughters, living with him in a cave, had no men around with whom they could have children. They got Lot drunk and slept with him. They each had sons who eventually fathered the two tribes, the Moabites and the Ammonites.

Abram saw the results of the volcanic destruction that that leveled the Jordon Valley. He returned home. There finally he and his wife in their old age gave birth to a son, Isaac. Abram became worried in his old age about whom his son could marry, He did not want Isaac to marry a Canaanite woman who would not be a worshipper of Yahweh. He sent his most senior servant back to Haran in northern Mesopotamia where some of Abram's kinfolk still lived. The servant found Rebecca, the granddaughter of Abram's brother, Nachor. She agreed to go back with the servant and there she was married to Isaac. Abram gave everything he had to Isaac, who became head of the tribe after Abram died.

Rebecca became pregnant with a pair of twins who seemed to be already fighting with each other inside her womb. The first to be born was Esau who became a hunter; he was the favorite of Isaac. The second was Jacob who became the keeper of the tents; he was the favorite of Rebecca. One day, Esau came home exhausted from hunting and was so hungry that, to get some of the food Jacob had cooked, sold to Jacob his birthright to be Isaac's heir.

Later, when a famine hit the land where Isaac lived, he moved his family and sheep into a Philistine area named 'Gerar'. Fearful that Philistines might kill him to get at his wife, Rebecca, he told them she was his sister. When Abimelech, head of the Philistines, heard about this deception, he was angry with Isaac because it was a serious crime to sleep with another man's wife even if it is done unknowingly. Thinking Rebecca was Isaac's sister, they might have done so. At first, Abimelech let Isaac stay and he gave an order that no man was to touch Rebecca. When Isaac became a very prosperous farmer and herder of sheep and cattle, Abimelech saw Isaac as a threat and ordered him to leave. Isaac stayed in the Gerar Valley but moved a little south. When Gerar shepherds quarreled with Isaac's shepherds over water rights, Isaac moved further south to Beersheba, where his shepherds dug a well and he built an altar at which to give thanks to Yahweh.

As Isaac approached death, Rebecca urged her favorite son, Jacob, to gain from Isaac himself his blessing to be the next head of their tribe. Jacob put animal skins on, so that to nearly blind Isaac, he would feel like Esau. Isaac put his blessing on Jacob. Esau was furious.

Taking Rebecca's advice, Jacob fled north to her hometown, Haran. Jacob saw Rachel, the daughter of Laban, the granddaughter of his father's brother, Nachor, and the cousin of Rebecca. Jacob agreed to work for Laban for seven years so that he could marry Rachel. At the end of the seven years, Laban tricked him into thinking he was spending his wedding night with Rachel when in fact Laban had snuck in Leah, Rachel's older sister, whom custom said should be married before the younger sister. Jacob was angry about being tricked, but after listening to Laban explain the custom about elder sisters marrying first, agreed with Laban to spend one week with Leah after which he finally would marry Rachel. He worked another seven years for his father-in-law, Laban. Between the two women, Jacob had many children. Leah gave birth to Reuben, Simon, Levi, and Judah. Rachel gave birth to Joseph, who would be Jacob's favorite.

Jacob decided to leave Haran and journey back down south to join his father, Isaac, in Beersheba. Laban tried to keep them at Haran, claiming that Rachel had stolen their household gods. She had, but she sat on them when her father searched for them. Jacob, inflamed by Laban's chase after them, continued the trip south. He heard that his brother Leah was up ahead with 500 of his men. One night, sneaking south, he met an unknown man who wrestled with him demanding that Jacob give him his blessing. Jacob refused to do so and the man broke Jacob's hip. The man also said that from now on Jacob would not be known as Jacob but as Israel (god-clutcher). When he saw Esau and his men ahead of him, fearing the worst, he prostrated himself before Esau seven times. Esau did not harm him but embraced him. He had no desire any longer to challenge Jacob's blessing from Isaac.

Jacob's older sons hated their youngest brother, Joseph, because he was his father's favorite and because he always told their father everything they were doing. They detested the many-colored coat Jacob had given Joseph and they resented the fact that Jacob always was pleased when Joseph gave interpretations of his dreams. They decided to kill Joseph by throwing him down a well and telling their father that a wild animal had eaten Joseph.

Joseph survived, however. Some Midianite merchants found Joseph and drew him out of the well. They in turn sold him to Ishmaelites leading a caravan of merchandise loaded camels down to Egypt. In Egypt Joseph was sold again, this time to a Lord who eventually made Joseph the superintendent of his affairs because Joseph helped make him very rich. Eventually, however, the Egyptian Lord threw Joseph in jail because he believed his wife when she charged Joseph with rape when Joseph would not succumb to her attempt to seduce him. Joseph soon was made the head supervisor of all the prison inmates.

One day the pharaoh had a very disturbing dream which none of his aids could interpret. His head waiter told the pharaoh about the prisoner, Joseph, who had become famous in prison for interpreting dreams. Joseph was brought to the pharaoh who told Joseph of his dream of seven healthy cows coming up out of the river followed by seven emaciated cows. Joseph interpreted the dream as a prediction that there would be seven years with great harvests to be followed by seven years of famine. He advised the pharaoh to prepare to save up food during the fat years so that there would be food to eat during the lean years. The pharaoh put Joseph in charge of all food production, preservation, and distribution. When the drought hit Egypt and all the surrounding areas, everyone came to Joseph asking for food.

The drought also hit the area where Jacob and his sons lived. He heard about food reserves in Egypt and sent all his sons except Benjamin to Egypt to buy food. Benjamin, like Joseph, was the son of Rebecca. The brothers went to Egypt, and not recognizing Joseph, begged for the right to buy food. He gave them food and hid in their bag the money they had paid him for the food. When the purchased food ran out and the famine continued, Jacob sent the brothers back to Egypt to buy more food. The brothers told Jacob that the man in charge of Egypt's food reserves required them to bring Benjamin along with them this time. They did not know how he knew about Benjamin. At first Jacob refused to let Benjamin go because he thought he was the only one of Rebecca's sons still alive, but he changed his mind when one of the older sons, Judah, promise to protect Benjamin.

When Joseph saw Benjamin, his own mother' son, he revealed himself to his brothers and told them to go back and bring his father, Jacob, to Egypt. He told them to live as herders of livestock because the pharaoh hated shepherds. Jacob died there in Egypt, but Joseph buried him at Goren where Sarai also had been buried. In time, Joseph, his brothers, and their whole generation died in Egypt. Their descendants, however, multiplied and became wealthy and powerful.

Eventually, a pharaoh arose who did not know Joseph and who feared the rising power of Joseph's offspring. He ordered that all their newborn sons be killed by throwing them in the river and that everyone else be enslaved. One Levite woman attempted to save her son by putting him in a papyrus crib and placing him in a river to flow downstream. A daughter of the pharaoh saw the baby, took him out of the river, and raised him as her own. She named him Moses.

When Moses grew into manhood, he learned that he was a descendent of the Hebrew ancestors: Jacob, Isaac, and Abram. He sensed the injustice of the Egyptian enslavement of his kinsmen. He killed one Egyptian who had beaten to death one of the Hebrews and he had to flee East before the pharaoh could kill him. He settled in the land of the Midianites, the very people who had pulled Joseph out of the well and sold him into slavery. Moses married the daughter of one of the Midianite priests who worshipped a god they called 'Yahweh'. Moses worked for his father-in-law as a shepherd.

One day when he was guiding his sheep past the Midianite's holy mountain, he sensed the presence of God in a bush on the mountain that seemed to be burning but was never turned to ashes. He heard him being called to recognize that he was standing on sacred ground. He sensed that this God shared his opposition to the injustice that the Hebrew slaves in Egypt were experienced. He heard a call to be an instrument of God's desire to liberate the Hebrews in Egypt and to lead them in an exodus from Egypt. His earlier anger over the unjust treatment of Hebrews now became a mission to liberate them. Justice demanded no less.

Moses was not sure that he could do what this godly voice of justice called him to do. First, how could he get pharaoh to let his people go? Eventually, Moses persuaded himself that pharaoh in the end would let his people exit Egypt, even though he did not know what would persuade him to do so. Second, he asked how he could get the Hebrews to accept his leadership? Why should they trust his belief that the God talking to him in Midian had the authority to appoint him as their leader? Moses, knowing that he was a Hebrew, heard the God, Yahweh. speaking to him on the holy mountain of the Midianites, tell him that he, Yahweh, was not just a god of the Midianites. He in fact was the God of the Hebrews, the God of the fathers - Abram, Isaac, and Jacob. He was told that he should say to the Hebrews that their god, now to be named Yahweh, was commanding him to serve as their leader. Moses accepted his assignment, and as a sign of his commitment to the Hebrews, he had his Midianite son circumcised.

The pharaoh who had wanted to kill Moses had died and so Moses approached the new pharaoh, who ridiculed Moses' request to let his valued slaves go free. Then one disaster after another hit Egypt. Fish in the Nile died, and the river's waters could not be drunk. Frogs left the Nile and were found in every house and field in Egypt, and when they died their terrible smell penetrated everything. Droves of flies descended on the dead frogs and all the Egyptians. The flies brought a plague that killed off Egypt's livestock. A hailstorm killed off all plant life. Locusts descended to finish off any vegetation that survived the hailstorm. Every time that a natural disaster hit Egypt, the pharaoh promised Moses that the Hebrews could leave Egypt, but then, when the disaster ended, he changed his mind. One final disaster caused the pharaoh to finally grant permission for the Hebrew to leave. All the young Egyptian boys began to get sick and die from the plague that hit Egypt. The Hebrews immunized their children, by placing a mixture of blood and marjoram on the lintel and door posts of their homes. Having been granted permission to leave, the Hebrews hurried to get out of Egypt before the pharaoh changed his mind again. They grabbed the bread that was still unleavened and hurried East to get across the Nile.

The pharaoh did change his mind and he had his army mount chariots and chase the Hebrews. The Hebrews were heading for the desert beyond the Nile, keeping an eye on the pillar of dust ahead of them during the day which became a pillar of fire in the light of the moon at night. The Hebrews went East along the dry shoreline of the Reed Sea, but, by the time the Egyptian chariots got there, water blown by a Westerly wind turned the shoreline into mud, trapping the wheels of the chariots and killing Egyptian soldiers who could not escape the wall of water being blown at them.

Escaping Egypt, Moses gave thanks to Yahweh for the Exodus. He and the Hebrews who worshipped with him knew that they now were free not because of anything for which they could claim credit. They sang with hearts overflowing with gratitude about Egyptian drivers and chariots overturned on the shores of the Reed Sea.

Moving east beyond the Nile into the desert that separated them from the lands from which Jacob had come, many of the exiles grumbled about the lack of water, the lack of meat or fish, and the powerful peoples already living in Canaan whom they would have to forcibly displace if the Hebrews were to have a place to live and thus fulfill the promise made to Abram, Isaac, and Jacob. Moses tried his best to forge them into a common people unified by their loyal worship of Yahweh, the God of their fathers. At Mount Sinai, Moses again felt the presence of Yahweh as he had at the holy mountain in Midian. He took his brother, Aaron, two of Aaron's sons, and seventy of Israel's elders to experience the holiness of Mount Sinai and to pledge loyalty to Yahweh and all the laws that Moses heard Yahweh requiring of his people. They were to serve as the priests who would preserve the boundary between mortal Hebrews and imageless Yahweh. Seeking to execute Yahweh's will, Moses carried two stone tablets to the summit of Mount Sinai on which could be engraved the laws governing the lives of those worshipping only Yahweh. Moses and the spirit of Yahweh made a new covenant with each other, a covenant that now applied the covenant with Abram to the Israelites saved out of Egypt.

Moses spend a long time on Mount Sinai absorbing in his heart the living presence of Yahweh. When he came down from the mountain, he found the exiles from Egypt worshipping the golden calf which was the icon of the God of fertility. Moses chastised Aaron for letting this happen. After learning from scouts that they were near to the land promised to Abram, Isaac, and Jacob, a land of milk and honey but already settled by powerful Canaanites, Moses knew that they were not ready yet to enter the promised land. Some wanted to replace Moses with a leader who would take them back to Egypt. Some were marrying women from the area of Moab where they now were residing, and they were worshipping the gods of the Moabites. Although Moses felt that Yahweh would be tempted to destroy all of them, as he did in Noah's age, Moses, striving to obey the call of Yahweh to build a faithful community out of the exiles from Egypt, decided to do what would fulfill Yahweh's will. He would stay with the exiles in the wilderness for a long time (forty years) until the generation who once lived in Egypt had died off and a new generation nurtured by Moses to worship Yahweh had replaced them. He would also stay in the wilderness until he died. He would transfer leadership of the

Israelites to his young nephew, Joshua, who, unlike Aaron, always had been faithful to Moses and Yahweh. Moses died and was buried in Moab, but no one knows where his grave is. This is where the story in J ends.

Than you, Beverly. A marvelous telling of a marvelous epic. J, of course, is just the Jerusalem version of the epic. The Northern E version, however, is very similar to the Southern J version, with one major exception. Reflecting the North's opposition to the monarchy of David and Solomon, they included in their version of the epic a story accenting that nothing that humans might proudly point to as their creation should be considered more important than faithfully worshipping Yahweh. No king, temple, or centralized empire government in Jerusalem ever must be allowed to be a graven image. In the story that E included in their version of the epic, E shows that faithfulness to Yahweh must even take precedence over obedience to human laws and customs such as the prohibitions against murder and human sacrifice and the cherishing of the life of one's son, even a son a whole tribe depends upon in order to live on in the future, even a son needed for the continuity of a community worshipping Yahweh. The story tells of Abram hearing Yahweh challenging him to be faithful to Yahweh even if it means the sacrifice of his son, Isaac. Abram shows how to respond to the dilemma that all worshippers of Yahweh face. On the one hand, Yahweh can be one's God only if loyalty to Yahweh takes precedence over everything else. On the other hand, Yahweh is one's God of worship only if Yahweh is seen as just and loving. Abram shows his faithfulness to Yahweh by his willingness to sacrifice his son. He shows his faith in Yahweh as a God of justice and love by trusting that innocent Isaac will not be sacrificed and that his descendants will live as a worshipping community so long as they remain faithful and full of faith.

J plus E still does not give us the written epic as it appears in the Bible. To appreciate the final written version of the epic one needs to examine what priests in Babylon, after their exile from Jerusalem by the Babylonians, did to the epic, hundreds of years after J and E were written. They edited the text to remove discrepancies between the two versions of the epic. They wrote two prologues to the written text of J/ E that they had brought with them from Jerusalem. I have asked one of my graduate students, Archebold Rilling, to tell us what the worshipping community of priests in Babylon was like and how their reaction to the destruction of Jerusalem and its temple influenced their editing of the epic and their adding of two prologues.

Thank you, Professor Hamann.

First, let me say something about what it meant to the priests in Babylon to worship Yahweh now that Jerusalem and the temple had been destroyed, what it meant to worship Yahweh in a foreign land, what kind of new covenant they formed with Yahweh. Second, let me try to explain why their new faith is really an extension of their old faith. It just had been given new life. The priests infused that new life into the old texts they brought with them from their old homeland. They studied those old texts, interpreted them, edited them, correlated and unified them. They brought with them the two written versions of the epic that Hebrews had used to define themselves as a people. Finally, let me try to interpret what they probably intended when they added to the epic a prologue based on old Mesopotamian creation myths.

Let me begin by considering the impact of the destruction of Jerusalem and its temple on their understanding of their worship of Yahweh. They knew that Yahweh is for them their only God. It was Yahweh and only Yahweh that they worshipped in thought, feeling, and deed. The faithful worshippers of Yahweh knew that they can be who they are as a people only because they never served any god other than Yahweh. Now in Babylon they became convinced of something else, something they felt called to proclaim to the whole world. "**Our God is the only God; there is no other god but Yahweh.**"

For many generations, ever since the time of Moses, they had named their God "Yahweh." It is true that there were earlier times when their founding fathers used other names, such as "El Shaddai." As Moses pointed out, however, names are not what matter. The god of their ancient fathers (Abraham, Isaac, and Jacob) is the same God that Moses told the Hebrews to worship under the new name, "Yahweh." It is true that J and E had characters in their epic use the name 'Yahweh' before Moses did, but they made it clear that it was Moses who took the name of the Midianite god, 'Yahweh' and declared that it was just another name for the God of the fathers.

Other people in Canaan, Assyria, and Babylonia gave different names to what they worshipped. They believed there were many gods. Sometimes, they worshipped only the one god they saw as the supreme king over the other gods. Sometimes they worshipped different gods at the same time, a god of fertility or a god of war, thereby treating as sacred what they prized and depended upon so completely. They did not believe that there is only one god to worship. Different names led them to think that there are different gods. Often, their tribal hubris led them to think that there was one god in particular who was their god, protecting them in their way of life, against all foreign enemies. Many of the Hebrew prophets warned against treating Yahweh as such a protector guaranteeing that Israel and Judah never would be conquered by foreign nations. The priests in Babylon knew that many of the kings and popular prophets in Israel and Judah were mistaken when they proclaimed that Yahweh would protect them from military defeat. Religious tribalism was so strong that the Hebrews and the nations around them, who thought that almighty God was their special god, often described the military battles between their cities and nations as battles between these gods. Many Hebrews did not understand that Yahweh does not play favorites. Yahweh, of whom no graven image can be made, is the one God that all people need to worship to live well.

The journey that the exiles in Babylon had to take to come to this new understanding was painful, but this pain allowed them to learn that they now must live with a new spirit, understanding in a new way the significance of their travels with Yahweh. They knew that they needed to form with Yahweh a new covenant in which they understood in a new way the blessings from Yahweh that are to fill them with gratitude and the mission that they are now mandated to carry out in Yahweh's name. Their new spirit allowed them to understand that the suffering they experienced, as Israel and Judah were destroyed and as they were scattered throughout the world, did not make their existence meaningless. Rather it made their lives even more meaningful by giving a new point and purpose to their existence as worshippers of Yahweh.

I think it will help us all if I rehearse again the story of the birth of the new spirit and the goal at which their worship of Yahweh aimed them. I ask all of you to imagine that I am an exiled priest in Babylon telling the faithful with me in exile what that spirit and goal is.

The priest speaks.

"We all know that we are not in Jerusalem anymore. We all know also that although we have no temple here we still have continued to worship Yahweh. We know now that we can worship God no matter where we are. We didn't, but we should have, understood what Moses meant when he said we should not worship any graven idol. Every idol is a graven idol. Every idol is something tangible. That is not Yahweh. Yahweh is not tangible, located at some specific place. We can worship Yahweh anywhere. Yahweh is fully present to us wherever we are. Yahweh is fully present to be worshipped wherever any people are, no matter what name they give to God.

"Since the time of our ancient ancestors, we have defined ourselves as God's chosen people, chosen to receive uniquely God's blessings and do God's will. Now we understand that we have a different kind of uniqueness. We understand that all people are unique in Yahweh's eyes. We falsely thought that we were chosen uniquely to escape slavery in Egypt, conquer Canaan, establish Solomon's empire, and be protected from the power of Assyria, Egypt, and Babylonia. For us here in captivity in Babylon, it doesn't make sense anymore to think of our God, Yahweh, as being a more powerful warrior than the gods of these other empires. Now we understand that God must be almighty, to us who worship Yahweh, in some other way, in a way that lets God be the God of all people.

"In worshipping Yahweh as the creator of heaven and earth, we acknowledge that we are not masters of all things. We gratefully accept as undeserved blessings the existence of the world around us and our own existence. In gratefully receiving these blessings we praise the goodness of God and the goodness of these blessings which guarantee that life itself is good and that goodness lies within ourselves no matter how much we live as our own worst enemies. We never can be the masters over nature, which, in our worship, we affirm when we proclaim that God has ordered things so that sun shines on the good and bad, the planting and the harvesting, the gentile rain and the devastating floods, the banquets and the droughts, the beautiful, strong dancers and the lepers, the births and deaths.

"Neither are we almighty masters who determine what is just and unjust. In worshipping Yahweh, we acknowledge God as our rightful, almighty judge. By worshiping Yahweh, as the almighty sovereign of justice before whose bar of justice all other social and political rules and laws are to be judged, we affirm that goodness and justice in Jerusalem is not different from what it is here in Babylon. There is one God and one justice, although the requirements not to harm people and to help people in need may make different specific demands in different locales. Finally, our God is not just the creator of nature, including our nature, and the judge of all people, but he also is the God who loves all people, forgives all, and gives us the mission of saving all people from their hubris and ignorance.

"In worshipping Yahweh as Almighty, we recognize that we do not have the power to destroy the goodness that lies deep within us. We thankfully accept the fact that our goodness cannot be destroyed no matter what we do. Our almighty God has the power to save us, despite what we do to ourselves. Yahweh is a God of love and mercy. No matter how corrupt we and those round us may have become, we always retain the ability to forgive ourselves and each other. We remember the evil we have done and that has been done to us, but we remember it as forgivable and forgiven. By forgiving others we free ourselves from the anger and resentment that would continuously chain us to past pain and would grow and dominate our future. Forgiving ourselves enables us to journey to future gardens flowing with spiritual milk and honey, and to a place where we can do, in our specific way, the will of God in carrying out Yahweh's ultimate purpose, having all people worship God. Only in such a life of worshipping Yahweh can we avoid always being unfaithful to ourselves and each other.

"Here in Babylon there are some writers who have written a series of poems that set forth in magnificent, inspiring language how we Hebrews are to understand what has happened to us and how we are to respond as a community still worshipping Yahweh. Using their poetic imagination in beautiful and powerful ways, they express what they have heard Yahweh say to them here and now in Babylon. They have not put any name on their collection of poems but have offered them to us as a gift that Yahweh inspired them to write. Some of these poets are members of the community of prophets that has continued to exist since Isaiah first founded it two hundred and fifty years ago. Perhaps it should just be added to Isaiah's original prophetic writing.

"The poets begin by giving a voice to Yahweh who can still speak to us, even though our Jerusalem temple is destroyed, and we are captives in this land that we once called a wilderness far from our homes. Yahweh's voice proclaims to us that here in Babylon, here with us, a new thing has begun. A whole new way of life is being born in this wilderness. We are not to let ourselves be made impotent and miserable by thinking only about what we have lost and how terrible it is to live in captivity. Without pretending that it doesn't hurt, worshippers of Yahweh now can find comfort in the fact that a new door has been opened for us, a new covenant will be made between us and Yahweh that will give new meaning and purpose to our lives as worshipers of Yahweh. We are about to begin the greatest adventure of our lives, helping to make something happen that is more important than anything we have ever done before. All the suffering that we have experienced in losing our land and our temple will be the spiritual flame that enables us to carry out successfully the new mission now being given to us.

"The covenant will be new, and the mission will be new. Back before the Babylonians conquered Jerusalem, the prophet Jeremiah told us that we needed to change the kind of covenant we have with Yahweh. It is not merely a contract between Yahweh and some tribe, empire or nation, that was re-enacted on festival days. It is a covenant that is to live in our hearts, in our attitudes towards the worlds in which we live and towards ourselves, in our dispositions to behave in ways showing our faithfulness to Yahweh's goodness and justice. Jeremiah rejected the understanding of the contractual mandates expressed by the popular prophets he condemned, popular because they echoed what most people wanted the covenant to mean. Jeremiah called for people to get Yahweh out of the game of militarily protecting one nation warring with another nation. These new poets of the exile are saying the same thing. Israel was not destroyed by the Assyrians and Judah was not destroyed by the Babylonians because Yahweh failed to live up to his half of the contract that we Hebrew made with Yahweh. They were destroyed because they were militarily weak nations warring against mighty empires. Yahweh did not fail us. We failed Yahweh by ceasing to see ourselves as a worshipping community and by choosing to live instead as a political nation engaged in geo-political power politics.

"In order to be Yahweh's instrument for inaugurating a new way of life where Yahweh rules as Almighty God, our poets tell us that we must understand what Yahweh is and is not like, and in what sense he is Almighty God. They proclaim that Yahweh is not one god among many gods. Yahweh is the everlasting God, the creator of the ends of the earth. Yahweh sits above the circle of the earth. Yahweh forms light and creates darkness. Yahweh is a righteous god and savior. Yahweh is the first and the last and beside Yahweh there is no other god. It is a huge mistake to say that Yahweh is like this or like that while the other gods are different and greater or lesser. There are no other gods to whom Yahweh can be compared. There are only idols made by workmen. Divine glory is to be given only to Yahweh. Besides Yahweh there is no other savior. Yahweh is not like anything in the created world and no idol made by workmen can be compared to Yahweh.

"Whether the peoples of the world know it or not, all genuine worship is of Yahweh only. Yahweh is the god of all people and places. We have learned that almighty Yahweh cannot be compared to a warrior god protecting some little nation. Yahweh's might must be of a different sort. Were Yahweh a warrior god, we would have to say that Murdock, the god of the Babylonians, was mightier than Yahweh since the Babylonian empire that Murdock supposedly protected defeated our nation. No, Yahweh has a different kind of power. Yahweh's power shows itself in people who, even though they are living self-destructive lives, are drawn to worship him in spirit and action. Sensing the presence of a loving God, they are saved from what they have made of themselves, saved for living joyfully and justly in a good world, and saved to be Yahweh's servant in bringing such salvation to all the people of the world. Yahweh's power is the power of a shepherd who cares for his flock, especially when, being frightened, they endanger themselves.

"These new poets proclaim that faithful worship of Yahweh mandates that we be a light to all nations, to open the eyes of the blind, and to bring out of prison those who sit in spiritual darkness. In the old days we usually thought that being faithful in our worship of Yahweh was a matter of living well as a people especially blest by Yahweh. Now in this day when everything is new, living well means living as Yahweh's servant bringing salvation to all people. Some of us Hebrews in Babylon still think that Yahweh will once again raise up the tribes of Jacob and restore a preserved Israel. We and these new poets now know that this is too light a thing for Yahweh and the worshippers of Yahweh to do. In this age and way of life in which everything is new, we are to serve so that Yahweh can bring salvation to the ends of the world. We are called to bring good tidings, publish peace and salvation to all the people of the world. As the poets put it, how beautiful upon the mountains are the feet of Yahweh's faithful servants who do this.

"In the past we were mistaken. We thought we would be doing Yahweh's will, and showing forth our God's glory and might, if we, as contractual partners with Yahweh, gained mighty victories in escaping from Egypt, conquering the Canaanites, and building a mighty empire. The destruction of Israel and Jerusalem shows that we were wrong. It is our very loss and suffering, however, that enables us to bring good tidings to all people, not just our own. In a sense we died when our Jerusalem and our temple died, but now worshipping Yahweh in a new way gives to us a new spiritual way of life that cannot be destroyed by any foreign armies. It gives us the most important mission for which any person could hope. This mission gives meaning and significance to our lives, despite what has been done to us. By proclaiming that our just and loving Yahweh is the creator of everything and everyone, we make it possible for all people to unite themselves as worshippers of the one and only God there is, celebrating life, despite anything that happens to us."

The Hebrew priests in Babylon editing J and E understood what these poets were saying. They knew that something new had arisen among them. They also know, however, that nothing is created out of nothing. What was then coming alive with them was the flowering of seeds that were planted by their Fathers centuries before. These priests were trying to preserve the many manuscripts that were written over many centuries, written even as destruction was occurring all around them when they wrote: the destruction of the empire of David and Solomon and the nations of Israel and Judah. These priests had been studying these manuscripts, striving to understand what they meant to their original writers and early readers, and what significance they still had to them now living as exiles in Babylon.

I hope that my comments here have helped you appreciate the religious atmosphere in which these protests did their editing.

Thank you Archibold. I think you are well on your way to writing your thesis. Let me add an historical note. Scholars have given a name to the poems about which Archibold was talking. They call them 'Second Isaiah' and exist in chapters 40-60 in the Book of Isaiah. They probably were written just before Persia conquered Babylonia and their king, Cyrus, permitted the Hebrews to return to Jerusalem. There also is a 'Third Isaiah', chapters 61-66, written after the Hebrews were back in Jerusalem.

In their editing of J and E, the priestly writers added short narrative material telling stories about names used in J being changed to names used in E: Abram to Abraham, Sarai to Sarah, Horeb to Sinai. A much more significant addition by these writers was their Hebrew reconstitution of Mesopotamian creation myths. Ironically, this last addition to the great Hebrew epic now appears as the first thing in the Bible, chapter one of Genesis.

In the priestly myth of creation, Elohim's creative activity is divided into six separate acts. First, with Elohim's spirit animating the primordial watery chaos, Elohim lights the chaos up so that there was day and night. Second, Elohim began the process of structuring the watery chaos by locating a primordial stuff (firmament) at the center of the chaos with water above the firmament (heaven) and water below the firmament. Third, Elohim enabled vegetation to appear on dry land. This land had existed below the waters that but now appeared, as the waters below the heavenly ferment became seas surrounding the dry earth and the heavenly ferment became a dome giving space between the heavens and the earth. Fourth, Elohim structured the heavenly ferment so that the sun, the moon, and the stars moved on the heavenly dome thus causing both day and night and the seasons. Fifth, Elohim acted so that the seas and the dry earth could bring forth living creatures: fish, animals, birds. Sixth, Elohim acted to create unique living creatures, humans who like Elohim were able to act and exercise control over the earth and all other living plants and creatures. Everything that appeared during each of Elohim's creative acts was something good because it was a product of the primordial chaos animated by Elohim's good spirit. On the seventh day, Elohim rested.

This creation myth was located by the priestly writers as the first of the four epochs into which they divided the history of the universe. They identified the age of Noah as the second epoch, the age of Abram, Isaac, and Jacob as the third, and the age of Moses as the fourth. Elohim is the name the priestly writers use in talking about events in ages one and two, El Shaddai in age three, and Yahweh in age four. The priestly writers turn to the four ages to legitimate four of their most precious ritual practices: resting to worship on the sabbath, offering sacrifices of gratitude as Noah did, circumcision as Abram did to Isaac, and the book of laws (the Torah) given to Moses.

When thinking about the great Hebrew national epic it is important to keep in mind that neither J, E, not P took the oral stories or written texts with which they worked as something that must not be altered in any way. J and E selected what stories in the oral tradition would be included. Some most likely were excluded. P edited J and E and added material to make the epic relevant to their situation in Exile.

Rev. Kennedy, let me turn the stage back to you.

Thank you, Professor Hamann. And thank you, Mr. Rilling. We will now adjourn to the lounge. I think we have several more hours before the rain bands from the hurricane hit us.

Chapter Five

Jacksonville Responds

Rev. Kennedy, may I talk to you a second before we go into the lounge?

Sure, Lydia. What's up?

Almost everything I heard today just went over my head. I really am not sure I belong here. These people are just too smart for me. I can't remember half of what the professors and their students said. I liked some of the stories. I remember hearing some stories like that. I always sent my kinds to Sunday School and sometimes when they came home they told we the stories they had been taught that day. I guess some of that stuck in my head. I try to do what I'm supposed to do. I go to church every Sunday. I had all my kinds baptized. I even talked my husband into being baptized, but he never goes to church. I listen when my preacher reads from the Bible on Sunday, but he never talks about the Bible the way today's speakers did. Do I have to know all this stuff?

No. Lydia. You don 't need to be a Biblical scholar to worship the Biblical God. The Hebrews talked about in the stories that make up the Hebrew epic weren't Biblical scholars. Most of them could not read or write. Like you, Lydia, they did the sorts of things you are doing. They participated in their religious rituals. They sang Psalms together. They tried to treat others fairly and kindly. They weren't very different from you. None of your fellow students here can remember in detail most of what they heard. Still what they do remember can help them greatly in avoiding certain kinds of confusion. I think this most likely is true of you too. Don't you wonder sometimes what preachers on radio or TV are talking about when they say that every word in the Bible is to be taken literally?

No, Reverend Kennedy, I am too busy to listen to that kind of stuff. I barely find time to read our daily paper. I find it difficult enough to get up to go to 11:00 services on Sunday, after not getting home until five in the morning from work. Besides, I know these radio preachers weren't there to see what God was doing. One good thing about coming here is that now if someone tries to force me to listen to that kind of stuff, I'll just tell them to come and join you here.

Good for you, Lydia. Now let's go into the lounge and have something hot to drink.

Folks, can I get you standing by the window to come over and take a seat on one of the chairs or couches. I hear that the bands of rain still are several hours away. You will get home safely in plenty of time. Besides, you probably already have gotten your homes ready to meet the hurricane.

O.K. Who has something to say?

Dorothy, I think you had your hand up first. So, let's begin with your question or comment.

I have more of a comment that a question. My comment may take me a bit of time to get it out.

Don't worry, Dorothy. I think we have plenty of time. It looks like people are just getting into drinking their coffee and tea.

As I said before, I was for a long time a math teacher. I deal with proofs and not with wild speculation. I was delighted to learn that different people had different creation stories and that they were not offering philosophical proofs or scientific explanations of the origin of the cosmos when they told those myths. For years I have been examining so-called proofs for the existence of God and I have found all of them to be logically unsound. I don't believe in any supernatural being or power that caused our universe to exist. Hearing analyses of Biblical myths and epics confirms for me what I already believe, that I can worship without taking these myths as proofs or scientific explanations.

Let me take a little of your time to share with you my objections to the traditional proofs of God's existence. During the break, I jotted down some notes to organize my thoughts. The old proofs all depend on misusing what we call "The Principle of Sufficient Reason." The principle has two forms and its use produces two different kinds of supposed proofs. The first form of the principle says that for everything that exists, but might not have existed, and for everything that happens, but might not have happened, there is a good and sufficient reason why it happened. Put another way, the principle says that for every contingency there is a cause that made it happen. All things existing in time, and all events occurring at a specific time, might not have existed or occurred. They are all contingent. Using the principle of sufficient reason, philosophers such as Aristotle and Aquinas tried to prove that a necessarily existent being must exist and be the ultimate cause of all contingent beings and events. All contingencies, they claimed, need a sufficient cause but if all causes were themselves continent then there would be no sufficient cause of anything. Only a non-contingent, or, in other words, a necessarily existing being, could be a sufficient cause for contingencies. They concluded, therefore, that there exists an eternal being which necessarily exists and is the cause of everything else.

Along with many other philosophers, I reject the claim that this form of the principle of sufficient reason is true. There is no necessary reason why a string of contingent causes could not continue forever in the same way that the series of negative numbers can go on forever. I have three other reasons for rejecting this form of the principle of sufficient reason, one logical, one linguistic. and one religious.

First, Aristotle and Aquinas used the principle of sufficient reason to explain continencies by claiming that assertions of such contingencies are logically deducible from the assertion that an eternal, necessary being exists and the assertion that all contingencies need a sufficient reason. Such a proof, however, would not provide an explanation of contingencies but rather would show that there are no contingencies. Everything deducible from a necessity must be a necessity. Making a necessarily existent God the cause of everything is to guarantee that everything is fated to be as it is. Aquinas, without knowing it, would then be committed to Calvin's principle of predestination and would face the objection that this would make God the cause of all the suffering in the world.

Second, missing from the minds of those presenting such an argument is any understanding of the human practice of explaining things. Not every contingency is something we need to explain. Only when some contingency surprises us do we have a reason to ask why it is so and not otherwise. When things happen in a way that we assume is generally normal for them, and when people act in the way we expect them to ask, we don't start looking for explanations, for reasons why. It is when we observe something out of the ordinary, something that conflicts with the general beliefs that govern our expectations, that we try to figure out why things are happening that way. We find a good and sufficient reason for this anomaly when we succeed in removing the conflict between our observations and our general beliefs.

Third, the very idea of such a philosophically necessary being is radically different from the idea most people have of the God they worship. The philosopher's god must be an eternal and unchanging being not affected by anything happening contingently in the world. Worshippers, however, do not believe that the God they worship is unaffected by the suffering of people in the world. They don't think their God is like the tangible things in space and time, but neither can they worship a God who is not present with them when they are in different places at different times. As we just heard, God was with Abram in Ur, Moses in Sinai, and the exiled priests in Babylon.

Let me also share with you my objections to the second form of the Principle of Sufficient Reason. The theologian Anselm and the philosopher Spinoza used this second form in their effort to prove God's existence. The second form of the principle says that not only all contingencies but also all possibilities need a sufficient reason for being possible. God for them is defined as that which is necessary for every possibility. However, they claimed, if it were possible that God did not exist, that possibility would require God to be the cause of that possibility. They argued that to even think that it is possible that God does not exist is to presuppose that God does exist. For anything to be merely possible, God must exist.

As I see it, the defect in this proof is the assumption that possibilities must be something like potentialities. I can sit here speaking only because I have the physical equipment needed for speaking and the linguistic training needed to speak. My vocal chords and acquired skills in using language give me the potentiality for saying what I do. My potentialities can exist, however, only if I exist. Spinoza assumes that all possibilities are God's potentialities and thus concludes that the possibility that God not exist cannot be one of God's potentialities. Logical possibilities, however, are not potentialities of anything. The physical possibility that a human can run a four-minute mile depends upon the person having certain muscle, lung, and heart conditions that make this something the person potentially could do. Logical possibilities, however, are not like such physical potentialities. Either they are necessarily possible, or their possibility depends on the social norms governing the use of words and sentences.

I don't believe there are any logical proofs for the existence of God.

But, Dorothy, that's not the kind of proofs that I hear creationists and evangelical fundamentalists giving. They are claiming that there is no way to explain the design of things in the world except by postulating a supernatural God who designed them and created them.

Yes, Chris, I realize that, but I wanted to share my thinking about these two kinds or arguments because I, as a mathematician, find them interesting. Although I have thought a great deal about the arguments you are talking about, I am no expert in the fields of biology or cosmology, which is what is needed to refute the creationists.

I realize, Dorothy, that you are no expert here, but we would love to hear what you have concluded after thinking about them.

O.K., Chris, let me try, if we have time for this. Do we, Reverend Kennedy?

Go for it, Dorothy.

As I understand it, there are three different kinds of design arguments for the existence of God. First, there is the classical argument that begins with the claim that the cells and organs in living things are intricately coordinated together and that the only plausible explanation for this is that they were designed this way by some intelligent creator. The Scottish philosopher, David Hume, charged that there exist many other possible explanations for this coordination. His claim did not have much impact on the popular mind. The rug was pulled out from under the argument for design when Darwin provided a physical, chemical, biological explanation for all the coordination in living things. Observable characteristics of things, he claimed, are passed on from generation to generation because the creature's DNA determines these characteristics and these DNA forms are passed on at conception from parents to their babies. Sometimes, for physical or chemical reasons, these DNA forms mutate, and new observable characteristics appear. In their efforts to reproduce, some of these characteristics produced through mutation give the creature an advantage in the competition among living creatures to reproduce. The intricate coordination that we observe is the outcome of thousands and millions of years of mutations and gained reproduction advantages. Scientists today disagree among themselves about the details about what exactly determines reproductive advantage but they all agree that the whole process is physical, chemical and biological, and that no supernatural designer needs to be postulated to explain the coordination.

The form of creationism that is more popular today among the people advocating it depends, I think, on a misunderstanding of the big bang theory defended by astronomers and cosmologists. By observing the speed at which galaxies are moving apart from each other, these astronomers have concluded that the expanding character of our universe of billions of galaxies, containing billions of stars, can be traced back to one big bang. Creationists argue that something must have caused this big bang because something cannot come out of nothing. Only something radically different from everything in the physical universe, they claim, must have caused the big bang. What is misunderstood is that, if the big bang theory is true, then there cannot be a time before the big bang when some supernatural god could have started the big bang. Talk about time makes sense only if some things move against a background of unmoving things, in the way the hands on a clock move around the face of the clock. If there is no motion, there is no time. Time comes into existence as things explode in the big bang. Cosmologists agree that the current expansion of the physical universe can be traced back to a big bang, but there are many different stories they tell about what such a big bang is. Perhaps our physical universe is only one among many universes, some expanding like ours until they start contracting until a big bang expansion takes place again. Perhaps the waves in our energy field that make up the sub-atomic particles that make up physical objects do originate out of nothing, as quantum mechanics suggests is happening all the time. Since cosmologists can't answer these questions now, we should not think that we can do so. The point is that the big bang theory does not require postulating a supernatural spark to send the galaxies on their expanding trajectories.

The third form of creationism is the one we hear being preached by evangelical fundamentalists who advocate what they call the literal meaning of the Bible's creation story. I totally reject such talk. First, as we have heard today, there is no one creation story in the Bible. There is J's story and there is P's story. Second, I am not willing to let these fundamentalists imperialistically determine the meaning of the word 'literal'. The literal meaning of what is written depends on what a writer is doing when writing certain sentences. As we have heard, Biblical writers often were reciting worship rituals, telling myths, writing poetry. Fundamentalists think that Biblical creation sentences are being used to report observable events that CNN cameras could have recorded if they existed back then. I believe they are being written to convey much bigger religious truths. We have no reason to think that J,

E, and P were offering explanations of events that could have been photographed. No one was around watching God create the world. The speech of J, E, and P, I suggest, was part of their worshipping and not their explaining.

I've said far too much. Let me get back to my tea. Luckily, I don't mind it being cold.

Thank you, Dorothy. You have given us so much more that we need to think about. I think we have time for one more question or comment. Mark, I see your hand up.

Thank you, Reverend Kennedy. I do want to ask two questions. As I said on our first day together I am a cultural Jew. I don't attend regularly any temple or synagogue. As a family we do celebrate Rosh Hashanah. Like, Dorothy, however, I don't believe in any supernatural god. I was so happy to hear our Jewish epic explained today. I don't think I have to believe in any supernatural god to believe the truths contained in it. I do have two questions, however.

Which came first, the chicken or the egg? I am referring to our religious rituals. Do we celebrate Passover because of what the epic says about exiting Egypt or did J include the story about Hebrew babies being saved from pharaoh's wrath to legitimate his celebration of Passover? Others in Canaan also had spring festivals. Do we honor the sabbath because P's creation myth talks about God resting on the seventh day after creating the world in six days, or did P edit old Mesopotamian creations myths in a way that legitimates his observance of the Sabbath? After all, Hebrews celebrated the Sabbath long before P added his creation myth to the Hebrew epic. I am inclined to think that the rituals existed before their legitimation and that, therefore, we need to critically think about why these rituals became a part of Hebrew religious life.

This leads me to my second question. If our epics, myths and religious rituals are really expressions of the life defining attitudes of Hebrew people, attitudes of gratitude, trust, justice, kindness, disdain for hubris, and forgiveness of oneself and others, then what is the difference between being merely a cultural Jew and being a Jew believing in God? Maybe I am more a Jew than I think I am.

Mark, you may be right about that. The issue may be not a matter of deciding whether a belief that God exists is true or false. Perhaps Judaism and Christianity are not a matter of beliefs about the existence of some being, but instead are a matter of faithfully living in a certain way. Many critically minded Jews and Christians think that the best way to reinforce the attitudes you have mentioned, and the best way to nurture children to have such attitudes, is to preserve certain sorts of talk and social rituals that are focused on a personal God. As you and Dorothy have pointed out, there is a danger in doing this, the danger of a metamorphosis of a god of worship into a supernatural God.

I presume that you want to label yourself "a cultural Jew" because even a God of worship is not real for you. For many Jews and Christians, however, living in a world of God talk and God worship makes God very real for them. God doesn't have to be a supernatural being for God to be real for them. Money is very real for people living in a monetary world, because of what they do in exchanging money and goods, but money can't be identified with coins, pieces of paper, or blips on a computer screen. The same is true of corporations, the U.S. constitution and presidency, and this university. Social practices give reality to the socially constituted objects of such practices. Seen this way, God is the object of religious practices of faithful worship and service. Mark, you believe that you can possess the same attitudes as those living a religious way of life, and you can nurture your children to have these attitudes, without talking God talk. You are correct that your form of cultural Judaism is very close to religious Judaism. Still, there is a difference. God is very real to them, even if God lives in their hearts and not in some supernatural dimension. They find God talk crucial for focusing the attitudes you mentioned. You feel no such need. Given your attitudes, however, I think that you would agree that there is nothing wrong when religious Jews live their religious form of life. I am assuming, of course, that they do not try to force anyone to talk as they do or to worship as they do.

I think you are sort-of right, Reverend Kennedy. I am eager to see whether Christianity's God can be viewed in the same way.

Let's wait on that, Mark. I would like to stay with the Hebrew Bible for one more week. Next week I would like to have you think some more about the Hebrew and Jewish religious way of life, especially as it concerns the pursuit of justice. For now, let's get out of here so we can be home when the hurricane hits. Drive carefully. Be safe.

Chapter Six

Jerusalem to Babylon to Jerusalem

A good day to all of you. I am sure that all of us are grateful for this clear and sunny day. I am never quite sure what to say after the kind of week we just have had. We were fortunate that we escaped the full force of the hurricane but so many Floridians south of us still haven't recovered from the damage and death inflicted upon them by the water and wind that hit them. I have placed a box at the back of the lecture hall if any of you want to contribute funds to help the poorest of the poor who seem to have been hit the harvest. I am sure that some of you have already done this.

As we continue to consider today the history and literature of the Bible, we will see that many of the texts we will be studying deal with issues with which we still are trying to handle. What does acting justly towards people in need require of us? How can one faithfully trust God when we in Jacksonville were so lucky but the people in Broward county suffered so many hurricane losses? The challenge that this weather hurricane makes on our faith may be more immediate and personal than the international hurricane causing havoc in our dealings with other nations, but the latter is just as dangerous, if not more so. Our faith seems to demand that we ask about what we should do to act justly to stateless immigrants seeking a permanent home and to innocent people being killed as collateral damage in our military actions against what our government sees as dangerous enemies. Just maintaining our faith seems to require that we find a way to continue living when we are so lucky, and many are so unlucky.

Today Professor Hill is going to help us understand the history of the Hebrews (Jews) from the time they returned from exile in Babylon in 530 BCE to the occupation of Jerusalem by Roman legions in 63 BCE. Professor Hamann and some of our university students are going to provide their interpretations of the Biblical texts that help us understand the religious attitudes and actions of Jews during this period.

Professor Hill.

You have presented a very demanding challenge to those of us dealing with Jewish history and literature from this period. But then, Reverend Kennedy, as you know, justice and the meaningfulness of life in the face of tragedy always present a demanding challenge.

To keep things somewhat in perspective, let's remember the time line with which we are dealing here. It took 250 years for the Hebrews to go from exiting Egypt to building the empire of David and Solomon. It took 200 years to go from Israel's independence from Solomon's empire to its destruction by the Assyrians in 720 BCE. It was another 125 years before Babylonia conquered Judah and 50 years after that before the Hebrews came back to rebuild Judah and Jerusalem. 200 years after their return from exile in 540 BCE, they were conquered by Alexander the Great and, 250 years after Alexander, Pompey and the Romans conquered Jerusalem. A hundred years later, in 70 CE, the Romans destroyed Jerusalem and dispersed the Jews throughout the Mediterranean world. In other words, we are dealing with a 1300 year stretch of Hebrew/Jewish history. Our country's history only goes back 250 years.

Our focus today is going to be on the 450 years of Jewish history from the time of the return from Babylon to the time the Romans conquered Jerusalem. In addition to the Biblical texts written during this era, we have a great deal of Persian,

Greek and Roman documents to work with in establishing this story line. Cyrus of Persia let the Hebrews go back to Judah in 538 BCE. Locating themselves in Judah led to their now being called 'Jews'. Their initial leader was the chief priest, Zerrubbabel, who started to rebuild the Jerusalem temple, only on a much smaller scale than it had been. They discovered that they were not welcomed by the Hebrews (people of the land) living there who had never been forced to go to Babylon. The returning exiles thought of themselves as the true Hebrew people, not the 'people of the land' or the Samaritans who were worshipping in their own temple in Shechem. They stopped the building of the new temple in Jerusalem for twenty years, but it was finished in 515 BCE. Sixty years later the Persians sent Ezra to Judah to stop the quarreling among Hebrews about the proper way to worship Yahweh. His efforts at reform did not succeed, until fifteen years later when Persia sent Nehemiah to be governor of Judah with the power to force everyone concerned to accept Ezra's reforms.

The Nehemiah/Ezra reforms proved very controversial. Nehemiah conducted a census that would list as a Jew only people who could verify that they had a Jewish parent or grandparent. DNA and not religious faith determined one's status as a Jew. He also made it illegal to marry anyone but a Jew. Ezra went even further and strove to forcible break up any mixed marriages already existing. They also required all Jews to faithfully support the new Jewish temple in Jerusalem. They adopted a legalistic treatment of the many ritualistic, dietary, and sabbath rules that J had included in Leviticus, in what came to be called the 'Holiness Code' and the 'Priestly Code'. In a ceremony that mirrored earlier covenant renewal ceremonies, Ezra set forth the new regulations governing the worship of Yahweh.

In the spirit of Second Isaiah's universalism, however, several short story writers challenged this attempt to define who a Jew is. The motives behind the attempt to define Jewishness were mixed. On the one hand, Ezra and Nehemiah were trying to prevent a repeat of the cosmopolitanism of Solomon. On the other hand, however, this was an attempt to empower the temple priests in Jerusalem at the expense of Jewish leaders outside of Jerusalem.

One great literary achievement of the era of the "Second temple" was the collecting together of the Psalms, some of which were sung way back at the time of David. The book of Psalms became the hymnal for worship in the Jerusalem Temple and in the synagogues sprouting up wherever there were Jews who couldn't get to the Jerusalem temple.

Much of what we know about the era after the return of exiles from Babylon is found in a massive historical works whose final written forms occurred around 400 BCE. These works covered the era of the Hebrew Confederacy to the destruction of Jerusalem by the Babylonians. (1st and 2nd Samuel, 1st and 2nd Kings, 1st and 2nd Chronicles). The story of the Jews after returning to Jerusalem from Babylon is found in the books: Ezra, Nehemiah. Crucial for understanding the writings of the Priestly writers in Babylon, especially the poems now called 'Send Isaiah', are the texts of the prophets who wrote for 250 years before the destruction of Jerusalem by the Babylonians. They warned about the two patterns of behavior that Ezra-Nehemiah were engaged in once again: focusing on ritual legalism and on preserving the Hebrew/Jews as a nation state. The prophets accented, instead, justice and forgiveness and on being a worshipping community. The kind of justice the prophets talked about was universalistic in character and went beyond a merely legalistic notion of punishing those who broke a nation's laws. This was tied to their claim that the identity of the Hebrew people was not to be tied to their identity as citizens of Israel or Judah. As we heard last week, this universalistic tone dominating the thinking of the Priestly writers in Babylon.

In addition to the opposition to the tribal legalism expressed in shirt stories and poems, there are two other historical movements that need to be considered to understand what was happening religiously in the Jewish world created after the return from Babylonian exile. First, we need to keep in mind that about the same time the books of Ezra and Nehemiah are written, Greek philosophical ideas began to spread throughout the Fertile Crescent and the Mediterranean. Plato philosophized until his death in 428 BCE. Aristotle, the tutor of Alexander the Great, wrote until his death in 322 BCE, and Alexander's legions deposited Aristotle's ideas in all the areas they conquered. The stoic philosopher, Zeno, lived until 260 BCE, and it influenced a Greek slave, Epictetus, and a Roman emperor, Marcus Aurelius.

The great issue that all of them contemplated was the meaningfulness of life given the injustice that seemed so apparent in the world. The Greeks recommended trusting human reason no matter what happens. The Biblical texts of Proverbs, Ecclesiastes, and Job were written to address these same issues from the standpoint of a worshipper of Yahweh. Their reflections not only indicate Greek philosophical influence but also the influence of the Egyptian text *Dispute Over Suicide* and the Babylonian text *I Will Praise the Lord of Wisdom*.

Equally significant for later Jewish religious life was the effect of the conquering of Jerusalem by Alexander the Great in 323, and the division of his conquered territories after his death into four distinct regimes: the Lysimachus and Macedonia-Greece Kingdoms north of the Fertile Crescent, the Ptolemaic Kingdom in Egypt, with its capital in Alexandria, and the Seleucid Kingdom in Mesopotamia and Syria, with its capital in Antioch. The latter two had a direct influence on Jewish life. The Ptolemaic Kingdom governed Judah from 323 BCE, when Alexander died, until 200 BCE when the Seleucid Kingdom conquered the Ptolemaic Kingdom. The Ptolemies in Egypt prized their rich, cosmopolitan library in Alexandria and they had exercised a mild, patronizing attitude towards the Jews. The Seleucid leadership adopted a very hostile attitude towards the Jews.

When King Antiochus of the Seleucid Kingdom in Syria conquered Egypt and took control of Judah, he demanded that worship of Zeus be a test of loyalty to his kingdom. He auctioned off to the highest bidder the office of chief priest in the Jerusalem temple. When Jews rioted and refused to accept the highest bidder, Menelaus, King Antiochus plundered the temple, sentenced to death any mother who circumcised her sons, anyone observing the sabbath, and any one possessing the Torah. In 168 BCE, he erected an alter in the Jewish temple and on it sacrificed to Zeus a pig, and he used his army to force Jews to eat pork.

This was the straw that broke the camel's back, and a Jewish rebellion against the Seleucids began. This rebellious spirit led to liberation from Seleucid rule but two hundred years later it led to a rebellion against Roman rule that led to the destruction of Jerusalem once again. After the sacrilegious desecration of the Jewish temple by the Seleucids, a priest in the hills north of Jerusalem, Mattathias, refused to participate in a sacrifice to Zeus and, when a Syrian officer and a Jew did perform the sacrifice, he killed them. Then, he and his five sons hid out in the hills for safety and carried out guerrilla attacks. On his deathbed, Mattathias commissioned his oldest son, Judas, to carry on. Judas did so with vicious attacks on Seleucids and Jewish assimilationists. He was given by his followers the title 'Maccabeus' or 'The Hammer'. Writing in a code that the Seleucids were not equipped to break, the book of Daniel was written to encourage Jews to continue the fight for liberation. Finally, with indirect support from Rome, a rising power in the West, Maccabeus defeated the Seleucid army in 165 BCE, rebuilt the temple, and initiated a century of peace for the Jews that lasted until the Romans conquered the area in 63 BCE. In celebration of the Maccabean liberation of Judah and the re-dedication of the temple, Jews instituted Hanukkah, the celebration of the Feast of Lights that continues among Jews until this date.

I know that this is a complicated piece of history to keep in mind, but I hope that it will help you somewhat to understand what is written in the Biblical texts that Professor Hamann and his students now are going to introduce to you.

Professor Hamann.

Thank you, Professor Hill. This is how we are going to proceed. I will give a short introduction to a text and then one of our students will present her or his interpretive reading of the text. Students from the political science department will present the messages of the prophets. Majors in English will interpret the three short stories: Ruth, Jonah, and Esther. Philosophy students will try to help us understand the 'Wisdom Literature'.

To appreciate the universalism that was enunciated by Second Isaiah, what led up to it and how it continued as a counterforce to the Ezra-Nehemiah accent on national tribalism, we need to examine the writings of the major prophets who wrote when Israel and Judah were separate kingdoms. Although there were differences between different schools of prophets, we will look at some of the writings of just six of the prophets who were what we today would call social critics: Amos, Hosea, Micah, Isaiah, Jeremiah, and Ezekiel. To do this, we need to know a little bit more about the historical context in which they lived and worked. They all lived between the time of the division of Solomon's empire into Israel and Judah (920 BCE) and the time 307 years later when Babylonia destroyed Jerusalem (587 BCE). This was a period that began in violence and ended in violence, as Israel and Judah fought each other, as both kingdoms formed geo-political alliances to stay alive as their powerful neighbors (Egypt, Syria, Assyria, and Babylonia) warred with each other. There were brief periods of time when both kingdoms enjoyed prosperity but during these years wealth was concentrated in the hands of dishonest and corrupt elites. The major social critic prophets condemned both the economic injustice rampant in both kingdoms and the geo-political maneuvering that led them to forget that they were to be a religious community and not one more minor, nation state.

It took a violent revolt, led by Jeroboam I, for the ten northern tribes to secede from Solomon's empire and form their new nation of Israel. Solomon had selected his son Rehoboam to succeed him. Rehoboam decided to be even more severe in treating Israelis than his father had been. Solomon had for years given favor to people from the two southern tribes and had subjected people in the ten northern tribes to harsh labor. Rehoboam bragged that whereas his father had ruled the north with a whip he would rule with scorpions. The northerners revolted and stoned to death Rehoboam's taskmaster. The revolt was temporarily put down and Jeroboam had to flee to Egypt. Rehoboam did not follow through and crush the rebellion, however, because he feared Egyptian interference. In 922 BCE, Jeroboam returned and established the Kingdom of Israel, built a capital at Shechem, and gained the widespread support of people in the north by recognized all competing religious groups: Moses' priests and Levi priests, and even worshippers of Baal.

For fifty years a civil war continued between Israel and Judah. It was their national identity and not their identities as worshiping communities that concerned them. In 878 BCE Judah formed an alliance with Syria to defend itself against Israel. Two years later, Israel, after a new general, Omri, had seized power, formed an alliance with Phoenicia. Omri's son Ahab married a Phoenician princess, Jezebel, to seal the alliance. From 876 to 850 the alliance produced an economic boom in Israel, but it also resulted in Jezebel being able to spread throughout Israel her people's worship of Baal, the god of fertility. It was in opposition to Jezebel's efforts that the prophet Elijah spoke.

For the next 240 years, the history of Israel and Judah was dominated by their efforts to form alliances to deal with the far superior power of the Egyptian, Assyrian, and Babylonian empires. In 853 BCE, Israel allied with Syria in attempt to stop Assyria. Assyria defeated the alliance and succeeded in killing Ahab, but then returned home to refresh its armed forces. Syria took advantage of the lull and attacked Israel. Israel and Judah formed an alliance to defeat Syria, which they did. As a result, Israel enjoyed peace for 50 years, became prosperous, and turned Judah into virtually a vassal state of Israel. From 786 BCE to 746 BCE, Jeroboam II ruled in Israel where the upper class enjoyed all the privileges of wealth. It was during this time that the prophets Amos (750 BCE) and Hosea (745 BCE) stepped forward to condemn the economic injustices upon which Israel's wealth was based. Israel's prosperity did not last.

Israel again formed an alliance with Syria to stop Assyria, but in 732 Assyria destroyed Syria and in 722 it destroyed Israel and dispersed Israelis throughout the Fertile Crescent. Assyrian armies came to the gates of Jerusalem in Judah but did not destroy the city. The army was called back home to deal with the rising threat of Babylonia. It was at this time that the prophets Isaiah (742-701 BCE) and Micah (722-701 BCE) criticized the economic practices of Judah and its alliance with Egypt to defend itself against Assyria and the rising power of Babylonia. From 640 BCE to 609 BCE, Josiah, King of Judah, attempted to reform Judah, but he had no control over the actions of the military powers surrounding Judah. Babylonia defeated Assyria in 612 and Egypt at Cardemish in 605. It destroyed Jerusalem in 587 and sent the leaders of Judah into exile in Babylon. Persia conquered Babylon in 539 and sent the exiles back to Jerusalem. For over forty years prior to the destruction of Jerusalem (626-587), the prophet Jeremiah criticized Judah for its injustices and its trust in military alliances. The condemnation by prophets of Israel and Judah for thinking of the Hebrews as national kingdoms rather than religious communities significantly influenced the priests in Babylon who saw the destruction of Jerusalem and its temple as verification of the prophets' criticisms. Very influential also was the reassurance given by the prophets that a Hebrew community of faithful worshippers always would survive. In Babylon, Second Isaiah spelled out what that community would be like.

Keeping that history in mind, let's begin by locking at what Amos wrote. Tom Paynter, one of our political science majors, will give his interpretation of the book of Amos.

Amos was a shepherd from Judah who came north to Israel during its prosperous days under Jeroboam II. He came to criticize the economic injustice that was widespread there among the wealthy families. As I read Amos, two themes stand out. First, he uses a universal standard of justice. He not only indicts Israel's ethical transgressions, but he does the same to the transgressions of her neighbors: Damascus, Gaza, Lyre, Edom, the Ammonites, Moab, and Judah. Second, to all Hebrews he makes it very clear that worshipping Yahweh means much more than going through the motions of participating in religious rituals. Acting justly is a necessary part of worshipping Yahweh.

Amos presents a long list of unjust actions of which wealthy Israelites are guilty. They exploit the poverty of the poor by forcing them to sell themselves into indentured service to gain a little silver or a pair of shoes. They act as though the poor don't even exist when they are of no use to the rich. While the poor enslave themselves to survive, the rich have winter and summer houses decorated with beautiful ivory in which they have feasts gorging themselves with lamb and veal and wine drunk from jeweled bowls. The wives of the rich are nothing but "cows of Basham" who are full of milk because they oppress the poor, crush the needy, and lie around on ivory beds while the poor give them food and drink. Government officials do not treat everyone as equals, but they enrich themselves by taking bribes from the rich and then give them special services. The rich get away with deceiving customers with false balances.

Having indicted them for their unjust treatment of the poor, Amos then loudly proclaims what people must do to be just. Seek good and hate evil. Hate evil and love good. "Let justice roll down like waters, and righteousness like an ever-flowing stream." He makes it very clear that acting justly in the marketplace is not something separate from worshipping Yahweh. Know that Yahweh, the creator of the world, the one who chose the Hebrews to be his special people, is a holy God of justice. One is only pretending to be worshipping Yahweh if one is not acting justly, no matter how much one is involved in Hebrew rituals. Speaking for Yahweh, Amos proclaims, "I hate, I despise your feasts and I take no delight in your solemn assemblies." Yahweh is not going to be satisfied with you offering sacrifices and singing psalms. Yahweh promises his chosen people that they will survive only if they live as a community genuinely worshipping Yahweh with attitudes of gratitude and thankfulness and with actions that justly deal with all people. Amos then adds a word of hope. You are not such a righteous people now, but Yahweh will not give up on you. By judging you and forgiving you, the goodness in all the poor being abused and in you, as in all Yahweh's creations, will allow a worshipping community to arise and replace the current, unjust situation in Israel.

Let me now give way to Roger Johnson. who will offer his understanding of the text of Hosea.

Hosea was a northern Israelite. He was the type of worshipper of Yahweh that Amos probably had in mind when telling the Israelites not to lose hope about Israel becoming a faithful, worshipping community. Hosea's words to Israel were an echo and amplification of the words of Amos. He proclaimed that Yahweh had a controversy with the inhabitants of Israel. Although Hosea also condemned them for "swearing, lying, killing, stealing … murder," his criticism is focused on another aspect of their current way of life. Their making of alliances with Egypt and Assyria, to protect their political kingdom, shows that they do not know that they can be Yahweh's community only if there are a faithful and righteous community. As a political kingdom, Hosea proclaims, the House of Israel will be destroyed by those whom they sometimes treat as military partners. Only as a people worshipping Yahweh is their continued existence immune to the military power of other empires. Hosea proclaims that Israel does not understand that it was only as a worshipping community, trusting that their God, Yahweh, is a compassionate and loving God, that they left Egypt as a child and learned to walk as adults thanking Yahweh for all of creation and for forgiving them as they continuously failed to remain faithful.

Hosea proclaimed that as a God of love and forgiveness, Yahweh is not a vengeful God punishing Israel by guaranteeing its destruction. He proclaims that worshipping God, after having broken one's religious contract with Yahweh, requires making a new covenant with Yahweh, one that gives Hebrews a harmonious way of living with all living things and peaceful life with all other humans. To do that, they are to abolish all military weapons and to cease to exist as a warring nation. Israel must cease trying to be a contending player in the game of war. If Israel tries to do that, it will be swallowed up by the military powers surrounding it. In that game, the House of Israel will be a pitiful player, but, as a community defined by worship of Yahweh, Israel can function in a way that nation states cannot even conceive. Sounding like Amos, Hosea points out that worshipping Yahweh requires much more than sacrifices and ritual performances. Worshippers must "Sow for yourselves righteousness, reap the fruit of steadfast love; break up the fallow ground, for it is the time to seek Yahweh that he may come and rain salvation upon you."

To demonstrate that judgement for unrighteousness does not mean one is fated for unending punishment, Hosea uses the example of his wife as an illustration of the kind of worship that Yahweh requires. His wife had run away turning to other "lovers" to meet the needs she felt Hosea was not providing. None of her "lovers," however, could give her what she wanted, any more than the House of Israel's use of military alliances could give it what it wanted. When Hosea's wife recognized that she was pursuing an unfillable fantasy, she returned to her home. Hosea welcomed her with open arms, so they could live harmoniously and joyfully with each other. Neither forgot what she had done but they both remembered it as forgiven. They did not pretend that the past had not happened, but neither did they let that memory evaporate the joyful possibilities available in their future life together. Hosea is saying to the Israelis that although they must accept judgement for their choice to abandon faith in worshipping Yahweh, choosing instead to worship the House of Israel, this knowledge of what they have done need not be a dead weight tied around their necks. It can be remembered as forgiven so that a new covenant with Yahweh can be established.

Let me turn the lectern over to Lloyd Phillip, who will try to help us understand the writings of Micah and his prophesies concerning Judah.

Hold on just a moment, Lloyd. I have a few things I want to say. First, I want to thank Tom and Roger for their insightful interpretations of the prophetic judgements on Israel. Before turning to the prophets writing about Judah, however, let me point out several things. First, we possess the writings of Amos and Hosea because around them developed prophetic circles of followers who preserved their pronouncements in written texts. Second, the prophets in Judah knew about the writings of Amos and Hosea when they did their work. Also, by the time they wrote, Israel had been conquered by the Assyrians and there was no Israel any longer. They wrote in that period of 130 years between the fall of Israel in 722 BCE and the capture of Jerusalem in 587. Their thoughts were dominated by four concerns. The destruction of Israel in 722 and the plight of the Israelis dispersed throughout the Fertile Crescent. The threat by the Assyrians in 703 to conquer Jerusalem. The temptation to form an alliance with Assyria to stop the growth in power of Babylonia. The attempt to form an alliance with Egypt to stop Babylonia. Both attempts were useless because Jerusalem was conquered by the Babylonians in 587.

O.K. Let's now hear Lloyd.

Thank you, Professor Hamann.

Micah was a prophet from a rural village just south of Jerusalem who was motivated to speak out between 721 BCE and 701 BCE by three sets of circumstances. First, he criticized landowners in Judah for their unjust treatment of farmers. Second, he responded to the Assyrian threat in 703 to destroy Jerusalem by predicting that Jerusalem would be crushed in the same way that Israel had been conquered in 722. Third, he proclaimed that the Hebrews of Israel and Judah, who fell under the hand of the Assyrians, would be reconstituted as a new kind of religious community by a leader like David who came from Micah's own rural home territory.

Large landowners in the area where Micah lived were coveting the land of small farmers and were forcing farmers, their wives, and their children to become landless people with no inheritance to give to future generations. They did this not only because large landowners were greedy but because these small farmers just wanted to work their plots of land peacefully and care for their families. They did not want to go to war for the large landowner against the Assyrians. Micah proclaims that the Assyrians will plow over Judah just as it had done to Israel. He attacked what he called the false prophets who supported Judah's war efforts and who proclaimed that Yahweh was a warrior God who would defeat the Assyrians.

Micah railed against the claim of the false prophets that the way to serve Yahweh and receive his protection was through offering sacrifices of calves, thousands of rams, rivers of oil, and even their first-born sons. This, Micah cries out, is not the way to worship Yahweh. To do the will of Yahweh is "to do justice, and to love kindness, and to walk humbly with your God." Don't think you can control Yahweh and force his hand to militarily protect you by offering sacrifices. You want to protect the monarchy of David, but you misunderstand what kind of kingdom it is that worshipping Yahweh protects or how Yahweh will provide that protection.

Micah proclaimed that there will arrive a new kingdom of David for the remnants already dispersed from Israel and soon to be dispersed from Judah. It will not be a kingdom of military warriors but a kingdom of humble, farming peacemakers who will motivate other nations to "beat their swords into plowshares and their spears into pruning hooks, nations shall not lift up swords against nation, neither shall they learn war anymore." This new kingdom of peace makers will come from the same, small, farming tribe from which King David came, Bethlehem. That this is the smallest of the twelve Hebrew tribes indicates that it is not military or economic power that makes life in this new kingdom of David successful. It is humility, justice, and kindness.

Micah's challenge to the remnants of Israel and Judah to be Yahweh's instrument for building a peaceful world is the one the priestly writers of Second Isaiah heard in Babylon.

To tell us what First Isaiah had to say, let me introduce Mary Jo Kutill.

Thanks, Lloyd.

Understanding the book of Isaiah is very much like getting to understand the first four books of the Bible. Scholars have distinguished different sections of the book written by different authors at different times. Second Isaiah (Chapters 40-60) and Third Isaiah (Chapters 61-66) were added by later members of Isaiah's school of prophets, one group in Babylon after the Exile and group after the return to Jerusalem. Also, but the little apocalypse in which Yahweh ends the whole world (chapters 24-27), the critique of foreign nations (Chapters 13-23), the copying of material from Second Kings (Chapters 36-39) and the comfort and consolation texts (Chapters 12 and 33) were probably added to what Isaiah himself wrote. This means that we should look only at Chapters 1-11 and 28-32 to learn what the Prophet Isaiah proclaimed to Judah.

Isaiah, in contrast to Micah, was a city dweller from Jerusalem, the city of David. He never mentions the Exodus or the covenant with Moses. It is the covenant with David that is his concern. He charged Israel and Judah with failing to live up to the spirit of that covenant. He proclaimed that the true essence of a Davidic Kingdom will be reborn in the hearts and minds of remnants of the Kingdom of Israel and those in Judah who remain righteous and loyal to Yahweh despite the threat posed by the armies of Assyria.

Isaiah had a religious experience in 734 BCE, the year that King Uzziah (Azariah) died from leprosy. He imagined that he was in a heavenly version of Solomon's temple, that Yahweh was sitting upon a throne surrounded by half human and half animal seraphim's. He experienced a call from Yahweh to be a prophet to the people of Judah. When Isaiah protested that he was not qualified to do this job, he heard Yahweh remind him that spokespersons for Yahweh must be people humble enough to know that they cannot on their own produce a community of people faithfully doing Yahweh's will. Isaiah humbly accepted the assignment and served as a prophet for forty years.

Like the prophets before him, Isaiah condemned injustice in Judah, substituting empty ritual formalities for faithful worship of Yahweh, and striving to live as a national state depending on military alliances rather than as a worshipping community faithful to Yahweh in attitudes and actions. Isaiah then enlarged Micah's vision of the Hebrews building a world at peace by sharing his vision of a new Davidic Kingdom being established by those disenfranchised by the Assyrians.

Isaiah, like Micha, issued a long list of indictments of the powerful in Jerusalem for their unjust dealings with other Hebrews: corruption, bribery, colluding with thieves, murder, proudly showing off jewelry acquired by spilling the blood of others. He criticized Israel for aligning itself with Syria to force Judah to join them in opposing Assyria and he criticized Judah for giving in to the pressure to join the alliance. Later, he criticized them for forming an alliance with Egypt against Assyria, an alliance or league that was a covenant with death. He declared worship of Yahweh could not be satisfied by putting on huge feasts and claiming that these showed their faithfulness to Yahweh. He proclaimed that worship of Yahweh required them to "cease to do evil, learn to do good, seek justice, correct oppression, defend the fatherless, plead for the widow."

Having leveled indictment after indictment against people in Judah, the consequences of which will be severe, Isaiah then goes on to offer hope. Acting unjustly will weaken Judah internally and forming alliances against a rising foreign power like Assyria will guarantee that that Assyria will see Judah as a threat to be destroyed. Isaiah calls for Hebrews to remember that worshipping Yahweh requires two things: first, acting justly and placing faith in one's worshipping relationship to Yahweh; second, humbly accepting the unwarranted forgiveness that makes it possible to leave the past in the past and to enjoy a blessed future as a religious community. Thus, Isaiah writes, "Come, now, let us reason together, says Yahweh: though your sins are like scarlet, they shall be as white as snow; though they are red like crimson, they will become like wool. If you are willing and obedient, you shall eat the good of the land."

Isaiah goes on to promise that the worshipping community that will be a "branch of Yahweh shall be beautiful and glorious, the fruit of the land shall be the pride and glory of the survivors of Israel, and the survivors of Jerusalem will be called holy." The new Kingdom of David will not have a mighty warrior as its King. Isaiah understood that just as humility was a requirement for him to hear Yahweh's call, so this kingdom's leader will be like a humble child, born of a young woman, eating only goat's curds and the honey of bees, but knowing how to refuse evil and choose good and thus be deserving of the title 'Immanuel', 'God is with us'. This child-like leader will lighten up the lives lost in darkness and these people will understand that warrior boots and bloody garments will be burnt to provide warming fires in the new kingdom. No longer dreaming of a military savior, the redeemed in Israel and Judah will see this leader as a wonderful counselor and a prince of peace. This leader will govern and insure peace, justice, and righteousness within the worshipping community and will bring peace between nations. Within the new Davidic kingdom of worship, the deaf shall hear, the eyes of the blind shall see, the poor will celebrate living in a world of justice, and the meek will replace the ruthless as the enjoyers of life. To make his point about worshippers of Yahweh being peace-makers, Isaiah quotes Micah to show the powerful influence that a worshipping community can have on warring nations. This new David will get nations to "beat their swords into pruning hooks; nation shall not lift up sword against nation, neither shall they learn war any more."

Thank you, Mary Jo. Ms. Ferne Cassidy, can you take it from here and share with us the prophetic judgements Jeremiah made during his long, forty year career. He did claim that he was called to be a "Prophet to the Nations."

Yes, Professor Hamann. Jeremiah responded to his original call to prophesize by speaking out again and again against Judah's useless efforts to act as a typical nation state seeking to make international alliances to stop Babylonia's successful conquering of the whole Fertile crescent. He paid a huge personal price for speaking truth to the power of the kings and popular priests ruling Judah. He not only was filled with sorrow over the destruction Babylonia caused in Judah, but he wished that he never had been born and heard any call to speak out against the behavior of Judah's holders of power.

Jeremiah, the son of a priest outside Jerusalem who was not involved in temple rituals, was only a teenager when he experienced a need to speak as a prosecuting attorney for Yahweh because Judah was not living up to the covenant (contract) it had made with Yahweh who had every right to contend with Judah for this breach of contract. This experience occurred around 626 BCE when there was a lull in actual warfare between Egypt, Assyria, and Babylonia, and Judeans like its King, Josiah, were considering strengthening and reforming the Kingdom of Judah.

Jeremiah was trying to establish worship of Yahweh as a founding consideration in the reconstitution of Judah. He approved Josiah's idea of reforming Judah, but he had objections to the way the King, with the support of temple priests, was trying to do this. Josiah wanted to strengthen Judah as a nation state by building a sense of nationalism centered on the royal house of David in Jerusalem and the ritualistic worship of Yahweh as stated in Leviticus and interpreted by temple priests. Jeremiah's idea of worshipping Yahweh was quite different. His understanding was grounded in the sentiments and practices of the line of priests in his family tree that went back to the shrine of Shiloh where the arc of the covenant was kept during the era of the confederation of 12 tribes. These priests were not supporters of centralizing worship in the Jerusalem temple whose priests accented a covenant with Kind David, whereas Jeremiah accented the covenant with Moses. Josiah was seeking to build a stronger Davidic national state and Jeremiah heard a call to reform a people so that they could be what Moses first tried to get the exiles from Egypt to be, a faithful community of worshippers of Yahweh in spirit and action. In his defense of Yahweh's indictment of Judah, he used Hosea's language to claim that Judah had been an unfaithful wife to Yahweh. The political and priestly leadership in Judah, he said, thought more about national and priestly power than about molding a community of worshippers grateful for life, striving to be just and kind, honest in confessing failures, and trusting in the compassionate forgiveness of Yahweh.

Josiah and his supporters believed that their reforms would issue in a great "Day of the Lord" in which they would enjoy national security and prosperous life. They presumed that Yahweh was a powerful bodyguard who would protect them as a nation, if they obeyed certain rules. During Josiah's long reign, a group of

Hebrew historians, whom scholars call "The Deuteronomistic Historians," wrote a history of Israel and Judah in which they claimed that material success occurred when a kingdom was lawfully pure. Jeremiah rejected this conception of Yahweh and this simple philosophy of history. He charged that Yahweh is not a God at hand who will obey our bidding if we tip him with sacrifices and feasts. Yahweh is not a chess master moving warring pieces around. Yahweh, as a god of worship, affects national policies, practices and material well-being by being worshipped through attitudes and actions by people who are involved in national life.

Jeremiah proclaimed that Judah's willed ignorance of the military dynamics of the era in which they lived is blinding them to the fact that just to the north is the might of Babylonia which will give them days of grief. There is a boiling kettle in the north tilting to pour destruction on Jerusalem. The temple priests, who are crying "Peace! Peace!", when there is no real peace but only a lull in the fighting, are false prophets, prophesizing lies in Yahweh's name. Totally misreading the dynamics of the military actions of the powers surrounding them, Josiah makes an alliance with Babylonia, who was marching to destroy the alliance that been made between Egypt and the remnants of Assyrian forces. Josiah was killed during the clash, and when Babylonia defeated the advancing Egyptian army in the battle at Carchemish in 605 BCE. Egypt itself was not yet destroyed. Egypt did not forget that Judah had supported their enemy, Babylonia. They turned Judah into a vassal state and reduced Josiah's son, Jehoiakim, into a vassal king charged with imposing harsh taxes to pay indemnities to Egypt. Being an appendage of Egyptian power, this made Judah the inevitable target during Babylonia's eventual march south to finish off Egypt. Babylonia did not forgive Judah for switching loyalties.

Before Babylonia destroyed Jerusalem, Jehoiakim had ruled as a tyrant, ruthlessly using forced labor to meet Egyptian demands. To pacify Egypt, he also permitted the introduction of worship of the Egyptian god, Ishtar. Because of Jeremiah's opposition to the international policies of Judah and the liturgical practices of the Temple priests, he was prohibited from entering Jerusalem or the temple. Therefore, he sent his assistant, Baruch, in with a written copy of his prophetic condemnations. King Jehoiakim took Jerimiah' scroll and section by section through it into the flames. Opposition in Jerusalem to Jeremiah and his indictment of Judah's practices got worse and worse when Jehoiakim was replaced as king by Jehoiachin. He was imprisoned and almost murdered because he counseled Judah not to fight against Babylonian armies even as they were assaulting the gates of Jerusalem. After Babylonia did destroy Jerusalem, sent the elite leadership of Judah off to Babylon, and appointed Zedekiah to be king, they came back to destroy Jerusalem because Zedekiah again conspired with the Egyptians. Here again Jeremiah condemned their foolishness.

Looked at from one point of view, one could say that Jeremiah had failed in all his prophetic efforts since he was a teenager. This is also how Jeremiah often felt. He never wanted the job of being a prophet. His faithful worship of Yahweh kept forcing him to do what he did. He got no material reward for what he did. Judah never permitted itself to be reformed in the way that he believed was necessary. Non-temple priests like his father never could eliminate the false prophets or their false propaganda about Yahweh being a military savior. Even they got swept up and exiled to Babylon. Judah and Jerusalem lay in ruins. He lived in constant fear of being arrested and killed for speaking truth to power. He had been imprisoned and dropped into a well to die.

Jeremiah, who had been the prosecuting attorney against those who had failed to live up to their covenantal responsibilities, now made his case against Yahweh. Why has nothing that I have tried to do born any fruit? Is it better to be faithful to Yahweh or is it better to just appear to be faithful, as the false prophets were doing? Jeremiah mused, I know that it was folly to oppose Babylon, but would it have been any worse if we had sided with them? Does it make any sense to be a community worshipping you, if the future is always determined by the powerful and not the righteous?

His moments of depression, however, did not destroyed his faith in worshipping Yahweh in thanksgiving and just actions. He heard Yahweh tell him that a new worshipping community will be formed out of the remnants from Israel and the exiles in Babylon. With these worshippers, it is their hearts that will be circumcised as the covenant with Yahweh will be in their hearts, in their gratefulness for the goodness of life (no matter what happens), in their kindness and just actions, in their facing the future remembering their past failures as forgiven.

It is not surprising, therefore, that Jeremiah had such a heavy influence on people in Babylon like the poets who wrote Second Isaiah and spelled out what the mission of Hebrews to the world was to be like.

Thank you, Ferne. Now let's turn our attention to the last of the prophets we will be hearing from today, Ezekiel. He lived through the days of Jerusalem's destruction and the early years of exile in Babylon. Mr. Elmer Czaplinski will do the honors.

Ezekiel was a priest from an aristocratic family of priests who served in the temple in Jerusalem. After being exiled to Babylon, he became a supporter of Levi teaching priests who traced their heritage back to Moses and who functioned in the synagogues founded by Jews dispersed into many countries outside Judah. In 593 BCE, five years after being exiled to Babylon, the 30 years old Ezekiel had a religious experience in which figures in Hebrew and Babylonian mythology combined in a vision in which he heard a call to be a prophet to the exiles in Babylon and those dispersed all the way from Egypt to Damascus and Antioch. In his vision he saw the Jerusalem temple and the Gate in Babylon dedicated to Instar, the consort of the Babylonian god, Murdock. He sensed the presence of Yahweh in many forms, sometimes humanlike and sometimes transcendent beyond all images. Yahweh was sitting on the throne of the ark in the temple in Jerusalem, being protected by a half-human/half animal cherub, and then Yahweh was riding in a heavenly chariot carrying the arc from the temple in Jerusalem to the exiles in Babylon where Yahweh would sit on a new throne. The protecting cherub became four creatures pulling the chariot. Over the chariot was a new throne, existing in a new sapphire strewn realm above the firmament that Yahweh as creator had turned into the world in which humans lived, a realm in which Ezekiel was sure that Yahweh existed as the Hebrew God of worship although totally unlike any observable creature in the world created from the firmament.

In the vision that inspired him to prophesize to the exiles, Ezekiel provided the understanding of worshipping Yahweh that the priests in Babylon, especially the writers of Second Isaiah, needed to continue to worship Yahweh in a foreign land and to live as Yahweh's chosen people serving as a saving light to all the people in all the nations of the world. The place where the presence of Yahweh can be encountered is not the physical arc in Jerusalem's temple but in every place where Yahweh's worshippers reside. The God that Yahweh's worshippers covenant with is not just the God that Hebrews have chosen from a pantheon of gods as their God. The god that Hebrews have worshipped as their God and the gods that the Babylonians have worshipped as their God is the one and only God there is, Yahweh. This God cannot be likened to anything picturable. In worshipping Yahweh, one is not dealing with anything in the observable world, but one is living with attitudes of thanksgiving and gratitude towards the goodness of everything in the world seen as Yahweh's creation.

Having universalized all genuine worship of Yahweh, Ezekiel also universalizes the problem of humanity's failure to worship God, humanity's hubris in thinking that it is the rightful master of nature and history. The Hebrew faithlessness, leading to acting unjustly and to placing ultimate trust in national power, is just one example of the general cause of human suffering. Ezekiel charges that way back during their days of slavery in Egypt, Hebrews already were being unfaithful to the God of Abraham, Isaac, and Jacob. He traces the cause of human suffering back to the Garden of Eden when humanity started trying to be masters of everything. For Ezekiel, the problem facing humanity is universal because, against the one existing transcendent God, all people are rebelling with their attitudes and actions. Furthermore, just as there is only one transcendent God, and one universal cause of human suffering, so there is only one universal way to remove this cause and to return to wonderful life in the Garden of Eden. People must come to understand the true cause of their misery, sense that things do not have to be this way, unconditionally surrender their desire to be God, celebrate the goodness of life even when their most prized possessions are destroyed, welcome into their minds and hearts an acceptance of loving forgiveness and a hope and trust for a beautiful life to come.

Ezekiel heard the call to proclaim to the Hebrews in Babylon and the Diaspora that the destruction of Jerusalem and the temple by the Babylonians should not cause them to feel despair or hopelessness. The suffering they are experiencing can be a springboard for the appearance of a people with a new heart and spirit, for the appearance of a new everlasting covenant, a new kind of Jerusalem, temple, and Arc, in which Yahweh will tabernacle with them no matter where they physically reside and no matter what other people do to them. He shared his imagined trip into a valley of despair and saw how, into the pile of bones lying there, new spiritual life can be blown. They will get up and be a new community of Israel. He warned not to think erroneously that this is some action that people can take and then be credited for taking. This new way of life will come to be only if people quit trying to run the show, get out of the way, and simply let it come to be.

Let the goodness of life impress itself upon oneself so that thankful gratitude can be one's attitude towards life. Let the beauty and infinite preciousness of every individual person fill one with a desire to be just and kind. Allow oneself to be one of the sheep that Yahweh, as one's shepherd, leads home into luscious pastures. Live as a worshipper in the company of other worshippers, each of whom becomes Yahweh's instrument in strengthening the faithfulness of others, as the spirit of Yahweh is nurtured in generation after generation. Having people strengthen and nurture each other is necessary for the will of Yahweh to be carried out, but it is not sufficient. Each person remains individually responsible to live faithful to Yahweh. The individual must let Yahweh's spirit enter his or her heart.

It is difficult to decide whether Ezekiel is a prophet to the exiles or an exile who prophetically is speaking to all mankind, a prophet who is a light to all the nations of the world.

Thank you, Elmer. I hope that it is now obvious that these prophets laid the ground work for the thinking of the priestly writers in exile in Babylon. The prophets came from many different walks of life. Amos was a shepherd in Judah. Hosea was from Israel. Micah was a farmer in Judah. Isaiah was a Jerusalem city dweller. Jeremiah was from a family of priests outside Jerusalem. Ezekiel was from an aristocratic family of temple priests. They played two functions in the life of Israel and Judah. They were social critics of unjust economic practices and national geo-political policies and they were visionaries of a form of righteous religious life not dependent on the good and bad fortunes of the national kingdoms of Israel and Judah. Amos indicted the unjust practices of wealthy city dwellers and Micah condemned the injustices suffered by rural people. Isaiah and Jeremiah spoke out against the Hebrews thinking of themselves primarily as citizens of political kingdoms relying on military alliances rather than as faithful worshippers in a religious kingdom. Hosea accented the power of forgiveness to give the Hebrews another chance to be such a religious community. Jeremiah picked up this accent and proclaimed that Hebrews could form a new covenant in their hearts and Ezekiel proclaimed that Yahweh is the God for all people, that a new religious way of life is available for all people, and that the Hebrews, chased out of Israel and Judah, have a unique opportunity to let themselves be used to establish that new world.

When Persia permitted the exiles in Babylon to go back to Jerusalem, the kingdom that was re-established was more like the old nationalistic kingdoms of Israel and Judah than the envisioned universalistic religious communities of Jeremiah and Ezekiel. In many ways it became even more tribal with its use of biological criteria to determine membership in the new Jewish community and in its insistence on obedience to the letter of tribally specific ritualistic laws. This abandonment of the dreams of Jeremiah, Ezekiel, and Second Isaiah, however, did not go unchallenged. Writers of historical, fictional short stories replaced the prophets as the new social critics.

Three students from our literature departments will present their analyses of three of these short stories. Susan Burk will deal with the short story, *Ruth*. Jean Fehland will introduce us to *Jonah*, and Marion Gerhard will analyze the story of Esther.

Ms. Burk.

Thank you, Professor Hamann.

The book of Ruth was written after the exiles in Babylon had returned to Jerusalem, had re-built the temple, re-established temple worship, and had instituted the rules that true Hebrews and worshippers of Yahweh must be the biological offspring of Hebrews and that Hebrews must never marry non-Hebrews.

Ruth, the protagonist in the story, however, was a Moabite and not a Hebrew, although she was the widow of a Hebrew. The writer of this work of fiction presented Ruth as an example of a person who was a genuine Hebrew in her heart and actions. Furthermore, it is people like Ruth who will give birth to the true, restored kingdom of David. In the story she is the great grandmother of King David, and just as the whole community of Hebrews were the offspring of Isaac's wives, Rachael and Leah, so the true worshippers in the restored Kingdom of David are Ruth's offspring.

The story of Ruth is set back in the time before David was king, back in the time of the old confederacy when the tribes were ruled by judges. The home tribe of a man, Elimelich, and his wife, Naomi, was Bethlehem. This also was the home tribe of King David. A severe drought in Bethlehem forced them to move to a foreign kingdom, Moah, just as Jacob had been forced to go to Egypt and the Hebrews had been forced to leave Jerusalem and go into exile in Babylon. Elimelech and Naomi dwelt in Moah for a long time, had two sons there who, when they grew up, married two Moabite women, Orpha and Ruth. Similarly, the exiles in Babylon stayed there for decades and many took Babylonian wives. Elimelech and both sons, Mahlon and Chilion, died in Moah. The drought in Bethlehem ended and Naomi was able to return to her home country, just as things had changed so that Moses could take the Hebrews back to the land of Jacob and the exiles in Babylon could return to Jerusalem.

Naomi advised her two daughters in law to stay in Moab where they had been raised. She even advised them to worship the God of the Moabites. Ruth, however, insisted on returning with Naomi to Bethlehem. She now totally identified herself with the family of her dead husband and Naomi. She declared that their people, the Hebrews, were now her people, and that their God, Yahweh, was now her God. It was in Bethlehem that she would live, care for Naomi until her death. It was there she would die because of who she now was, a Hebrew – not be birth but by choice.

When they returned to Bethlehem, Naomi and Ruth proceeded to integrate Ruth completely into the life of the people of Bethlehem. It was an old law of Moses that grain harvesters would allow the poor to follow behind the harvesters and to 'gleam' grain from the stalks that had not been cut. Naomi advised Ruth to go to the fields of one of her husband's close relatives, Boaz, and gleam behind his harvesters. She worked harder than anyone and took the grain she gleamed and gave it to Naomi. Boaz noticed her diligence in gleaming and her faithfulness to Naomi. He ordered his harvesters to leave behind them more stalks to be gleamed. Eventually Boaz invited Ruth to eat with him and the harvesters. He noticed that she saved food from the meal and took it back to Naomi. No woman born a Hebrew ever showed more of the spirit of a Hebrew daughter.

Naomi, recognizing how fond Boaz was of Ruth and wanting to have the land owned by her dead husband to remain with her kinsmen, recommended that Ruth put on her finest clothes, wait until Boaz fell asleep after eating and drinking, then pull his sleeping blanket off his feet and lie down at his feet. This she did. At midnight his feet got cold. He woke up rolled over and saw Ruth lying at his feet. She proposed to him by inviting him to spread her skirt over him. He informed her that he could not marry her until the closest next of kin to her father in law, who by custom had a right to replace her dead husband, had turned down the opportunity. Boaz called a meeting of all the elders and told the eligible kinsman about Ruth and that he could inherit the land of Ruth's father in law, Naomi's husband. Elimelech, if he would marry Ruth. Recognizing that Inheriting Elimelech's land would mean losing his own inheritance, the eligible kinsman turned down the offer. Having thereby becoming eligible, Boaz married Ruth who gave birth to a son who became the grandfather of King David.

The story tells us that Hebrews left Bethlehem for Moab, returned to Bethlehem, and laid the foundation for the glorious Kingdom of David based on faithfulness and not on blood. Elimelech and Naomi took the light of the Hebrew faith to a foreign nation and it gave new life and strength to a Hebrew Kingdom of Yahweh. By telling a story, the author of the book of Ruth challenged the directives of Ezra and Nehemiah.

Thank you, Ms. Burk. Ms. Jean Fehland now will give us her analysis of the book of Jonah.

I will try, Professor Hamann. I know most of you have heard the story. I just hope we don't get bogged down on whales swallowing Jonah. It wasn't a whale but a big fish. Besides, it is a fictional short story.

We do not know who the author of this story is. Scholars, using linguistic evidence, surmise that it was written near the end of the rule of the Persians who had allowed the exiles to return from Babylon to Jerusalem. Alexander the Great had not yet ended the power of Persia. The story gives expression to the turmoil that existed in the minds and hearts of the exiles living in Ezra and Nehemiah's new tribal Jerusalem and temple, while also remembering Second Isaiah's proclamation that people can experience the presence of Yahweh anywhere. Yahweh is the God whom Hebrews thank for the ordered world of nature that replaced the primordial waters. The author of *Jonah* illustrates that Yahweh calls Hebrews to be a saving light to all nations. The Jonah story affirms that such a missionary effort works.

The story is set back in an age before Israel was destroyed by Assyria and the people living there were dispersed throughout the region. The author of the story transfers back into Jonah's mind his own feelings. He writes that Jonah is troubled with the mixed feelings of a returning exile from Babylon. On the one hand, he worships Yahweh as the one creator of the whole world and as the compassionate God who calls all worshippers to be God's servants helping all people to come into Gods kingdom of love and joy. On the other hand, he worships Yahweh as the special God of the Hebrews whose presence can be experienced only in the holy temple in Jerusalem. When Jonah, while worshipping Yahweh, hears the call to be a light to the people of Nineveh, the capital of the very Assyrian Empire that will destroy Israel, he thinks he can escape the presence of Yahweh by running away from the temple and sailing off to Tarshish, the Phoenician city at the Western end of the Mediterranean Sea. He soon realizes that this does not work because wherever he goes, on a ship in a raging sea or in the belly of a fish, there he continues to experience the presence of Yahweh.

Jonah paid the fare to get on a ship headed for Tashish, but his ship soon was floundering in a massive storm that had sprung up. The sailors on the boat worshipped other gods that supposedly were their tribal protectors. They prayed to their gods to save them from the storm, but it did not work. The storm raged on. They asked Jonah to pray to his god, Yahweh, to keep them from perishing. Jonah knew that although worshipping Yahweh meant giving thanks for the whole natural world, with its orderly land and raging seas, Yahweh was not a first-responder God. He confessed to the sailors that he had heard a call from his God to go to Nineveh to tell them of the loving compassion of the one God to whom everyone should express thanks that there was no primordial chaos but rather an ordered world of dry land and watery seas. Still influenced by his practices back at the temple to offer sacrifices to Yahweh, he volunteers to sacrifice himself to quiet the seas. Thus, despite his resistance to do so, Jonah's willingness to be a suffering servant to save others turns him into a light to the nations. The sailors accepted Jonah's offer to sacrifice himself and tossed him into the sea. The offering in their minds was really to Jonah's God, Yahweh, whom they believed was willing for his worshippers to make such a personal sacrifice. In the story the sailors accepted the sacrifice and began to trust Yahweh and make their own sacrifices to him.

The story does not end there. The debate in Jonah's mind continues. Jonah, while floundering in the raging storm in the sea and in the belly of the fish that swallowed him, still fails to grasp Second Isaiah's new understanding of Yahweh. At first, he thinks that he cannot experience Yahweh's presence where he is because he can't get back to the temple in Jerusalem. Then, for a little while, Jonah stops debating with himself. He convinces himself that his God, Yahweh, could not be confined to a single place. He turned in prayer to Yahweh because he believed that even in the belly of a fish he was in Yahweh's holy temple. The fish spit him out on dry land. In thanksgiving for life, the created world, and the mission he had been called to carry out, Jonah promised that that he would serve as a light to the nations.

Promises, however, are easier made than kept. Jonah heard for a second time the call to go to Nineveh and enlighten them. He went, and they responded positively. They began to believe in God and turned away from violence, the violence that eventually would destroy Israel. That can happen in fiction. Assyrians, of course, never became Yahweh worshippers. The writer of the story of Jonah was not narrating for history a record of actual events that could be fact checked. He was trying to communicate a bigger truth, one that Jonah never does understand.

The character Jonah became unhappy that the people of Nineveh, who were his foreign enemy, experienced the mercy and love of God. This is just what he feared would happen and the reason why he ran off to Tarshish. If anyone could experience the love of Yahweh, then what meaning was there to be found in his life as a Hebrew. The writer of this story raised the question that many in his age were asking, "If Yahweh loves everyone, what is the point of being a Hebrew?" The writer was addressing the concern of his readers. They had suffered so much for being a Hebrew. They had experienced the Assyrian destruction of Israel, the Babylonian destruction of Jerusalem, their dispersal throughout the world. If Yahweh loved everyone equally, then their miserable lives had no special worth, and it would have been better to die than to live.

Jonah pities his own existence and he pities the plant that died after temporally providing him with shade from the scorching sun. The plant was not his enemy and he could pity its death. His self-pity made it impossible, however, for him to rejoice over the people of Nineveh enjoying the blessing of feeling the love of Yahweh. Jonah pitied himself because he still saw his God as the private possession of him and his tribe. Rather than thanking Yahweh for the opportunity to do a great thing for other people, he could only pity himself for not being allowed to be special and above all others. Second Isaiah's new universalism called him to go to Nineveh, but his old tribalism never allowed him to appreciate the significance of his call. By writing this fictional short story, its creative writer gave voice to a bigger truth. The tribe of Jews is special, not because of material benefits it will receive, but because, through its worship of God even when suffering, it can show people the saving love of God, even people residing in enemy nations.

Thank you, Ms. Fehland. Ms. Marion Gerhard will now explain why the short story, *Esther*, is in the Bible, even though the words 'Elohim' and 'Yahweh' appear nowhere in it.

Ms. Gerhard.

Thank you, Professor Hamann.

Scholars tells us that the book of *Esther* is in the Bible because by the time that the Jewish leaders made the decision about what gets in the Bible the celebration of the Feist of Purim had already been very popular for hundreds of years, a day of celebration that began when, according to the story *Esther,* Jews in Persia celebrated being saved, by Esther and her father, Mordecai, from murder. The point and purpose of this work of fiction, however, is to express opposition to Ezra's tribalism by showing that a Jewish woman married to a Persian king can be a faithful and important worshipper of Yahweh.

The setting of this work of fiction is Persia during the reign of Xerxes I from 486 BCE to 465 BCE, a hundred years after the fall of Babylonia and just around the time that Ezra and Nehemiah were rebuilding Jerusalem. It probably was written sometime just before Alexander the Great destroyed the Persian empire around 330 BCE.

Esther is an orphan who was adopted by her deceased father's nephew, a man named Mordecai. He is described as a descendent of Kish, the father of Saul, who militarily unified the twelve tribes in the ancient confederacy and laid the foundation for David's Kingdom. The conflict that is the centerpiece of the story is between Mordecai and the King of Persia's grand vizier, Haman, a descendent of the Amalekite king defeated by Saul and whose tribe had been antagonists of the Hebrews since the days of Moses when the Amalekites battled against the Hebrew exiles coming out of Egypt. The ancient Battle between the evil Amalekites and the virtuous Moses and Saul is updated in this story as a battle between the faithful Jew, Mordecai, and the evil vizier, Haman. Haman had persuaded the King of Persia to require all Jews to assimilate into a Persian way of life or suffer the penalty of death. Esther heroically saves the day by persuading the king to change his mind and by tricking Hamann into ordering his own destruction.

The story begins with Xerxes ordering his Persian wife to come and show off her beauty to the King's guests and her refusing to make such a spectacle of herself. For disobeying his order, and fearful that other wives of princes would follow her example, the king proclaimed that all women must honor their husbands, He began looking for a replacement for the queen. He brought into the harem in his palace all the beautiful young virgins in the empire. Esther was one of those chosen to be in the king's harem. Only when sent for were any of these women allowed to come to the king. Eventually Esther was called in to be with the king. He fell in love with her and made her his queen. Even as queen she could go to the king only went he sent for her to come.

One day, as Mordecai was sitting at the King's gate, he overheard two of the King's eunuchs planning to assassinate the king. He reported this to Esther. She reported it to the king on one of her invited visits. The two men were hanged.

Meanwhile, Haman had been trying to get all the Jews in Persia to give up being Jews and following Jewish laws and instead to accept becoming assimilated into Persian life, obeying its laws and showing proper courtesies to their royal superiors, including himself. Mordecai refused to do either, and he led the Jews in their desire to remain faithful Jews. Furious over Mordecai's refusal to show him proper respect, he decided to punish Mordecai by punishing all Jews in Persia. He persuaded King Xerxes that the Jews are a subversive threat inside the kingdom. Haman got the king to issue an order that all Jews were to be killed and all their property would become the king's property. Being a rich man himself, Haman gave the king added motivation by promising to pay into the king's treasury ten thousand talents of silver for every Jew killed.

Mordecai asked Esther to help save the Jews. At first, she was hesitant to break the rule forbidden her to go to the king uninvited. Mordecai reminded her that if the order went into effect to kill all Jews, it would apply to her also. Esther devised a plan to save the Jews, knowing full well what happened to the last queen who disobeyed an order by the King. She also knew, however, that if someone entered the inner court uninvited and the king held out the golden scepter to the person, the person would not be killed. She went uninvited to see the king and he held out the golden scepter and asked what it is she wanted. Haman was also present. She requested that the king and Haman come to a dinner that she had prepared for them. They came and dined. She then invited them to come again the next night. They agreed to do so.

Unable to sleep, the king ordered that the book of memorable deeds be brought to him to read. He saw the entry about being saved by Mordecai from assassination by the two eunuchs. He asked what reward had been given to the person who saved his life. He was told that nothing had been done. The next day he asked Haman what should be done to a man whom the king delights to honor. Haman, thinking the king was talking about himself, told the king that this man should be honored by being given a royal robe and one of the prince's horses, and then paraded around the whole city to be honored. The king ordered Haman to do this to Mordecai. Haman was taken completely by surprise.

Afterward, Haman feeling humiliated, was brought by eunuchs to Esther's dinner for the king. The king asked Esther what she desired. He would grant any petition she requested. She asked that the order to kill the Jews be rescinded because she too was a Jew and would have to be killed. The Jews, she said, had been purchased to be murdered. The king asked her who was buying the deaths of her and her people and she answered "Haman." When the king, filled with anger toward Haman, temporarily left the room, Haman ran over to Esther sitting on a couch and bent over her, pleading for his life. The king returned, thought Haman was attacking his queen, ordered that Haman be hanged on the same gallows prepared by Haman's wife for Mordecai. Haman's ten sons were hanged with him.

The king gave to Esther Haman's house and issued an order that no Jews anywhere in the empire were to be harmed and that they may arm themselves and annihilate anyone who acts violently against them. The Jews killed five hundred of their enemies. They then gathered together and made that day one of feasting and gladness. The king ordered that every year on this day there should be a similar celebration of the day that the Jews were saved.

This, the story says, was the beginning of the Feast of Purim.

A Jew, an orphan, a woman, a member of a Persian king's harem, a queen married to a non-Jewish Persian King, a faithful and heroic savior of Jews, a founder of the Feast of Purim. This is who Esther was. The writer of the story is saying that something is drastically wrong with the laws of Ezra and Nehemiah which forbid her from being a faithful worshipper of Yahweh.

Thank you, Ms. Gerhard.

We have looked at the prophets who prepared the way for the universalism proclaimed by the exiled Hebrews in Babylon and then at the short story writers protesting the threat to such universalism posed by the tribalism reintroduced into Jerusalem after the exile. The practices of Ezra and Nehemiah posed an institutional threat to the new Hebrew spirit given birth in Babylon.

A very different kind of intellectual and existential threat was posed by the Greek philosophical ideas spreading throughout the Mediterranean world. During the century before Alexander the Great swept through the Fertile Crescent, the writings of two Athenian philosophers, Plato (428-347 BCE) and Aristotle (384-322), succeeded in Greece in getting trust in human theoretical and practical rationality to replace worship of the gods in the Greek pantheon of gods. Throughout the history of the Hebrews there always had been a place in the life of Hebrews for the Sage who gave practical advice about how to live well as a farmer or merchant. As the new age of Greek rationalism began to seep into the thinking of Jews dispersed throughout the Fertile Crescent and Egypt. Jewish writers began to wrestle rationally with the issues of the meaning and point of human existence and the justification for the attitudes of gratitude and hope inherent in worshipping Yahweh, given all the senseless suffering occurring in the world.

The book of Proverbs in the Bible offers dozens of pieces of practical advice comparable to what is found in Benjamin Franklin's *Poor Richard's Almanac*. The book of Ecclesiastes questions whether anything, including the worship of Yahweh, can give a good reason for anyone not regretting being born. In the poetic portion of the book of Job, Job puts Yahweh on trial for permitting so much suffering and injustice to exist in the world and he offers refutations of the arguments presented by Yahweh's defense attorneys.

Students from our philosophy department will share with us their critical analyses and responses to these three books. Mr. Bruce Jensen will help us think about the book of Proverbs.

Thank you, Professor Hamann.

The book of Proverbs contains wise pieces of advice, some of which go back as far as Solomon. Many in fact are reworkings of things said in the Egyptian book, *Instruction of Amen-em-opet* (1,000-600 BCE), and the Babylonian book, *Counsels of Wisdom*. Many of the saying were written after the exile in Babylon. They basically consist of four kinds of sayings: advice on how to behave, recommendations of virtuous character traits, declarations that moral virtues depend upon worshipping attitudes towards Yahweh, personifications of wisdom.

Here are a few of the pieces of advice that would be prudent in any kingdom or age. "He who tills his land will have plenty of bread, but he who follows worthless pursuits has no sense." "A hot-tempered man stirs up strife, but he who is slow to anger quiets contention." "The sluggard does not plow in the autumn; he will seek at harvest and have nothing." "Make no friendship with a man given to anger, nor go with a wrathful man, lest you learn his ways and entangle yourself in a snare." The following pithy sayings in *Poor Richard's Almanac* would be right at home among these proverbs. "Three may keep a secret if two of them are dead." "Speak little, do much." "Content makes a poor man rich; discontent makes a rich man poor." This kind of wisdom is universal and not particularly religious.

Virtues and vices are character traits, habits of acting and feeling in a certain way. Aristotle had suggested building up good habits by being reasonable and not overestimating or underestimating one's evaluations of the objects of one's feelings. Virtuous habits lie at the golden mean between the vices of extreme reactions; it is a matter of living with moderation in life. Courage is the virtuous mean between cowardliness and foolhardiness. Temperance is the virtuous mean between indulgence and self-denial. Modesty is the virtuous mean between bashfulness and shamelessness. A modern version of recommended virtues is found in the Boy Scout's pledge to be trustworthy, loyal, helpful, friendly, courteous, kind, obedient, cheerful, thrifty, brave, clean, and reverent. The virtues praised in the Proverbs are habits like diligence and sobriety and the vices are laziness, drunkenness. One proverb reduces the vices down to six: haughty eyes, lying tongue, shedding innocent blood, devising wicked plans, bearing false witness, sowing discord. Repeatedly, the collectors of these proverbs declare that being virtuous will lead to successful living and acting from vices will result in personal ruin.

Throughout the collection of Proverbs, a Jewish accent is given to the claim that virtuous living is rewarded with good results and having vices is punished with personal disasters. The Jewish writers put this claim in the language of fearing God guaranteeing a secure life at ease and without dread of evil. The writers of the Provers were reproducing at the personal level what the Deuteronomic historian was promising at the national level to Israel and Judah. Be faithful and things will go well; be unfaithful and face destruction. "The fear of Yahweh prolongs life, the years of the wicked will be short. The hope of the righteous ends in gladness, but the expectation of the wicked comes to naught." This was the position that Jeremiah rejected, and it seemed to the exiles in Babylon to have been refuted by the destruction of Jerusalem. The writers of the book of Proverbs, however, attempted to give this position new life by utilizing the Greek treatment of rationality and the personalization of wisdom as Sophia.

Greek philosophers such as Plato, Aristotle, and the Stoic philosopher, Zeno, all claimed that the universe was rational and good through and through. Plato wrote that all truths are eternal and unchanging, like mathematics, and they are all organized in a single coherent whole in accordance with a principle of Goodness, a whole that any person could know if they placed their ultimate trust in human reason. Aristotle wrote that all observational beliefs are knowable to the rational person who understands that they are the way they are because of an unchanging, perfect principle governing all change. Zeno argued that reason enables humans to see that the only thing they can control in the world is their attitude towards the world and to see that it is rational to live by such an attitude because the world is rational and good. There is a good reason why everything is at it is. For many Greek thinkers, the rationality of the world was personalized as Sophia, wisdom itself.

The authors of Proverbs united such talk about rationality and wisdom with Hebrew and Jewish talk about God as the creator of the world. They wrote, "Yahweh by wisdom founded the earth; by understanding he established the heavens." Speaking of Wisdom, they wrote, "Yahweh created me at the beginning of his work, the first of his acts of old. Ages ago, I was set up, at the first, before the beginning of the earth. . . When he established the heavens, I was there. . . when he marked out the foundations of the earth, then I was beside him, like a master workman; I was daily his delight." Drawing upon the Greek personification of reason and wisdom, the authors of Proverbs re-states the claim of the Deuteronomic historians. "Long life is in her (wisdom's) right hand and in her left hand are riches and honor. Her ways are ways of pleasantness, and all her paths are peace. She is a tree of life to those who lay hold of her; those who hold her fast are called happy." 3:16-18

Even while the authors of the book of Proverbs were reassuring people that virtue receives its rewards and vice its miseries, that being wise pays off and being foolish leads to personal ruin, other writers challenged the reasonableness of such blind faith in wisdom and human reason.

Mr. David Bissell is going to give his take on the book of Ecclesiastes.

Thank you, Bruce.

The book of Ecclesiastes was written by one person, called "The teacher," sometime after Alexander the Great's empire had been divided into three kingdoms but before the Maccabee revolts took place. It might have been written by a Jew in the diaspora in Egypt. Its themes are very similar to those found in the Egyptian text, *Dispute Over Suicide.* The teacher's confession of his despairing search for meaning in life is like what is written in the Babylonian text, *I Will Praise the Lord of Wisdom.* In his despair, the teacher writes that the lives of people are so bad and insignificant that it might have been better if no humans ever had been born. Jonah's asking the same question about his life becomes the universal human question in Ecclesiastes. Clearly, the teacher is disappointed in life. The questions that need to be asked by those of us analyzing this book are: What were the expectations that he had which drove him to be suicidal when they were not fulfilled? What were the assumptions he was living on which led him to have those expectations?

The Teacher starts out be charging that everything is vanity, that it is vain for any person to do anything, because the same sorts of things keep happening again and again. The sun rises and sets again and again. The winds blow and the water in the rivers flow season after season. One generation of people is followed by another generation of people. Nothing new happens. We are caught up in constant repetitions of actions and none of them make our lives significant: being born and dying, planting and harvesting, killing and healing, breaking down and building up, weeping and laughing, mourning and dancing, casting away stones from one's garden and picking up stones for one's walls, embracing people and keeping one's distance, seeking and losing, keeping and throwing away, tearing and sowing, speaking and staying silent, making war and making peace. Same O; Same O.

The teacher says that he has repeatedly tried to find meaning in life and to understand the crazy madness of everything that is happening. He finds that also to be vain because his search for such wisdom provides no answers. He thought that perhaps simply gaining pleasurable experiences would be enough to make life worth living. These, however, are there only for a moment and then gone; they do not make a whole life significant, a life that ends in death. Even if I build houses and gardens that live on after me, this does not make my life significant. My works will not make me stand out as significant in the eyes of others because within a short period of time no one will even remember that I lived and built something. Neither does it help to think that I can reason and search for wisdom and that would make me superior to other animals and thus significant. Humans and animals alike eventually return to the dust from which they came. Being able to reason does not change that fact. Actually, being able to search for an ultimate meaning to life, and always failing, makes the whole business of human reasoning and living senseless.

What makes human living even more ridiculous, writes the Teacher, is the fact that wisdom and virtue do not prevent people from suffering, and being wicked does not prevent people from gaining pleasure, ease of life, wealth, and power. He writes, "In my vain life I have seen everything: there is the righteous man who perishes in his righteousness, and there is the wicked man who prolongs his life in his evil-doing." Furthermore, life makes no sense because not only do the righteous not prosper or the wicked suffer, but so much happens by senseless chance. "Again, I saw that under the sun the race is not to the swift, nor the battle to the strong, nor bread to the wise, nor riches to the intelligent, nor favor to the men of skill; but time and chance happen to them all.

Thus, finding no meaning in life, the Thinker writes that he thought to himself, "the dead who are already dead are more fortunate than the living who are still alive; but better than both is he who has not yet been, and has not seen the evil deeds that are done under the sun." The thinker concludes that since he has been born and is alive, he will quit seeking some big meaning in life but instead will "eat, and drink, and enjoy himself, for this will go with him in his toil through the days of life which God gives him under the sun."

The thinker's feelings of despair seem to be the result of frustrated expectations that themselves are based on a certain way of evaluating things. Let's reflect on these one by one. He is bored with his life because nature is governed by laws that cause things to repeatedly happen in the same way and because he is required to live by social norms and traditions that mean that he repeatedly does the same sort of things day after day. He wants to have something new happening in his life. He would find things significant if they were fresh and original; he finds repetition valueless. It seems to me that he is wrong on his facts and on his evaluations. Freshness and originality is happening all the time. Experiencing the new does add significant spice to life, but so can living in an orderly world permitting one to have certain expectations.

One of the great insights of the Buddhist tradition focuses on the constant changes in life. Buddhists point out that things in the world are very fragile and subject to change at every moment, but that is what makes experiencing them so valuable. The cherry blossoms are there for a moment but knowing that they soon will be gone makes viewing them so beautiful and sad. Patterns may govern the way sorts of things occur again and again, but what happens to things are singularly unique and can be experienced as such. People may go out every morning to care for their flowers, but every time they do so they see them in a fresh way and they value each of their experiences with them.

People are singularly unique in an even more profound and significant way. As the Biblical creation story puts it, people are images of the imageless God. We are not just a certain sort of thing, a physical and biological sort of thing or a mere occupant of a social role – a male student who is a citizen of the United States. Each of us is singularly unique, seeing the world from a unique point of view, acting in the unique ways determined by our endorsement or rejection of the social norms governing the human worlds in which we live. When, at some moment, we, as singularly unique persons, encounter other people in their singular uniqueness, something new occurs and we have a singularly unique challenge to ethically respect them in their uniqueness. Only by ignoring our own indescribable uniqueness, and the indescribable uniqueness of people we meet face to face, will we think that we are going through meaningless routines.

Focusing on our need to respond individually to the norms and routines that make up the social worlds into which we were thrown can lead us to sense how significant such norms and routines are to us. It is only because we do many things routinely that we escape the madness of having to choose each moment what to do. Only then can we find the time and mental space needed to do things creatively. It is only because we obey norms of language usage, that novelists, poets and thinkers can write what has never been written before and never will be written again. It is only because most people routinely drive in the United States on the right side of the road that any of us have the freedom to drive where we choose to go. It is only because of nature's repetitions that we enjoy seeing the first robin in spring, driving through hills bursting with fall colors, or ski down mountain sides – experiences that never get old no matter how many times we do them.

One of factors that plays a major role in the Thinker's frustration with life is his belief that there is an absence in human, social history of any progress. This is a frustration that many of us share today as we examine the last century of wars, economic domination and exploitation, and social revolutions that turn into despotic tyrannies. The questions we need to ask, however, are, "Is it true that historical progress never occurs?" "Why do we ever expect the kind of progress we find absent? "Do historical patterns, if there any, make the lives of individual persons insignificant? Is my personal life insignificant if I can't contribute to historical progress towards a certain sort of heaven on earth?"

Let me make several responses to these questions. First, are we letting ourselves get frustrated too soon? Are we focusing our attention so much on the big issues of war and peace, justice and injustice, that we blind ourselves from seeing the little improvements in social life that are occurring? Even if our big concerns did not blind us to these little improvements, the small steps being taken might seem little to us but huge to the people aided by these improvements. Human sacrifice has ended almost everywhere in the world. So also has polio. Millions who were starving now are not. Women in many countries of the world have gained the right to vote. In some countries same sex couples can marry. Most African Americans in southern states in the United states now can vote. Spousal abuse now is illegal in the U.S., as is child abuse. The list goes on and on. The Teacher's frustrations and our frustrations may be based on unreasonable expectations. We individually may not be able to create heaven on earth, but we do seem to be able to contribute to making human life in certain areas for many people a little less hellish. The Biblical story of Adam may be communicating a universal truth. All humans in all periods of history seek to dominate nature and other people. The Prophets also may be right that worshipping God means always having to combat injustice. We also have the voice of Second Isaiah, however, telling us that, even as we suffer because of the injustice in the world and because of our attempt to resist it, our call to do so makes our lives significant and meaningful.

There is still the trump card that the Thinker's skepticism can play. Even if one can enjoy moments of life, and even if one can contribute to lessening injustice in the world, still one ends up dead. Given human mortality, what's the use of living? I suggest we change the question around? What is the motivation that lies behind the expectation that mortality frustrates? Isn't it the desire to be god, the desire for the power to control everything and to be dependent on nothing? Biblical writers continuously point out that God has the sun shine on the good and bad. The prophets condemned the idea that the Hebrew Kingdoms were God chosen nations that would be protected from other warring empires. They condemned the popular prophets who thought that faithfulness to rituals would buy divine protection. Isn't that desire to be God an unreasonable desire? Isn't the desire to ward off death really a desire to be God. The Thinker is not willing to be simply a person in a natural and social environment. He wants to be Lord and Master over that environment. He won't just let life and death be. He wants to maintain total control over everything. He thinks that his individual life is meaningful only if he as an individual can overpower death itself. He thinks that immortality and only immortality can give him what he so desperately wants

Let me give my reasons for thinking that the Thinker's desire and evaluation of human life is incorrect. We may be singularly unique in the way we respond to our inescapable location in a natural world of birth and death and in a social world of norms and routines, but we are inescapably biological and social. We may fantasize about shedding our earthly skin and social status, but this is a fantasy we have not thought through. We have no idea what it might be like to be a disembodied person with no eyes to see anything, no tongue to taste anything, no ears to hear anything. We have no idea what it would be like to be outside of time with no experiences happening one after another. The philosophers Plato and Descartes tried to imagine being such an eternal, bodiless soul, but what they came up with was something like a mathematical mind that was as immaterial and unchanging as numbers. They heavily influenced Christian thinking, but they and their followers were unaware of what later philosophers like Kant and Wittgenstein pointed out. Even imagining bodiless souls or minds presupposes that the people doing the imagining are embodied people. What people who want to control everything don't realize is that if they were immortal they still would not be independent and in control of things. They still would have to contend with other people wanted to run the show. They still would be subject to the commands of God or the requirements of Aristotle's unmoved mover.

If one understands that one is essentially embedded in a physical and biological world and in a social, historical world, then one can also understand that our social and individual identity does not begin with birth or end with death. So much of what makes us what we are is determined by the social and cultural history we have inherited from the past. Recognition of this is probably one of the reasons

Hebrews identified people by listing their ancestral relatives. We are who we are because Moses, Plato, Jesus, Thomas Jefferson, Abraham Lincoln, and FDR lived. They live on in us. We are who we are because of American slavery, genocide of Native Americans, American sexism, racism, and homophobia. Our singular uniqueness is determined by how we have responded to this historical inheritance. Without that inheritance there would be nothing to which we could respond. This is the reason why a sense of history is required to know ourselves. The same is true of our identity on into the future. People in future generations will be what they are because of the social and cultural practices and institutions we leave as out legacy. People live on in their social and cultural children. The more we can nurture in our children a sense of history the more they will know of our continued life in them.

There is one final factor that led to the Thinkers frustration with life. There is no guarantee that good people will be rewarded for their virtue and there is no guarantee that having vices is materially unreasonable, since such people often prosper, often because of their vices. Here the Thinker is operating on the assumption that virtue should pay, and vice should not. He is disappointed that in fact this is not true. He believes it should be true. Is it reasonable, however, to believe as he does? Is it necessary for this to be true for our individual lives to be meaningful and significant?

The assumption that life is fair, despite all counter evidence, or that life at least ought to be fair, is an assumption that people have made in every age, especially in our own. When a mother working two low paying jobs to care for her fatherless children is shot to death in a drive-by shooting, many of her friends claim that there must be a good reason for what happened even though we don't know what it is. So many people seem to believe in heaven and hell because they believe that somehow there must be rewards for the virtuous and punishment for the villains, even if this does not happen during their lifetimes. Parents of murdered children often claim that the demands of justice have finally been met when the murderer of their child is sentenced to death; they could not live in peace until this justice was obtained. They can find peace, and life can be meaningful again for them, only if they can again believe that things are as they ought to be, that injustice is justly punished. A tornado rips through one family's home and leaves untouched their neighbor's house, and often the survivors either cry out, "Not fair" or "God must have some reason for doing this." People resent villains getting away with murder and shirkers living well while hard working people barely can get by.

The book of Proverbs calls upon people to reason together. Is there any good reason, however, for people to believe that life is fair or ought to be fair if their personal lives are to be meaningful? I suggest that It is only when people do not believe that life in and of itself is meaningful that they feel that it is necessary to go outside life to find something that can make life meaningful. They postulate the existence of a God or a superior power to guarantee that there is a good and justifying reason for everything happening in the world. There is so much injustice and so many senseless accidents in life that it is very understandable that they convince themselves that there is some supernatural crutch they can depend upon, as they try to walk through lives that seem filled with so much injustice and unfairness.

It is perfectly possible, however, that if one did not assume that life ought to be fair, and if one just let what has happened in life be what it is, free of evaluation in terms of fairness, free of the resentment that frustrated expectations of fairness generate, then one would be living a life one could joyfully celebrate. Tending the flowers in one's garden then can bring joy even after one's house was blown away. Of course, one will do what one can to lessen the hellishness in life, but one will let one's failures and one's successes just be. Repeatedly, Biblical writers call for people to be grateful for the existence of the world and human life, even when famines and wars are occurring. The prophets and the priestly writers in Babylon tell us to live grateful lives of service even though one's past life has been crushed and one lives as captives in a foreign land. The philosopher Nietzsche spent his life in pain, but he also celebrated just being alive and he said that he would welcome living his life of physical pain again and again for all time. The Lutheran pastor, Dietrich Bonhoeffer, up until the moment Hitler ordered him killed just before the end of World War II, counseled inmates in Nazi concentration camps not to despair or commit suicide but to cherish life right up to the last minute.

Let me finish here. Val Kroening is going to deal with a great deal of this in his analysis of the book of Job.

Val?

Thanks, David.

It is the poem at the heart of the book of Job on which I want to focus. The prose prelude and postlude were added later to take the edge off the radical truth the poet was trying to convey. The folktale about Job existed for centuries before the writer of the poem at the heart of the book was written. The similarity of many of its lines to those written by Second Isaiah has led scholars to conclude that Second Isaiah probably was influenced by the poem about Job. The poem's questioning of the Deuteronomic thesis that God rewards the virtuous and punishes the unrighteous is very similar to Jeremiah's, suggesting to scholars that it probably was written after Jeremiah and before the writings of the priests in Babylon. Its story line, themes, and literary form show that the Job poet was influenced by similar Egyptian and Babylonia writings. In the so-called *"Babylonian Job"*, a rich man, who loses his wealth and power and ends up sick and in trouble, defends his innocence and claims that the Babylonian gods have treated him unfairly. In the Babylonian *Dialogue about Human Misery,* a man who has suffered all his life debates with a friend about the justice of the gods' treatment of him. In the Egyptian *Protests of the Eloquent Peasant* the same issues are dealt with in a poem sandwiched between a prose prelude and a prose postlude.

Job takes God to court. He brings a lawsuit against God for breach of contract. "I desire to argue my case with God." Job charges that God has promised in the covenants he made with Abraham and Moses to care for his people, but he has broken this contract. Job issues a general charge and a specific charge. The general charge is that God's chosen people have not found a land of milk and honey in which to live. They have been treated unfairly by those not faithful to God who have grown rich and powerful because of their unrighteousness. Other nations worshipping other gods have crushed them and chased them into exile. God has not protected those who have been faithful worshippers of him. The poem begins with a lament in which Job, speaking for many like himself, curses the day he was born for then he and they would not have been troubled by the wicked, lived in misery and fear of the call of cruel taskmasters, or been fooled into hoping for what God had promised.

Job's specific charge is that he himself has suffered greatly even though he has done nothing wrong, either in the eyes of men or the eyes of God. He is an innocent man who has tried to protect the vulnerable from unjust treatment by the wicked, but God lets him be punished as though he were guilty of terrible crimes. His skin is hard and broken and painful wounds cover his body. His mind is cursed during the day by being filled with feelings of bitterness, and his nights are filled with misery and terrible dreams. He is a laughing stock in the eyes of supposed friends and his spirit is broken. He cries to God for relief and justice, but he hears only silence. "Behold, I go forward, but he is not there; and backward, but I cannot perceive him; on the left hand I seek him, but cannot behold him; I turn to the right hand, but cannot see him."

There is no doubt that Job believes in God; otherwise he would not be bringing this lawsuit against God. He is not asking that God be punished for breaking the covenants. He desperately is crying out wanting to understand why so much misery, injustice and dashed hopes exist, given that God is so powerful and so good. The poet has Job confess, "God is wise in heart and mighty in strength." "With God are wisdom and might... In his hands is the life of every living thing and the breath of all mankind." "God stretches out the north over the void, and hangs the earth upon nothing." Job is taking God to court because he presumes that God has a good reason for all the misery and injustice in his life and in the world overall. He wants to hear God tell him what that reason is, because as he sees things there is no good reason. If this misery and injustice is a matter of God punishing evil doers, then the one's being punished have a right to hear what it is they have done wrong. Job feels despair because he hears no indictment from God and, as far as he can see, he has done nothing wrong. The same is true of many other innocent people suffering so much.

The poet provided God with three defenses attorneys, three "friends of Job." Each tried three times to convince Job that he really was not innocent, and that God was not guilty of unjustly punishing him. Their defense of God really consisted of trying to convict Job. He must have done something wrong. Each time, however, Job replies that they have not and cannot justify their indictment of him; he is innocent and does not deserve conviction and punishment.

Eliphaz charges that we can observe that only evil people get punished and that no mortal men are pure. He tells Job that his very doubt that his suffering is deserved punishment shows that he is not faithful in his heart to God. Your putting God on trial proves that you do not show proper respect for God, and such lack of faith is evil and deserving of punishment. Bildad points out to Job that immortal God cannot act unjustly, just as mortal men cannot be anything but a maggot and worm, having been born of unclean women. Zophar claims that God knows what is hidden from humans; he knows what they have done wrong even if they can't discern it. God also sees things from a perspective other than any that humans can take. Zophar claims that God sees that in the long run the temporary profits of evil doers will be lost with their children who will end up suffering, and God sees that the temporary pains of the righteous will be short.

Job is not persuaded by any of these charges and arguments. To Eliphaz, Job replies that he has shown in his actions his faithfulness to God. He has been kind and did not accept any bribes or deceive anyone. Furthermore, his case is not exceptional. Everywhere bad things happen to people whether they are righteous or wicked. If it is sinful to search to learn God's reasons for these things happening, then why does God make it possible to ask such questions? To Bildad, Job replies that if everyone ends up being punished because they necessarily are nothing but worms and maggots, then why would a just God punish them. He made them that way. To Zophar, Job addresses the question, "Would you lie for God?" Every time I point out cases where the good suffer and the evil prosper, you reply that there is some bigger reason that justifies it, even if you don't know what that reason is. This is just white-washing God and not a matter of showing that my case against God is unjustified. None of you have provided a reason why our good and powerful God would let such apparent unfairness exist.

The debate between Job and his "friends" ends up with no one offering or finding a justifying reason for the pain and suffering in the world or for the unfair distribution of the burdens and benefits of human life. If the story ended there, this would be a poem expressing justification for Job's despair. The poem does not end there, however. Rather, it goes on to challenge the appropriateness of seeking such a justification. Job, who had been striving to hear from God why things are as they are, now hears God challenge Job's whole project of striving to find such an ultimate reason. Job is challenged to simply accept and cherish the natural world as an unwarranted gift given to him, as a basically good creation of the God he worships. Job is challenged to cherish life even if there is no big reason why people's lives are as they are. Job responds by saying that he will stop the whole process of seeking a kind of wisdom that would offer such answers. He repents his search for such wisdom that is not wisdom at all but is instead an attempt by humans to maintain intellectual mastery over everything, even God. He will accept his place in nature and history, a place that is both lowly and marvelous, continuing to worship God in attitudes and actions no matter what happens.

The poet writing Job rejects the Deuteronomic Historian's conception of God and the Wisdom tradition of seeking rational explanations for everything in nature and history. This was too radical an idea for the Jews who read his poem. They added a preface and postlude to the poem. They gave, in the form of a myth, an explanation for Job's suffering and anguish, by having God's messenger, Satan, persuade God to test the faithfulness of the worshipper of whom God was so proud, Job. They persuaded God to take away from Job all his riches and to subject him to suffering and anguish. These editors of his poem then had all Job's blessings restored to him when he proved faithful. These editors inverted the big Truth the poet was trying to communicate. Job's virtue, patience, is rewarded. The poem itself, however, stands as a refutation of the literary book ends within which it was placed. There is no big reason, discoverable by the "wise," for why things are as they are. They just happen. Despite that fact of life, do not lose faith in life but cherish it as a wonderful gift from a good and loving creator.

That professor Hamann is what the political science department is able to add to your course.

I thank you, Val. Let me also thank David and Bruce from the political science department, and Susan, Jean, and Marion from English, and the five presenters of the prophets: Mary Jo, Fern, Lloyd, Roger, and Tom. You gave us so much to think about.

Reverend Kennedy left a few minutes ago to ready things for you over in the lounge. Therefore, let's adjourn to the lounge.

Chapter Seven

Jacksonville Responds

If you would take a seat, we can begin. I wasn't surprised to see you chatting excitingly with each other. So much material was covered by Professor Hamann and the university students. I am sure that you had many things to say to each other. By the way, you probably noticed that Professor Hamann was losing his voice by the end. I gave him some Chinese herbal tea that works wonders for me when I have a cold. If any of you would like some, I think I have with me enough for a couple of people. Some of you probably got drenched during the hurricane last week. I stayed inside and just watched the power and beauty of nature at work. Looking outside right now at our magnificent sunny day, I keep thinking that nature's power is at work in quiet ways that we hardly notice. As Job said, such power affects the virtuous and unrighteous alike. Having experienced both manifestations of nature's, I am so glad that we are here able to celebrate being alive and together, recognizing that we can just let things be that we cannot control.

I've got to take my wife's advice and stop talking so that you have a chance to share your ideas with all of us. Who wants to begin? Christopher, I see your hand up.

Yes, Reverend Kennedy. As I listened to narratives of the writing of the many texts that make up this portion of the Bible, one scene kept flashing through my mind. Often my evangelical, fundamentalist friends have said to me, "This is what the Bible says." I keep wanting to say to them that the Bible is not a person who says anything. As we have just herd, the Bible is made up of many texts of many different kinds. Specific persons, molded by their social and cultural inheritances, have written them on specific historical occasions in specific social situations. Some of the texts have embodied in them texts written by non-Biblical writers. Some of them are edited texts of earlier Biblical writers. Some of the texts are epics and others are historical interpretations, prophetic pronouncements, short stories, or poems. As we have just heard, to understand these texts we need to understand the point and purpose of people writing them when they did.

I am sure that my friends would then say that they were all written by people inspired by God. Therefore, the whole Bible has been written by God. Listening to the speakers today it is very apparent to me that all the Biblical writers were inspired by the God they worshipped. We must be careful, however, not to work with the wrong picture of what such inspiring is all about. The Biblical writer is not simply some telegraph operator whose fingers and brain are connected by an invisible wire to some supernatural being who sends energy impulses that cause the writer's fingers to write the words making up his text. As I see it, in the same manner that Bill Mauldin was inspired by the plight of ordinary infantrymen to create G.I. Joe cartoons, the Biblical writers perceived human life through the lens of the attitudes and actions that constituted their worship of God. Their inheritance of hundreds of years of Biblical traditions, their perceptions of what was happening to and around them, and their creative response to their inheritance and perceptions produced those attitudes and inspired them to write what they did. What makes the Bible a sacred book is not magical telegraph impulses but the righteous character of people who wrote the Biblical texts. Given that critical thinking is America's other national deficit, I am not very hopeful that my evangelical, fundamentalist friends will be able to hear what I am saying any more than Job's friends could hear him.

Thank you, Chris. And thank you for not abandoning your friends even if the bubble in which they live insulates them from the kind of critical thinking you are doing. When Second Isaiah heard God call him to be a light to the nations, he didn't hear any promise that his enlightening words could penetrate the blinds that had been erected to keep out such light.

Ms. Zhang, I think I saw your hand raised. We would love to hear your reactions to what you heard today.

I also heard something that many people today seem unable to hear, although to me it seems indispensable if we are to find a way of life that gives us peace of mind even while we do the frustrating work of opposing injustice. When I heard of Job deciding to stop talking and to quit looking for some big explanation and justification for human suffering, I could not help but think of the Buddha calling for Golden Silence. There are no big supernatural reasons why things are as they are. Don't look for one. Stop talking about ultimate reasons why, or final justifications for human suffering. Things just happen. No one is there to be blamed if typhoons occur or children get cancer. As Job also found out, searching for the meaning for life in something outside of life is one of the things that causes people so much mental anguish. As I see it, the enlightenment Job gains is not that much different from the enlightenment Siddhartha Gautama gained while meditating under the Bo tree and that led to his being called "The Buddha", the awakened one.

Craving to find ultimate explanations and ultimate justifications is just one more of the cravings that create in people the kind of despair and suffering that drives them to be suicidal. People generally cannot accept just being in the world; they crave to be in control of the world. They constantly compare themselves to other people and they must be superior. They crave for whatever is needed to be superior. This leads to personal despair when one fails to be king of the hill. It also leads to continuous, frustrating social conflict as each person seeks superiority over every other person. What people need to do is to let everything be as is independent of our comparative evaluations, but this is just what people generally and for the most part won't do. We want to be in control of everything: other people, nature, guilt and shame for past misdeeds, fear about future pains, disabilities, and death.

Let me add a warning. The injunction from Job and the Buddha to just let things be must not be misunderstood. It does not imply passively doing nothing in the world, such as not resisting injustice or failing to be kind and compassionate. People are not trapped in an iron cage of fate. It is our comparative evaluations and our dependence on them in building our sense of self-worth that drives us into despair and the misuse of other people and nature. For the Buddha, we freely cause out problem and we can freely eliminate this problem, but it is going to take a great deal of hard work to unravel the onion that our comparative evaluations and cravings have caused. His point is that we don't have to make ourselves and other people miserable. We know that we can't completely control what is going on in the world, but I suggest that we can make a difference and we need not see ourselves as failures when we have not achieved everything that justice and compassion requires us to do. When we have done something, we need to let ourselves be the half-pealed onion that almost all of us remain. We need to forgive ourselves even as we forgive others no matter how much of their onion remains.

What I heard today helps me understand why I never became a Christian even though I was married to a person whom I would say was a good Christian. There are different ways of letting things be in their suchness and of avoiding subjecting them to human comparative evaluations. I meditate. My husband prayed. The attitudes and commitments that resulted were very similar even though the rituals were significantly different.

Thank you, Zhang. You have made a very important point. Being a light to the nations does not mean that one bringing the light is superior to the one being enlightened by the light one brings. By lighting up the nations to which one goes, one makes it possible to see what they are in their suchness and thus to be enlightened by them. Being Second Isaiah's light to the nations must never be a matter of imperialistically destroying who they are or of turning them into a clone of oneself. Not domination but dialogue is what is needed. I think that Buddhist-

Christian dialogue would enrich the religious lives of people living in either tradition. Zhang, I think that you are living proof of that point. Val gave voice to Job and you heard the Buddha.

Mark, I think you have something to say.

I would like to address the issue dealt with by all the prophets, but especially Amos. That is the issue of economic justice. Amos points out that it is unfair to have a huge differential between the rich and the poor. The poor work so hard and remain poor. The rich do little except lie and cheat and they get richer. Amos made a point that all of us know too well. The rich can maintain their domination over the poor because there are ways to bribe government officials to use their police and military power to keep the poor in line. In our day, the bribes take the form of guaranteeing that elected politicians keep their jobs by funding re-election campaigns and by pouring billions of dollars into media outlets favorable to the candidates they support. As a result, laws get passed aiding the rich to get richer and laws protecting the poor and vulnerable do not get enforced when they are passed.

On all of this I think Amos's moral criticisms are right on target. I think it is important, however, not to misidentify the problem. Without denying that it is unfair to place so many burdens on the poor and to make it so difficult for them to reap significant benefits, I would suggest that it is not inequality of wealth per se that is the problem. Equalizing burdens and benefits among all people might not be the best way to aid the poor who are being exploited by the rich. If some people are permitted to gain more wealth and power for themselves by being entrepreneurs, working harder, taking on more responsibilities, being more imaginative, and taking more risks than others, then they might increase the benefits and reduce the burdens to be distributed to the poor. Don't misunderstand me. I am not suggesting the huge differences now existing between the rich and the poor are needed to motivate such entrepreneurs.

Mark, I couldn't agree with you more. I'm a farmer's wife. I know the risks we had to take in trying out new ideas. Sometimes it worked and sometimes it didn't. When it did work, we made more money and we enjoyed our land and animals more, and we produced better quality food and lower prices to everyone buying our products. As I said, I've spend my spare time reading a lot of books on economics and I am convinced that everyone is better off in our competitive economy if people can get ahead through hard work and taking risks. In the abstract, one might wish for a noncompetitive economy, but I don't know of any such economy functioning on a large-scale basis. I don't think we have any choice but to try to seek justice with competitive economies. People are different. For many reasons some people get ahead while others don't. No one gets helped if some people aren't permitted to try to make their lives better and better. Making everyone equal just isn't a very good idea.

I agree, Anita, but the issue is how much better must people be allowed to be to increase the size of the pie and improve the lives of the poor. Many of us are convinced that the difference between the rich and the poor today is much larger than is needed to motivate people to increase the size of the pie. I would suggest that we consider an idea put forward by one of America's best, twentieth century philosophers, the late John Rawls. He advocated that, as a general moral principle of fairness and justice, inequalities in burdens and benefits should exist only if they serve the best interests of the least advantaged in society. Given the differences existing in different societies, the changes constantly occurring in the worlds in which people live, and the limitations of human knowledge about what inequalities really do serve the best interests of the poorest among us, there is no mathematical formula that can be applied automatically to determine what inequalities are fair and just. People need to keep debating about the best way to reach this moral goal. For the debate to be morally profitable, of course, the debaters need to be as well informed as possible and as skillful as possible at critically evaluating what are presented to them as facts.

Excuse me, Mark, for interrupting. but I think we need to step back from talking about ideals of fairness. I think we need to look at what is really going on and what it is reasonable to expect that we can do to make our world more just.

That's O.K., Scott. You have had much more personal experience with people who are under the thumb of the rich and powerful than I have had. Go ahead.

Professor Rawls' principle of justice makes sense, even as a goal to aim at, only if it can be operationalized. Tremendous inequality exists today. Is it possible to change that? I have no confidence that we can turn to government to politically change current economic practices or the unfair results they are producing. As you, today's Amos, have said, the economically powerful have so many ways to bribe our politicians. From what I hear, more and more poor people have lost faith in their governments and their politicians. That is probably one of the big reasons so many people in America and other countries are attracted to strong leaders who ignore the niceties of traditional politics and promise to power their way to results. Although I spent my life in the military, and although I am a strong supporter of the command structure in the military, I think it is disastrous to abandon the messiness of political democracy to "efficiently get things done." It is too bad that so many people in the West don't have the sense of history that the Chinese always have possessed. We are so focused on the latest jobs report or stock market fluctuations that we forget about the strong men in the past who trampled on the institutions and practices of political democracy but were temporarily popular for getting the trains to run on time or for restoring national honor: Lenin, Mussolini, Hitler, Mao, Putin.

When I first joined the military, I took an oath to defend the constitution of the United States. I am totally convinced that democratically elected civilians must always be commanders in chief of the military. I don't think, however, that the military is what threatens American democracy today. The military-industrial complex does pose such a threat, however, more so now than when President Eisenhower warned us about it. That complex is not the only threat. Rewarding entrepreneurs who produce nothing except new devices for banks speculating with their depositor's money is what is causing the wide gap between the rich and the poor. Our democracy is being weakened and seriously undermined by the economic inequality existing in our nation. Marx was wrong about many things, but about one thing he seems to have been right. Political democracy is not enough. Economic democracy also is needed. Property and wealth needs to be defined and distributed to serve the best interests of the least advantaged in society. In an economic democracy the interests of workers, consumers, managers, owners, stockholders, the disabled, the young and the very old, all need to be given equal consideration. It is going to take some very creative social engineering to create such an economic democracy. I am not sure it can be done. I am sure about what will happen if we don't try.

I know that I seem to have been talking in a circle. Economic democracy also is only another ideal goal to aim at. How does it get operationalized, given the great economic inequality that now exists? Let me make these two recommendations. First, pursing the dual goals of political democracy and economic justice might be more successful than pursuing just one of them. Rich and poor alike have shown their willingness to sacrifice themselves in the pursuit of political democracy. Exploited workers for centuries have fought for economic fairness. I recommend that you read Howard Zinn's book, *A People's History of the United* states, to see how true this is. What not enough people recognize is that people need to be enlightened about the need to pursue both goals, if there is to be any hope of successfully pursuing either one of them. People dedicated to the attainment of real political democracy need to recognize how today's holders of economic power are dominating the political process. People dedicated to attaining economic justice need to critically evaluate the propaganda power of the con artists who are promising them the moon. The pursuit of both goals will check the weakness in pursing only one. The practical challenge, of course, is finding an Amos or a Micah who can effectively tell people what they need to hear. My hope that such voices can be found is always darkened by my fear that they may end up like Jeremiah.

My second recommendation echoes what Reverend Kennedy has already said. Don't demand of your dedication to justice and fairness the attainment of heaven on earth. Making some people's lives a little less hellish makes this life-long project worthwhile. Work to elect some candidates who do not take PAC money. Support legislative compromises which move life an inch or two towards the goals of democracy and fairness. Support scholars and journalists who are trying, as best they can, to tell the truth. Think of progress in terms of generations and not in terms of election cycles. Remember also, however, that long term progress occurs only through short term efforts.

I contend that constitutional changes are needed to guarantee women's rights, to make the second amendment talk about gun ownership morally relevant to today's world, and to end treating corporations as though they were human persons. I know, however, that the constitution can be changed only in a manner permitted by the constitution. In a constitutional democracy, sovereignty does not lie with the people but with the constitution. Our forefathers decided that all citizens would be better off if each of them did not claim political sovereignty over themselves, but rather they transferred that sovereignty to the constitution. We can debate whether the creation of a nation state in such a manner is a morally fair thing to do to everyone affected, but the reality is that this is where we now find ourselves. It is in this social and historical world that we must seek justice. Realism requires us to be patient, to keep working for the decades needed to make constitutional changes.

Scott, let me add just one thing to what you have just said. As a Buddhist who was married for a long time to a Christian, I think religion has a role to play in helping motivate people to dedicate themselves to the pursuit of justice. Most people who are acquiring increasing amounts of political or economic power are not motivated to do so by a desire to increase the size of the benefit pie so as improve the well-being of the least advantaged in the world. They are doing it because they want to see themselves, and to have others see them, as being superior to others. This what Buddhists see as the most basic cause of human suffering. This, I think, is what the Hebrews called "acting from Hubris," having a god-complex, wanting to control everything. Buddhists believe that people will act compassionately towards others if they come to understand that they are being enslaved by a desire to top everyone else who in their eyes is important. Hebrews believe that loving God and loving God's creations are inseparable. I believe that pursuing political and economic ideals makes even more sense when the people pursuing them are religiously motivated to end such cravings and hubris.

I think that both Buddhism and Christianity can provide such motivation. Being compassionate towards others is letting them be in their "original suchness" before they are evaluated as better or worse. Such compassion is more likely to develop if people come to understand that the whole game of trying to be king of the hill never produces satisfaction. Someone is always trying to knock them off the hill. They never find peace of mind. I hear Job expressing a similar idea. His mind was never at peace until he let go and let God be God. I can endorse his final action because the Hebrew God is a God of justice and love. For the Buddhist and the Hebrew, letting things just be is not only a way of avoiding producing unjust and unsatisfying results. It also is a way of receiving the great benefit of finding joy and beauty when nature is permitted to simply be and when one lets oneself and others be what they would be if we were not always evaluating each other and seeking to be better than everything else. To be worthwhile in our own eyes does not require thinking that we are better than others. I am not less than others if they deservedly have more money than I do. I am not less than sighted people if I am blind. We are not less that the young athletes or homecoming queens at this university because we are past 60.

People keep asking, "What is religion good for?" It seems to me that we can see that it is good for so many things if we just worked with the right kind of currency in measuring its worth. As First and Second Isaiah, Jeremiah, Ezekiel, and Job keep pointing out, being religious will not prevent natural disasters, illness, national and cultural destruction, but if can lead one to celebrate being alive no matter what happens in one's life. That celebration, I think, can serve as a powerful factor motivating people to work for political and economic justice.

Zhang Binyan, may I say something.

Of course, Ms. Yamaguchi.

As I see it, most people's principles of justice are tribally specific. Philosophers may talk about universal principles of justice and preachers may talk about every child being equally precious in God's eyes, but that is not how most people think. So many American church goers think of America as God's chosen nation. Rather than being proud that as consumers they have lifted hundreds of millions of people out of poverty by buying products manufactured in China or Indonesia, most Americans now want the U.S. government to think only about American jobs. They approve of the United States going to war in other countries to protect America's national interest. Too many Americans, it seems to me, to protect American borders, sovereignty, and the American standard of living, are willing to let millions of refugees and Central American victims of criminal violence live on in their misery. More and more Europeans seem to be adopting the same nationalistic sense of justice.

More and more I am beginning to think that justice and nation states cannot live together in moral harmony. For many people, the God they worship is defined in terms of national interest. Given what I heard today, I don't think that is the God that Jeremiah and Isaiah worshipped. I think that all the wars of the 20th century could have been avoided if nationalism had not blinded people to the call to be fair to all people. National military alliances, the very thing condemned by the prophets, led to World War I. The French demand for reparations guaranteed the rise of Hitler and World war II in Europe. The model of Western imperialism gave birth to Japan's deadly march to build its empire in Asia. Western imperialism in China, and its support for the corrupt businessmen and politicians supporting Western interests, made it almost certain that Mao's revolution would succeed. America's addiction to fighting communism prohibited it from moderating Mao's policies to build a new communist nation and it led the U.S. to the war in Vietnam against Ho Chi Men who was a fan of Jeffersonian democracy. Protecting the interests of the French, British and Americans in Middle Eastern oil led to the wars in Afghanistan and Iraq. Whatever the value there is to having nation states, if seems to me, that value is far outweighed by the deaths, suffering, and injustice that nation states have and are causing.

I am not sure how to operationalize a pursuit of universal justice that would lessen the unbelievable harm that nation states have caused. I am sure, however, that if religion is going to have any impact here, it is going to need something more and different from what is going on in Christian Sunday morning rituals.

Yes, Ms. Yamaguchi, more and different practices surely are needed. I agree. That doesn't mean, however, that worship rituals should be done away with. If they are of the right kind, they can focus our attention on a Biblical God to worship and of the demands of justice and love that doing God's will requires. Not every worshipper can think things through as clearly as you have done. You have raised a vital question with which all of us must wrestle: How can we be a citizen of a specific nation and still pursue the demands of universal justice? Put in a less political tone: How can we live as a certain sort of social and cultural person, and be a universalist in worship and the pursuit of justice? Your question is just right: How can we operationalize a universalistic religion and ethics?

Chris, let me make these suggestions.

Sure, Mark. I know that you want to operationalize the movement towards a more just world. Besides, as a lawyer you probably have thought more about political philosophy and the justification for nation states than we have.

No one has thought about this issue enough, Chis. We are all just beginning to scratch the surface, but I think I can say something in response to Ms. Yamaguchi powerful indictment of nation states.

The first thing we need to keep in mind is that, when thinking about social institutions such as the nation state, we never start with a blank slate. Nation states were not created out of nothing and we can't correct the problems in our current system of nation states by thinking that we can wipe clean the current system of nation states and implement a new socially engineered blueprint that we think would be fair to all human beings. Although there were philosophers in the 18th century who presented social contract theories to legitimate the nation states that were historically emerging, these were not theoretical explanations of how nation states originated. Thomas Hobbes argued that people would be living in a hellish state of combat and fear of death if they, as individuals, did not transfer to the state the sovereignty they possessed in a state of nature prior to the existence of states. Historians have given complex explanations about how kings maneuvered to get domination over medieval lords by transferring to the state a monopoly over the legitimate use of violence and then assigned to themselves ownership of that monopoly. The point I want to make is that any effort to operationalize opposition to injustices perpetrated by the state must begin where we historically are right now with powerful states who have powerful police forces and armies at the disposal of the government officials who are right now acing as the agents of the state perpetuating nationalistic resistance to universalistic claims for justice.

There are also, however, forces working in our social world today that limit the power of nation states. Some of these forces seem to be making the problem of worldwide injustice even worse and some of them seem to be on the side of the good angels working to decrease injustice. More and more global corporations have appeared. They respect national interests and rules only when it is in their own best interests to do so. Their interests, unfortunatly, usually are not justice's interest. They bribe rulers of certain nation states by opening plants in their countries and providing jobs for their citizens in exchange for being free of environmental restrictions, worker's benefits, and existing tax rates. To protect their global economic interests, they often use their power over governments to get them to use their police and armies as extensions of their corporate organization. Despite their focus on short term profits, however, sometimes there are unintended consequences of their actions that support the goals of universal justice. Global mass media corporations sometimes increase awareness of the superior well-being of workers in countries from which these corporations are moving their plants. Following along with economic globalization there also is cultural globalization. Sometimes cultural factors ignoring national boundaries become factors resisting the unjust treatment of people by the policies and actions of nation states.

Perhaps the most powerful global force lessening nationally caused injustices is the development of international law. The best evidence of its power in restricting the unjust treatment of people by nation states is the viciousness of the attacks against it being waged by nationalists today in the name of preserving national sovereignty. Although world courts have no police power to punish nations violating international law agreements, the decisions of the courts can influence the opinions of the public in these nations. Little by little, especially in democratic nations, people are beginning to accept as normal and proper the requirement that nations respect international law. The opponents of international law are correct in seeing it as a threat to national sovereignty. The supporters of universal principles of justice think that the right kind of weakening of national sovereignty is a good thing. As respect for international law increases, the belief that national sovereignty trumps all other considerations decreases. Although narrow interpretations of national interest sometimes can lead politically democratic nations to go to war, they are less likely to do so if a respect for international law and demands for economic democracy exist in those nations. International law tends to focus more on the well-being of people than on the profits of global corporations, and this lessens the probability that political democracies will go to war, even when big money still dominates elections and governmental actions.

Working, in the name of peace and universal justice, to increase the power of international law does not mean that nation states will disappear. Many human problems are local problems best addressed by national and local governments. International law, and not a world government, may be the best way to work towards meeting the requirements of a universal understanding of justice. Given the complexities involved, and the historical differences in the political, economic, and cultural factors involved, there won't be anything like a mathematical algorithm that one can use to eliminate the vagueness of the border between international law and national sovereignty. Slowly, case by case, the vagueness of the border will be reduced.

In practical ways, decisions will have to be made and re-made to settle when individual differences should or should not trump one's social and cultural traditions, when cultural differences between communities in a nation should or should not trump national laws, and when unique national interests should and should not trump international law. I am a cultural Jew who wants to preserve and participate in some traditional Jewish practices, but I don't want to surrender my autonomy to some body of Jewish leaders. Neither do I want any national government to attempt to force people, who prize cultural practices different from those prized by the groups holding ruling power in the nation, to assimilate into a homogenized version of life of the dominate group. Here I am with Mordecai. Yes! Assimilate when justified national life requires it. No! Don't assimilate when social and cultural differences are just differences.

The same holds true of national differences. Americans couldn't be Japanese if they tried, and the French don't have to become Americans for both nations to respect international law and the wellbeing of all people, not just their own citizens. I think that the universalism of the exiled priests in Babylon has played a major historical roll in infusing in human consciousness a sense of justice that is universal and respectful of the priceless worth of every human being. I worry when the political leadership of a nation state ceases thinking in universalistic terms and starts thinking about protecting the practices of some one specific religion. As we can see right here, America is not just a Jewish/Christian country. It is also a Hindu, Buddhist, Islamic, Native American country. I worry about Iran, Israel, Turkey, Egypt, and Burma centralizing religious and political power in a single institution. We need to add this to our worries. In critiquing tyranny, we used to warn about centralizing economic and political power in the hands of a dictator. Now we also need to worry about centralizing economic, political, and religious power in a single person or institution. I don't want our nation to go where some Christians want to take the United States.

Mark, I apologize for having been silent when over many a beer many of my friends said, "Who needs lawyers." We need you. Thank you. Let me add one variation of what you said, if I may?

Of course, Scott.

There are two thoughts that came to mind while you were speaking. The first thought has to do with respecting cultural differences when they do not conflict with the justified requirements of higher authorities. I have served on military bases on which there were officers and enlisted personnel who belonged to very different religious traditions. Chaplains from very different religious traditions were assigned to the chapels on these bases. They always faced the problem of both respecting religious differences, not forcing their own religion down the throats of those cherishing a different religion, and not watering religion down to empty clichés supposedly acceptable to everyone. I don't say that they always were successful in negotiating their way through this minefield, but the requirement that everyone respect military order helped.

I find a similar problem existing in American life at home, one that may be much harder to handle. As I said earlier, I grew up in a poor, rural Black community in the South and when I retired I returned to a Black urban community here in Florida. I don't doubt that there are many historical, economic, and psychological reasons for racial prejudice against African Americans. The same is probably true of discrimination against Hispanics, Native Americans, and Asian Americans. What I want us to think about is not just the racism by Whites against people of color, but also the racism of Asian Americans against Blacks, of Mexican Americans against Haitians or Puerto Ricans, of Hispanics against Gringos, of African Americans against "Whites" or "Orio Blacks, and of many people in many of the above groups against Jews.". Some liberals love to say, "We are all Americans; this is the land of the great melting pot." We may all be Americans, but we are different kinds of Americans, and we don't want our way of life melted down into someone else's way of life. To preserve their racial or ethnic identities, some intellectuals and politicians talk about supporting "Identity Politics." Sometimes this helps in making us feel at home in our cultural shoes, but sometimes it makes people forget that all hyphenated Americans remain Americans. Just as I can't shed my Black cultural skin, so I can't shed the skin I share with all Americans. Respecting universal justice, it seems to me, requires that I live with both kinds of social and cultural markings. The problem is that so many of us do not know how to do that and do not want to do that. We don't know how to let innocent differences just be. I think Zhang Binyan was right on target. Most people need for there to be some group they think is inferior to them for them to think they are worth something at all.

Let me share my experience with you. In the military some of us learned to let differences just be differences. You had to trust the person fighting next to you whether that person was a guy or a gal, a Brown or a White, a person with African lips or Asian eyes. Some of us not only let differences be differences but we learned to prize some of those differences: different food, music, dress, sports, and religious practices. I love to sing, sway, and yell "Amen, in an African-Episcopal-Methodist worship service, and I love to silently pray during an Episcopal mass. Many people in America remain proud members of cultural tribes. There is nothing wrong with that if they also have, as many do, a passion for justice, for the just treatment of all people regardless of their social and cultural status and way of life. As Mark pointed out, that is the universal sense of justice that became the heart of the new Jewish way of life born in Babylon. Preserving the justified aspects of a shared American way of life does not require an all or nothing treatment of any of the specific features of the ethnic ways of life in America: eating ham or sushi, singing and dancing in church or singing and dancing in a beer hall, easily expressing your opinions in class or respectfully holding your tongue, wearing black to a funeral or wearing white as the Chinese do. The racist homogenizers often say to new immigrants, "You're in America now; become an American." Their racism blinds themselves to the fact that being an American means letting people with innocent differences be different. Besides, their fears are unfounded. Very quickly the children of immigrants lose so many of their parents' cultural traditions that the parents feel the need to set up schools to teach their children the old language and ways.

The second comment about today's lectures and conversations that I want to make deals with the condemnation of military alliances by the Hebrew prophets and with Yoshiko's concern about such alliances leading to the horrors of war. It seems to me that the prophets were correct in rejecting the identification of the Hebrew religious community with the community of people treated by their kings as subjects of Israel or Judah. For me, being a citizen of the United States and a member of its Armed Forces is very different from being a Christian. Every day of my life I must negotiate how to live as both. We Christians, as Christians, belong to a world-wide community and we must never stop feeling the tension between being a Christian and being an American. Just as universal principles of justice may require Americans to obey international law, so worshipping the Christian God may require obeying the principles of universal justice legitimating international law. In the pursuit of justice, international law leaves ethical room for nations to act as nations. I realize that it is possible here to make tragic errors of judgement, but, it seems to me, that the demands of justice may require nation states to go to war against other nation states and to form alliances with other nation states to carry on this pursuit of justice. As a Christian I am always skeptical about whether a nation is engaged in a just war. Sometimes, however, I find that my very Christianity and pursuit of universal justice requires me to conclude that a certain kind of war is justified as the least evil option available, even as it requires me to beg forgiveness for the horrible, often unintended consequences that follow.

Two things I heard today reinforce my belief that war sometimes is justified. Mark pointed out that we need to contextualize the situation in which decisions about war and peace need to be made. Nations do exist. Some of these nations, usually non-democratic nations, do make war on other nations for national self-interest reasons. Sometimes, the only way to stop them is through military force. Sometimes, the only effective way to exercise such force is through forming military alliances with other like-minded nations. Sometimes, the mere existence of such alliances is sufficient to prevent wars of national aggression. Usually peace-loving Christians must face the dirty fact that they live in terrible situations in which they are damned if they do and damned if they don't. One can't keep one's hands clean. Seeking forgiveness seems to be an everyday requirement.

Ms. Yamaguchi has given us another big reason for recognizing that this is true. When war breaks out neither side is innocent. As she pointed out, in all the wars that occurred during the past century the nations being attacked must bear some responsibility for creating conditions that motivated the attacking nations to go to war. The attacking nations, of course, were not compelled to go to war. They bear responsibility for choosing that way to deal with their problems partially caused by the nations they chose to attack. That everyone bears responsibility for what happened does not mean that attacked nations should not resist. Isaiah and Jeremiah were probably right in judging that Israel and Judah, even with their alliances, were too weak to blunt the attacks by the Assyrians and Babylonians. Our alliances, however, ended the horror of the attacks by Nazi Germany and Imperial Japan. In hindsight, could World War II have been fought differently with fewer casualties? Probably, yes. Imperfect politicians and warriors, with limited knowledge and at times less than virtuous motivation, however, were the only kinds of people available to wage the war. Ms. Yamaguchi probably is right in claiming that many of the wars fought since 1945 have not been just wars, even though many of our killed and wounded warriors are to be honored for their sacrifices during those wars. We are born into a messed-up world and no one gets out of it with clean hands. Universal justice is demanded of us and universal forgiveness is what we need. I am a Christian and I was a warrior because my worship of my God demands justice from me and offers forgiveness to me.

Thank you, Sergeant Washington. Thanks to all of you. Your responses to today's presentations show how relevant today is what the Hebrew prophets, priests, creative writers, and wise sages said over 2,000 years ago.

Let's close shop for today. Next week we will examine what Christians added to the Hebrew Bible.

Chapter Eight

Jerusalem's Quarrel with Rome

Welcome back again. Thanks for coming in this morning. This is our final day together learning about Biblical history and literature. Today we will hear from scholars and their students who have studied the texts included in what is called by Christians "The New Testament of the Bible." These texts are written in response to what was happening to Jews in Palestine when it was under the control of the Romans. Because there are so many kinds of texts in the New Testament, today's format will be a little different. We will take a fifteen-minute break in the middle of the presentations. When the presentations are finished, we will go to lunch together. The university has prepared for us an excellent light lunch. After lunch we will return here to the lecture hall for a Q & A. session. Since this will be our final session, I would like each of you at that time to share your thoughts about what you have heard.

Let me begin by making some general remarks about the texts making up the Christian New Testament. Many of these texts were written by a Jew (Saul/Paul) who became convinced that the crucified Jesus of Nazareth was the saving messiah whom all people need. Paul's letters and two other texts, Q and Mark, were written before the Romans destroyed Jerusalem in 70 CE. The other three texts that we will consider (Matthew, Luke, and John) were written after that date. Some were written for the Jews exiled by the Romans from Palestine and some were written for non-Jewish Greeks and Romans who had become Christians. To understand the historical contexts in which these texts were written, it is crucial to focus on the year 70 CE when the Romans destroyed Jerusalem and its temple and dispersed Jews throughout the Roman empire. Just as a new understanding of their worship of Yahweh was gained by Hebrew exiles after the Babylonians destroyed Jerusalem and its temple, so the events just preceding and following the Roman destruction of Jerusalem and its temple gave birth to a new Christian version of the understanding gained by the exiles in Babylon.

Professor Gloria Kiely, an expert here at the university on the New Testament, will begin today's presentations by analyzing the fateful events that immediately preceded and followed 70 CE. Then she and some of her graduate students will examine Paul's letters and the Christian "Good News" texts that expressed the Christians new messianic faith.

Professor Kiely.

Thank you, Reverend Kennedy. I want to do two things today. First, I will sketch a history of the events that function as the backdrop to the texts making up the New Testament. Second, I will locate the writing of these texts in that historical narrative. When I have finished, six of my students will share their readings of the major texts that make up this collection of texts: Letters of Paul, the Synoptic Gospels of Mark, Mathew and Luke/Acts, and the Gospel of John. Let me begin.

Jerusalem, O Jerusalem. How often you have been destroyed and how often your exiles have given birth to new communities of faithful worshippers of God. In 586 BCE the Babylonians destroyed Jerusalem and its temple and Hebrew exiles in Babylon gave birth to a universalistic understanding of themselves and their worship of Yahweh. In 70 CE the Romans destroyed Jerusalem and its temple. In the 30 years preceding this date and in the 30 years after it, communities of Christians were born which understood themselves as the living, worshipping messianic body of Yahweh. If we here today in Jacksonville, Florida are going to understand the texts written by some of these new Christians, then we are going to have to understand what was happening in and around Jerusalem and Rome during the hundred years leading up to 70 CE and the 65 years following it. We can name 65 BCE as a good beginning point for this period and 135 CE as a useful ending point. During these two hundred and fifteen years, and the violence, chaos, horror, hope, and fear dominating it, Christian communities were born that gave operational meaning to Second Isaiah's call for Hebrews to be the religiously enlightening light to the world.

The evidence that historians possess to support the narrative they have constructed of this period is of various sorts. There are numerous Roman manuscripts that show how Roman power and ideas dominated events in Galilee and Judea. There is some information embedded in the texts written by Christians just before and after the Roman destruction of Jerusalem, but these texts were written for religious reasons to support Christians in the new communities being founded and not to provide data for future historians. The most Important evidence comes from the Jewish historian, Josephus, (37-100 CE) writing in Alexandria, Egypt. To get a non-Christian narrative of events occurring at this time, I often recommend to my students that they read the historical work of fiction, *Zealot: The Life and Times of Jesus of Nazareth*, written in 2014 by the Muslim, Reza Aslan, I think you will find it an exciting, eye-opening read. Let me begin my sketch of this history.

In 168 BCE the Maccabean revolt had produced an independent Hebrew kingdom that came in 140 BCE to be governed by a Hasmonaean Dynasty. Sepphoris in Galilee was the administrative center for the kingdom. A single person functioned as King of the Jews and Chief Priest in the Jerusalem temple. This position was handed down from father to son. In 65 BCE a civil war broke out between two brothers, Hyrcanus and Aristobulus, both claiming the two positions. They asked Rome to settle the dispute and end the war. Pompey did that in 63 BCE when he invaded Jerusalem, made Judea a Roman protectorate, dismissed both brothers' claims to be king, made Hyrcanus High Priest, and infuriated Aristobulus whose subsequent little revolts were savagely put down by the Romans. The

Hebrew/Jews never again would have an independent nation until modern Israel was created in 1948.

Pompey and Julius Caesar fought a civil war over Rome's throne and Pompey was killed by Caesar's armies in Egypt in 46 BCE. Two years earlier, Caesar had given Roman citizenship to a Judean aristocrat, Antipater, for supporting him against Pompey. He also appointed him as administrator for Rome over all of Judea. Just before being assassinated in 43 BCE, he appointed his son, Herod, as governor of Galilee and his other son, Phasael, governor over Jerusalem. Herod, only 15 when he began to reign, ruled until his death in 4 BCE. Phasael committed suicide in 40 BCE when the son of Aristobulus besieged Jerusalem and killed the High Priest, Hyrcanus, appointed by Pompey. Rome authorized Herod the Great to use Roman legions to put down the Jerusalem revolt and end forever all remnants of the Maccabean, Hasmonaean Dynasty. In 37 BCE Rome gave Herod the title "King of the Jews." He also was called "Herod the Great."

For 39 years Herod did in Judea what Rome wanted him to do: collect taxes, Hellenize and Romanize new construction, place the Roman Eagle over the portal to the temple, pick priests sympathetic to Rome and have them make sacrifices to Caesar in the temple, and above all else ruthlessly crush rebels who protested Roman rule. Rome showed favoritism to rich landowners, rich priests, and the religious practices of Herod and his priests. Appealing to the wide-spread discontent of the poor and landless peasants, rebel bandits appeared and stole from the rich and gave to the poor, claiming the end of the world was soon to come. The leader of one of these bandit groups was named Hezekiah and he claimed that he was the messiah who would liberate the Jews from the Romans and end the oppression of the poor. For all practical purposes, he declared war on Rome. Herod endeared himself to Rome by capturing and executing Hezekiah and clearing Galilee of the rebels. Rome might call him "King of the Jews" but the Jews never agreed. Law and order, nevertheless, in the Roman sense of the words, did reign during Herod's rule for thirty-nine years.

When Herod died in 4 BCE, all hell broke loose. Caesar Augustus divided Herod's kingdom among three of Herod's sons. Herod Antipas got Galilee, Archelaus got

Judea and Samaria, and Phillip got the area north of the Sea of Galilee. Resentment against Rome and Herod was widespread. Rioting rebels burnt down one of the palaces of Herod Antipas, some of his troops mutinied, one of his slaves, Simon, claimed he was the messiah and plundered royal palaces. Augustus reacted with traditional Roman ruthlessness. Roman legions put down the rioting and crucified the rebel leaders, Archelaus was exiled, a Roman was appointed governor of Jerusalem, and in 6 C.E. Judea became a Roman province governed directly by Rome.

The unrest and violence did not end, however. Hezekiah's son, Judas the Galilean, took up his father's militant messianic mission and joined with a group of "Zealots" who were totally committed to ending Roman rule and made resistance to Rome a religious duty. Judas broke into the armory that Herod had built in Sepphoris and, using those weapons, began a guerrilla war in Galilee, plundering the homes of the rich and the Roman sympathizers. When Rome, in support of its taxation efforts ordered a census, and the Chief Priest in the Temple, Joazaz, supported the census, Judas and his followers set about killing all treasonous Jews. Following his father' example, he proclaimed that he was the messiah reclaiming for the Jews the throne of David. He was captured by the Romans and, together with two thousand of his supporters, was crucified.

The dream of liberation from Roman occupation never died. Neither did the resentment felt towards the rich and the priests using their positions to become wealthy. Private resentment turned into public opposition a generation later. Five different Roman governors had ruled the land, now called by the Romans "Palestine," before Pontius Pilate arrived in 26 CE. Pilate's immediate predecessor in 18 CE had named as Head Priest, Caiaphas, the son in law of an earlier wealthy High Priest, Ananus. Pilate and Caiaphas formed a working partnership for 10 years, until Pilate was recalled to Rome in 36 CE. To many Jews at the time this was an unholy alliance. Pilate disliked the Jews in general and had no hesitation in crucifying anyone who was or was perceived to be a threat to Roman rule.

The Jews in Jerusalem and Judea were not of a single mind. Very different attitudes toward the Romans existed among them. There were Jews who served as roman agents and tax collectors. There were the rich Sadducees who cooperated with the Romans and disappeared from history when Rome destroyed Jerusalem and dispersed the Jews. There were the Pharisees who attempted to remain neutral on Rome as they focused on enforcing their legalistic interpretation of the Torah. There were the zealots who were militant nationalistic rebels and opponents of the rich and collaborators with Rome. There were the Essences who rejected both Roman rule and military opposition to Rome and who dropped out of society, choosing to wait in the wilderness for the end of the world. In addition to these groups inside Palestine, there were five million Jews living outside Palestine.

The law and order alliance of Pilate and Caiaphas soon took its toll. Around 30 CE John the Baptist was perceived as a threat who was becoming too popular. Herod Antipas executed him. When soon after that Jesus rode triumphantly into Jerusalem like a new king and attacked the money operations in the Temple upon which Rome depended for revenue, Pilate crucified him as a rebel. In 36 CE Pilate slaughtered the followers of a man who claimed to be the messiah and was called "the Samaritan." This slaughter was even too bloodthirsty for Rome. Pilate was recalled to Rome and Caiaphas was dismissed as high priest. In the absence of these two who had done so much to keep the lid on things, even more leaders of opposition to Rome appeared. Rome killed them off one by one. In 44 CE Theudas claimed that he was the messiah who would save the Jews even as Moses had done. In 46 CE, two sons of Judas the Galilean attempted to get revenge for the killing of their father and grandfather. They were crucified by the Romans.

The governors sent be Rome to replace Pilate only made things worse, virtually guaranteeing that a full-blown revolution would occur. In 48 CE Roman soldiers insulted worshippers at the temple and riots occurred. Governor Cumanus ordered legionaries to end the riots. The Roman soldiers butchered the crowd and tore up the Torah. Resentment among Jews rose to a fever pitch. When Cumanus did nothing to punish Samaritans who had killed Jews passing through Samaria, Jewish bandits went to Samaria and killed every Samaritan they could find. Cumanus was replaced by Felix who suppressed the bandits only to have them replaced by the Sicarii, the daggermen, who believed the end of the world was coming and who began assassinating rich priests not opposing Rome. The leader of the Sicarii. Menahem, was the grandson of Judas of Galilee. In 56 CE one of the Sicarii killed the High Priest, Jonathan, a son of Ananus. A reign of terror followed with Sicarii attacking the whole ruling class of Jews, and Romans massacring rioters. New governors were sent by Rome, but things got worse. The last governor, Florus, in 66 CE stole the money in the Temple treasury. The captain of the Temple police, Eleazar, backed by Menahem and the secarii, ended all sacrifices to Rome, killed the priests supporting Rome, burnt the censor ledges used for taxation, and virtually declared independence from Rome. Rome sent only a small force of soldiers to put down the revolt. The Jews repelled them and got the remaining Roman soldiers to agree to surrender on condition that they be allowed to leave for Rome. Once surrendered, however, the rebels slaughtered all of them. Rome prepared for a massive show of force to put down the revolution,

Emperor Nero ordered General Vespasian to put down the revolt. Vespasian collected the Roman soldiers in Syria, and his son, Titus, did the same with the legions in Egypt. With 60,000 trained warriors at their command, Vespasian moved down from the north and subdued all the cities in Galilee while Titus coming from the south did the same to the villages in Judea. Before they could attack Jerusalem, Vespasian had to return to Rome and he became emperor, since Nero had committed suicide. Waiting for the Roman army to attack, chaos ruled in Jerusalem. The alliance between Menahem and Eleazar fell apart when Menahem declared himself the messiah and King of the Jews. Eleazer had Menahem killed and all the Sicarii exiled from Jerusalem. Refugees, fleeing from Roman armies, flooded into Jerusalem, exacerbating the food shortage. In Jerusalem there were 18,500 untrained Jewish fighters who were supposed to hold off 60,000 trained Roman warriors. Dissention spread among the Jews with some wanting to negotiate with the Romans and others wanting to fight to the death. One group of peasants, the Zealots, convinced that the end of the world was coming, and that God would destroy the Roman threat, terrorized the compromisers and those they felt were not sufficiently loyal to the revolution.

In 70 CE the Roman armies overwhelmed the Jewish forces in Jerusalem, stormed through the streets killing everyone they met, burning to the ground all the buildings in Jerusalem, saving the Temple as the last structure to be set on fire. In 73 CE a small remnant of Sicarii fighters, holed up in the fortress, Masada, committed group suicide rather than surrender to Roman soldiers. Vespasian, who was now emperor of Rome, didn't only want to put down a military rebellion. He wanted to destroy the Jewish religion which he believed would always nurture new generations to think that they were too good to be ruled by Romans and would continue to think that they would receive divine help to destroy the rule of Rome. Vespasian acted with vengeance. All Jews were expelled from Jerusalem. All Jews were required to pay taxes to support the Roman gods and the Roman way of life. Eventually, in 135 CE Rome removed from all its maps and official documents the name 'Jerusalem'. The temple in Jerusalem no longer served as the center of Jewish worship. The Torah replaced it in the many small synagogues established by the Jews exiled by the Romans from Jerusalem.

It is in this historical setting that a small number of people maneuvered their way through the violence and chaos of their age as they became what they said was the living body of the messiah promised by the prophets and the exiles in Babylon. The Christian texts written to sustain the life of these messianic communities present many problems to us as we strive to interpret them. The earliest stand-alone texts were letters written outside of Palestine to Greek Christians by a Christian convert from Judaism (Saul/Paul) from 50 CE to around 60 CE. This was a time when inside Palestine Roman soldiers were desecrating the temple and burning the Torah, Samaritans and Jews were killing each other, the Sicarii were slaughtering rich Jews and the high priest, Jonathan, and Menahem, their leader, was anointing himself as Messiah and King of the Jews. Our knowledge of Saul/Paul's life before he started writing letters must be gleamed from two sources. First, in his letters he mentions events that had occurred earlier in his life, especially his conversion experience from Judaism to Christianity around 37 CE, several years after the death of Jesus and when Saul/Paul was in his early twenties. Second, claims about his life are made in the book of Acts, not written until around 90-100 CE, thirty plus years after Paul was put to death in Rome just before the Romans destroyed Jerusalem. The book of Acts is the second half of a book, Luke/Acts, written to celebrate the birth of the first Christian community in

Jerusalem and its spread throughout the whole Greek and Roman world, while chaos and violence dominated life in Palestine.

Although Paul mentions almost nothing about events in the life of Jesus, he makes the centerpiece of his understanding of Christianity the claims by early Christians that Jesus was crucified and that a messianic age has begun with the resurrection of God's messiah following the death of Jesus. As we have seen, in the decade between 26 CE and 36 CE, when the alliance of Pilate and Caiaphas dominated events in Judea, many persons were crucified for claiming to be the messiah or King of the Jews. In 36 CE Pilate lost his job because of the bloody way in which he executed the followers of "The Samaritan" who claimed to be the messiah. Paul insists that faith in a resurrected messiah is crucial for faith that Christians will be resurrected.

We do have four other Christian texts, called by Christians "The Good News" (The Gospels), which present narratives of the life of Jesus. Interpreters of these texts, however, are faced with two major problems. First, there is the intertextuality that appears in Mark, Mathew and Luke. There are many passages in Mathew and Luke that are very similar. The authors of Mathew and Luck seem to be unaware of each other. Some of their shared passages are identical to passages found in the book of Mark. Both seem to have had a copy of Mark from which they copied material. There is another set of shared passages which do not appear in Mark. It seems that there was another text, now lost, from which both copied. Scholars have reconstructed that text and now call it "Q," for the Latin word "Quelle," which means 'Source'. If you want to do so, you can read the texts making up Q, by reading Marcus Borg's book, *The Lost Gospel of Q: The Original Sayings of Jesus*. John, the fourth Gospel, is radically different from Q, Mark, Matthew, and Luke. It is not so much a narrative about the life of Jesus as a religious narrative locating faith in the messiah in the worshipper's faith in creation itself.

That there are five texts, written by different authors at different times and places and to different sets of readers, creates the second problems for interpreters of the New Testament. The writers of these gospels, all inspired by their new Christian faith, had different purposes in writing and different major points to make. They were writing for religious reasons and not trying to record what modern historians would call an "objective" account of the life of Jesus. Given the point and purpose of his work, one writer included items in his narrative stories about events not even mentioned by the other writers. Even in the case of shared materials, small literary differences often seem to indicate major differences in perspective. These writers did not treat each other's writings as sacred and untouchable. They rearranged material, edited material, and added new material when it helped them achieve the point and purpose of their writing.

Scholars have different opinions about when exactly these texts were written, and thus what their historical contexts were, but they have achieved a consensus about dates. Q probably was written sometime before the Jerusalem revolts that led to the Roman destruction of Jerusalem in 70 CE, perhaps even before the Samaritan-Jewish bloody battles in 52 CE and the appearance of Menahem and the Sicarii in 56 CE. Mark probably was written after the Jewish rebellion began in 66 CE but before the destruction of Jerusalem in 70 CE. The book of Mark makes no mention of the destruction of Jerusalem and the temple, but it does seem to be written to protect Christians from the punishment that Rome unleashed on Jews after the revolution began.

The book of Matthew was written to Christians in Antioch, Syria a little after 80 CE, when Jewish leaders exiled from Jerusalem by the Romans agreed at the Council of Jamnie to issue the "Birkat-Haminim" directive forbidding Jewish synagogues to allow Christians to use their buildings to conduct their Christian worship services. This is what Christians in Antioch had been doing and so Matthew felt the need to explain to these Christians how Christians are both continuing Hebrew traditions and living in a resurrection, messianic age.

The author of the book Luke/Acts, divided into two books by later Christian leaders, wrote soon after Matthew to explain to Hellenist Christians in 90 CE why Christian communities have been flourishing for fifty years even as Judaism had been floundering. He charged that the religious spirit of Moses, the prophets, and the Babylonian exiles had been transferred from the Jews to Christian, messianic communities.

The author of the book of John wrote around 100 CE in Alexandria, Egypt to encourage Christians who were being persecuted and killed by the Romans. Christians were refusing to live in a Roman way of life because they now saw themselves living in an age when for them the end of the Roman World had come, and they were living in a new world as members of the body of the resurrected messiah.

I have asked some of my students to give their interpretations of these texts. Mr. Ted Eckerle will begin by interpreting the letters of Paul.

Thank you, Professor Kiely. To understand the letters of Paul it is necessary to understand two things about the man because all his letters are expressions of his life and his experiences. First, we need to understand his conflicting relationship to the leaders of the Christian community in Jerusalem prior to the Roman destruction of the city. Second, we need to understand the religious conversion experience that changed him from a Jew persecuting Christians into a Christian who spent his life converting people outside Palestine into being Christian. Let me begin with his conversion experience and then consider his interactions with the Jerusalem Christian community. After that, I will examine directly some of the letters he wrote.

Saul was born five to ten years after Jesus was born, as the son of a rich Jew with Roman citizenship living in the port city of Tarsus on the Southeastern edge of modern day Turkey, just a short distance west of Antioch. As a teenager he went to study under Pharisee teachers in Jerusalem. Several years after the crucifixion of Jesus, Saul went to hear a speech being given in Jerusalem's public square by a Christian named Stephen. Stephen was addressing a mixed crowd. Some of his listeners were Christians and some were Jewish priests and Pharisees. The leaders of the new Christian community were James, the brother of Jesus, Simon Peter, and John They were the converted Jews who had been the companions of Jesus during his lifetime. Some of the Christians were converted Jerusalem Jews (called "the Hebrews") and some of them were diaspora Jews who had come to Jerusalem to participate in Temple rituals and then became Christians (the Hellenists). Stephen was one of the Hellenists who had been picked by the Jerusalem leaders to help secure financial funds from the Hellenists to support the Hebrews whose leaders believed that they should only focus on preaching the Christian "Good News" and not work as laborers.

Stephen, after telling the great Hebrew epic, echoed the universalism of the Babylon priests and prophets, and chastised those Hebrew Christians who were horrified when he proclaimed that Christian Hellenists, who had not been Jews, only needed to be filled with the spirit of Moses's law to join the Christian community. He claimed that it was not necessary for them to obey the Jewish requirement that Jews be circumcised. Some of the Hebrew Christians, and the non-Christians Jews like Saul who were present, were infuriated and stoned Stephen to death and drove the Hellenist Christians out of Jerusalem. Saul saw Stephen courageously retell the great epic and claim that the spirit of Yahweh lives in the spirit of worshippers and not in the stones of a temple. He saw Stephen forgive those who were stoning him as he released his spirit into the hands of the God he worshipped. The next day Saul accepted a commission from the Pharisees to pursue the Christian Hellenists, who were running to Damascus to find protection, and bring them back to Jerusalem for judgement and punishment.

It was on the road to Damascus that Saul had his religious conversion experience and became the Christian Paul, the missionary to the Hellenists Christians, some of whom had been Jews but many were people in the Roman Empire who had not been Jews but who also were looking for liberation from Roman power and the Roman way of life. Seventeen years after his experience, Paul wrote in his letter to the Galatians that it was in this experience that he heard the voice of the one whom Stephen and the Christians called 'Jesus Christ', Jesus the messianic savior. In his many debates with the leaders of the Jerusalem Christian community, he always claimed that his experience was as authentic as the experiences that they reported having had with the resurrected Jesus Christ. He, therefore, had as much authority to do his work among Hellenists, Greeks, and Romans as they had to do their work among the Hebrew Christians. He mentions several times that, unlike the Hebrew

Christians who had no laboring jobs, he always worked as a tent maker even as he preached the Christian good news.

In Galatians, Paul writes that after his conversion experience he went south into Arabia and then back north to Damascus in Syria where the Hellenist Christian, Ananimas, shared his Christian beliefs and expressed his conviction as a Christian that Paul was uniquely qualified to take the Christian good news to the people outside Judea, and that he should do so. Writing more than forty years after Paul's experience, the author of the book of Acts gives two accounts of Saul's experience that differ with each other and with Paul's account in his letter to the Galatians. The accounts in Acts make no mention of a journey to Arabia. In one of Luke's accounts, Saul supposedly hears Jesus Christ tell him to go to Damascus. In the other account he doesn't hear this instruction, but nevertheless his traveling companions took him there. The writer of Acts has Paul's companions share Saul's religious experience. In one account they also hear the voice of Jesus Christ and in the other account they hear no voice but see a brilliant light surrounding them. Paul in his letters never mentions his companion's experiences. Luke never tries to reconcile these different accounts. He wasn't there. He is only including everything that he heard.

The controversies leading to Stephen's death contribute to Paul problems as he tries to continue and extend Stephen's claim that people do not have to become Jews to become Christians because the true Hebrew and Jewish spirit is now resurrected in the faith of people who become Christians. Following old Jewish ritualistic and dietary rules is not necessary. Paul keeps referring to his conversion experience to legitimate his mission and his equal standing as a Christian leader to those in Jerusalem. It was as a Pharisee that he was converted to Christianity. Now, as a Christian, he wants to make it very clear that it is necessary to change the traditional expectations of Pharisees about what a messianic savior would be like. In the eyes of many Jews, in a time when many people were claiming to be the messiah, pretenders were proven to be pretenders when they were unable to prevent Romans from crucifying them. Paul knew that a crucified Jesus could not be taken as a messiah. The Jesus Christ whom he heard in his conversion experience, however, was not simply one more crucified man. Jesus Christ was a very different kind of messiah, one who would not lead an army to overthrow Rome but one who could instill in people the best of the Hebrew spirit, a spirit not subject to the power of Rome or the crucifixion of a man.

Not until 40 CE, three years after his conversion experience, during which time Paul had been converting people to Christianity, did he go to Jerusalem to meet with the Christian leaders living there. They had heard of his conversion and his preaching in Syria and were delighted. They did not yet know, however, the details of what he was preaching. After this meeting, the Jerusalem leaders sent a man named Barnabas, who was a close confident of James, the leader of the Jerusalem community, to go with Paul as his companion and "helper."

Ten years later, Paul reported back to the leaders of the Jerusalem community. It seems that the Apostolic Council running the Jerusalem community had summoned him back to justify the claims that they had heard he was making about being the deciding voice when it comes to missionary activity to the gentiles. This meeting took place just after Pilate and Caiaphas had been dismissed and numerous rebels were appearing and claiming to be the messiah. Paul wrote in his letter to the Galatians that he was challenged by what he called "false believers," who demanded that all Christians show loyalty to the temple and the Torah. Paul refused to give in to them. To outsiders, this controversy among Christians would appear to be something unbelievably petty, given what was going on politically in Galilee and Judea. Fortunately, at least on the surface, a compromise was reached with James who decreed that Gentile Christians did not have to be circumcised. Once Paul left, however, with Barnabas staying behind, the Jerusalem Apostolic Council sent their own missionaries to Thessalonica, Galatia, Corinth, and Philippi to "correct" Paul's teachings. Almost all of Paul's letters were written after the meeting in Jerusalem in 50 CE. He always insisted that it was his conversion experience that legitimated his work, not the approval of the Jerusalem Christians.

In 57 CE, Paul was summoned back to Jerusalem, chastised by the leaders, and forced to participate in a purification ceremony in the temple. He was recognized by a mob of Jews as he was leaving the temple, where just a year before the High Priest had been assassinated by the Sicarii for being insufficiently Jewish. The mob would have beaten him to death if Roman soldiers had not stepped in and saved him. After keeping Paul in jail for three years, his claim that as a Roman citizen he had a right to be tried in Rome was honored by Judea's last governor, Titus, and he was send to Rome. For a short period of time, Paul was free in Rome and he tried unsuccessfully to carry on his missionary work. The Jerusalem Apostolic council had sent Peter to Rome a few years earlier to keep the small Christian community there from being contaminated by Paul's teaching. Both Paul and Peter were executed by Nero in 66 CE, as the Jews were revolting in Jerusalem.

With this as the immediate historical setting, let me look at a some of Paul's letters to various Christian communities. Let me begin with the first letter he wrote in 50 CE to Christians in Thessalonica, just after his second meeting in Jerusalem. The purpose of the letter was twofold. First, he reminded them to remain steadfast in loyalty to what they had become because of his evangelical work with them. His good news, he wrote, placed no hindrances in their way (no circumcision) and the genuineness of his preaching is verified by the spirit that now animates their lives. He apologizes for not having visited them recently. He explains that those opposed to his message to the Gentiles have hindered him. He charges that his opponents are filed with a satanic spirit that would bind them to old, useless and counterproductive Jewish requirements.

Paul's second purpose in writing the letter was to urge them to wait patiently for the end of the world. This eschatological belief is a constant in all of Paul's letters. It also was a constant in the thinking of all the rebels in Judea and Galilee. Neither these rebels nor Paul, however, were Greek metaphysicians with a well thought out theory about what such an end would be like or what new kind of world would replace it. It is clear, however, that Paul meant that the age of Roman rule would come to an end and a new Christian way of life would replace it. There is no indication that they thought that the mountains and seas would disappear, and a new physical universe would appear. The story of Noah guaranteed that such would not happen. It was the current world of human suffering and subjugation that would end. For Paul, belief in the destruction of Roman type worlds is entailed by his belief in God's creation of the universe and by his belief in the resurrection of Jesus Christ after the death of Jesus of Nazareth. Paul believed that he heard on the road to Damascus the voice of the messianic Jesus Christ. This belief cannot be divorced from the belief he gained from Stephen that the great Hebrew national epic would find its climax in an eschatological end to ungodly ways of life and in the birth of a genuine Kingdom of God. Even as the prophets and the priestly writers in Babylon spelled out the nature of the good, just, and universal God that Hebrews worshipped, so Paul was spelling out the messianic dimension of the nature of the God that Hebrews and Christians worshiped.

Let me now turn to Paul's letter to the Thessalonians. A new world, Paul wrote, is partially here now and is coming in its fulness as soon as the Christian community lives as the body of Jesus Christ. Don't lose faith that God's kingdom on earth eventually will come, even though the Romans still are in power and threaten the Christian community. As Isaiah and Jeremiah said again and again, the community of worshippers of God can't be destroyed by military might. Paul reassures the Thessalonica Christians that even their Christian brethren, who have physically died, will be resurrected in the coming Kingdom of God. Paul is not clear, however, about what kind of kingdom he is writing, other than that the resurrection kingdom of God is one in which the spirit of Jesus Christ rules in people's heart. He reassures the Christians in Thessalonica that the spirit that was in your fellow Christians who have died will live on in this resurrection community. He tells them that neither they nor their deceased family members will be reborn with physical bodies that are male or female. They will be reborn with spiritual identities (bodies) living on in the continuous life of the Christian community. Paul, therefore, wrote that Christians should not sit around waiting for total liberation from Roman rule. They should continue to live in the Roman world, but they should live there as Christians in the Kingdom of God worshipping God in the name of Jesus Christ.

Soon after his first letter, Paul wrote a second letter to the Thessalonians telling them again not to quit their jobs, thinking the world is going to end. The ungodly human Roman world that now exists, he writes, will die only when it fully matures, and its leader proclaims himself to be God above all gods and when his followers are deluded into worshipping this false God. This, of course, is what the Roman emperor was doing. By such delusional hubris, Paul claims, Romans will find themselves excluded from the presence of the true God of worship which alone allows people to cherish life rather than perish in meaninglessness. The conflict, between the expectation that the Roman way of life will end and the reality that ruthless Roman power is not going away, is a conflict that haunted early Christians for the rest of the first century CE.

Paul's first letter to the Corinthians was written just a few years after his letters to the Thessalonians. Earlier, Paul had spent eighteen months in this cosmopolitan Greek port city. Corinth was famed for the sexual delights it offered sailors, its Greek philosophers and mystery religions, and its temple dedicated to Isis, the mother goddess of nature. Paul wrote to address four problems that had arisen among the Christians in Corinth. First, Christians were splitting into competing factions, jealous of each other. This was a problem that has haunted Christians ever since. Second, some Christians were introducing Greek philosophy into their Christian thinking and others were introducing the practices of the Greek mystery religions. Third, some Christians were participating in common non-Christian Corinthian practices: bringing law suits against each other and engaging in sea-port kinds of sexuality. Fourth, some Christians had written Paul seeking answers to two questions they had about how they should live. They occupied social roles, such as parent or craftsman, that carried with them specific duties. Yet, Paul had said that the world was going to end. Are they still obligated to fulfill those duties? Second, in what ways was life going to be different when one is resurrected from the dead? Writing as their pastor, Paul addressed each of these problems.

The factionalism developing in the Corinth1an community was not due to different doctrines or liturgical practices but rather because the community was dividing up into groups each of whom claimed a different person as their leader. Some, influenced by the people sent by the Jerusalem community to Corinth, said that Simon Peter in Jerusalem was their leader. Some claimed that Apollos, a Jewish Christian from Alexandria who been serving as their pastor after Paul's preaching had converted them, was their leader. Some claimed that Paul was their leader. Finally, some claimed that only Jesus Christ was their leader. Paul insists that the Corinth community must remain united under the leadership of the only one that matters, Jesus Christ. He again writes that what legitimizes both him and the Jerusalem apostles is their personal encounters with Jesus Christ. He had an experience of hearing the voice of Jesus Christ and the apostles in Jerusalem had experiences of seeing Jesus Christ. His experience is just as good as theirs. Although he is not a Jerusalem Apostle, he is a different kind of apostle called to carry on a specific assignment to the Gentiles.

With respect to Apollos, Paul writes that there is no reason to see him as a competitor to Paul for leadership of the Corinth community. The two of them simply have different jobs to do. Paul points out that his job is to be an evangelist who preaches, converts, and begins Christian communities. Apollos functions as the one who serves as the pastor to the community, leading it in the liturgical practices of baptism and re-enacting Jesus's last supper with the Apostles in a way that the community experiences itself becoming the living body of Jesus Christ through the eating of bread and the drinking of wine. Although Christians are freed from old Jewish ritual requirements, these two rituals are crucial for Christians. By being baptized, he wrote, you express your desire to have your old way of life die off so that the new Christian way of life may begin. In celebrating the last supper, you celebrate being the new temple in which the spirit of God dwells. As Jeremiah said, a new covenant with Yahweh will dwell in your heart. This is what is now true with you.

Paul wrote to the Corinthians because he understood that as newly converted Christians they are still like babies only able to drink milk, that they do not yet understand in a mature way how drastic is their conversion to Christianity. It is not surprising that Corinthian Christians would divide into camps with different leaders. The city was filled with philosophers saying that they belonged to Plato or Aristotle or Epicurus or Zeno the Stoic. Paul wrote, therefore, to tell them that Christianity is not one more human philosophy. Paul claimed that Christians, like Job, should reject the idea that they can trust their intellects to solve the problem of human living. They should recognize the hubris of humans worshipping their own intellect. They should possess a living understanding that it is by worshipping, in their hearts and actions, God, in the name or manner of Jesus Christ, that their old Greek/Roman life will die off and they will be resurrected in the living body of Jesus Christ.

Furthermore, even though some of the new Christians are trying to incorporate into their new worship practices remnants from the practices of the Greek mystery religions, speaking in tongues, eating food offered to idols, it is crucial, Paul wrote, to remember that it is not the practices but the spirit in which they are carried out that matters. Food offered to idols is just food and cannot hurt the Christian eating it, but it can hurt others who do not know that one is not thereby worshipping what doesn't exist, some supposed god embodied in or symbolized by the idol. Having the ability to speak in tongues is irrelevant to possessing the Spirit of God and Jesus Christ. The test of the Christian genuineness of practices is the spirit in which they are done and the grateful attitudes and just and loving actions giving expression out of that spirit. The behavior that certainly is not expressive of the Christian spirit is engaging in seamen's wanton practices of casual sex or, even worse, having sex with one's stepmother. Christians also are not the people who are greedy, or verbally abuse others, or are drunkards or robbers. Paul charges that, when people professing to be Christians behave in these ways, let no one count them as members of Jesus Christ's body. Don't waste your time criticizing such outsiders because they are judged by God's universal and timeless principle of justice. Also, however, don't just pretend they do not exist, but rather proclaim to them that the worship of the Christian God can liberate them from meaningless life and into joyous life as a resurrected member of the temple of God and Jesus Christ.

Paul does his best to answer the questions of the Corinthian Christians about how they are to live now as worshippers filled with the spirit of Jesus Christ while waiting for the Greek/Roman way of life to be replaced by a Kingdom of God way of life. His recommendation: Be in the world but not of the world. You occupied social roles before you were converted and you occupy roles now having become Christians. You were men and women, husbands and wives, slaves and slave owners, gentiles and Jews. When non-Christian worlds cease to exist for you, and you live only in the Kingdom of God filled with the spirit of Jesus Christ, things will be different. Historically changing, perishable, social roles and identities will not exist then. They do exist now, however, and Christians must learn how to live with them while also living by the spirit of Jesus Christ.

Although in the kingdom of God justice and love rules between fellow Christians and no one is the master or slave of another, slaves who become Christians face special problems. Paul recommend that if they can do so, slaves should gain their freedom. If, however, their masers are not Christians and they will not free them, then they should accept their status as slaves. This may seem like harsh advice today, but one must remember that in Paul's age, unlike America's slave era, there were no free northern states to which slaves could run. Also, Romans were merciless in their treatment of runaway slaves. Paul was not endorsing slavery. He was offering pragmatic advice to slaves facing no good options.

It is also very easy to misunderstand Paul's advice to new Greek Christians, who are expecting the end of their whole old social world, on the matter of sex. His advice was based on his desire that people not be anxious about what to do because such anxiety would hinder their present joyous life in the Kingdom of God as they look forward to the end of all Greek and Roman laws and customs concerning sex and marriage. To the unmarried, Paul wrote, there is no Christian mandate to do one thing or another. Decide for yourself whether you can live best as a worshipping Christian by staying unmarried or by getting married. Paul says he decided to stay unmarried because he judged he could do his job as an evangelist best by staying unmarried. He advises those married to non-Christians not to choose to leave their spouses who still might be converted. To those in the Christian community married to another person in the community, he recommends that they stay married. There is nothing about living in the Christian community that warrants tearing apart a married couple who have over the years forged mutual bonds of affection and expectation, and who have most likely parented children to whom there exist bonds that should not be broken.

Believing that it does not make them any less Christian if they do so, Paul recommends that the Christians in Corinth continue to honor the traditions he grew up with, men not covering their heads when praying and women covering their heads when praying. For years afterwards, Hebrews have had reasons for preserving these practices that developed, because of their creation myth, as ways of honoring God who created man and of honoring God's creation in which men are born of women and men and women become one flesh when married. More surprising is his advice to continue the custom of women remaining silent in the temple, given that two women, Aquilla and Priscilla, played major roles in his original evangelical work in Corinth. Underlying all these recommendations is Paul's expectation that non-Christian ways of life soon will die and that then a new Christian way of life will exist for Christians as resurrected living members of the body of Jesus Christ. Unless customs threaten the core of the new Christian way of life, Paul seems not to want to rock the cultural boat. Unfortunately, in the centuries that followed what Paul wrote about slavery and women, so-called Christians quoted Paul to legitimate practices diametrically opposed to a Christian way of life.

Much of the advice that Paul gave in this letter depends upon his answer to the most complex question the Corinthians asked him. What are we to make of all this talk about the resurrection of the dead to new life? Paul used various metaphors and analogies in attempt to give his Christian interpretation of talk about the resurrection. His metaphors and analogies are better in clarifying what resurrection from the dead is not than they are in showing what it is. He made it very clear that faith in the resurrection is crucial for people being able to live the Christian way of life. He claimed that it is as resurrected spiritual bodies that we shall live in the kingdom of God. It is as images of the Jesus Christ who spoke to him on the road to Damascus that we shall live in the kingdom of God.

People who have not died, but have become resurrected Christians filled with the spirit of Jesus Christ, are not merely physical bodies of flesh and blood. As members of the Christian community, as members of the living body of Jesus Christ, they are observable images of Jesus Christ. The story about Adam is a story about the creation of bodily people who like all animals will physically die, but the story about Jesus Christ is the story of people who at long last are filled with a spirit that gives them a kind of life that does not perish when the physical body dies. Resurrected spirits, spiritual bodies, live on in the Kingdom of God, in the spiritual body of Christ that is the Christian community. The resurrection of Jesus of Nazareth as Jesus Christ was not a matter of resuscitating a dead corpse. It was a matter of demonstrating through the creation of a living body of Christ that neither the power of Rome nor the physical inevitability of bodily death can prevent the creation and continuation of the messianic community of worshippers of God in the name of Jesus Christ. Paul was not writing as a Greek metaphysician theorizing about a supernatural way of living; he was a Christian evangelist aiming to strengthen new Christians in their efforts to live a Christian way of life.

One of the most powerful parts of this letter to the Corinthians is Paul's characterization of life in the Christian Kingdom of God as life dominated by love. His hymn to love in Chapter 13 is one of the most quoted texts in the New Testament. Paul, like Amos, points out that it is not religious rituals such as striking gongs or cymbals or speaking in tongues that is at the heart of Christian life. Nor is it prophetically critiquing what Christians are doing wrong. Nor is it just a matter of being a martyr who is burned to death by Romans or a mob. It is even not just a matter of faithfully waiting for the Roman age to end.

Living in a community that is the body of the resurrected Jesus Christ is a matter of living with self-sacrificing and self-fulfilling love towards other people inside and outside the community. It is being patient and kind towards those who are just learning to become faithful Christians and towards those who can be moved by one's love to become another member of the body of Jesus Christ. It is not jealously craving what other people have or are, recognizing that Christians worship a God in whose eyes no one is or needs to be better or worse than others, either in wealth or physical beauty or skills. It is not boasting that one is better than other Christians or that one is saved but outsiders are not. Boasting will not help them be saved. Lovingly living in the new Christian kingdom of God is a matter not being irritated by others or resentful or angry when they do harm to you. It is a matter of not rejoicing when someone harms someone you do like or is your enemy. It is a matter of rejoicing when people treat each other justly and lovingly. When one lives with love in the new Christian community, love towards each other and towards life itself, then one can endure anything, one can believe that life is good no matter what, one can hope for the end to ungodliness and the coming of the Kingdom of God in all its fulness. One can trust that there never will be times or circumstances when this kind of loving is an inappropriate way to live. Before we were resurrected to life as the body of Jesus Christ we didn't understand what living well as a human being was all about; we were like an ignorant child. Now we understand what the game of life is all about and now we understand who we are, loving members of the body of Jesus Christ. In loving we gain that understanding.

Paul wrote a second letter to the Corinthians but permit me to pass it over and turn to Paul's letter to the Romans, his most systematic presentation of his understanding of Christianity. There are other letters that Paul wrote, but it is the book of Romans that has had such a dramatic influence on later Christianity through the writings of Augustine and Martin Luther.

The letter to the Romans was written while he was being held in Jerusalem by the Roman soldiers who had rescued him from the Jewish mob that was revolting against anything threatening their traditional temple worship practices. He was waiting to be sent to Rome and be tried as a Roman citizen. He had never been to Rome and the Roman church there was not established by him, but he wanted to go there. He hoped he could get provisions in Rome for an evangelizing trip to Spain. He wrote this letter defending his kind of ministry to Non-Jews. He felt he had to legitimate his work because he knew that the Jerusalem Christian community, which had just forced him to participate in a temple purification ritual, already had sent Peter there to represent their interpretation of Christianity. As Professor Kiely pointed out, he didn't succeed in influencing Roman Christians in his short time there. He and Peter were killed by Nero in 66 CE as Jews were revolting in Jerusalem. Augustine and Luther gave the letter an influence it never had in the city to which it was addressed.

The letter to the Romans is not a letter written to solve practical problems existing in communities Paul had established. It is written in a theoretical style common among Greek thinkers at the time. Paul begins by stating his primary thesis and then explains what his thesis means by saying what it does not mean. Then, in the light of what he has ruled out, he restates his thesis. To provide further understanding of his thesis he provides a concrete example of what he means. Then in the light of this example he states his thesis again. Finally, he uses his thesis to answer objections to his prior ministry that he presumes are circulating in the Roman Christian community.

Paul states his thesis early in his letter. The righteousness of God (as a good creator, judge of injustice, merciful forgiver, and savior of people from human hubris and for life in the Kingdom of God) is revealed to Christians when without any kind of proof they faithfully respond in a living way to the good news that one is part of the resurrected body of Jesus Christ and filled with his loving messianic spirit.

To explain what such a life of faithfulness is like, Paul writes what it is not like. It is not living according to the flesh rather than living faithfully in the messianic spirit of Jesus Christ. Living according to the flesh is trying to control things rather than surrendering control and accepting a new messianic way of living. Living according to the flesh is rebelling like Adam against being controlled by worship of God. Living by the flesh is living immorally like the rich and powerful who do not care for the poor and weak. Living by the flesh is living a Roman way of life worshipping Caesar and military power. It is living a way of life in which one worships various gods supposedly open to bribes by humans offering them sacrifices. It is living a way of life in which one thinks that participating in traditional Jewish rituals is enough to be worshipping God. Amos and Hosea already had rejected such assumptions of sufficiency, and Jeremiah and Ezekiel had already pointed out that faithfulness to God must include faithfulness of attitudes in one's heart and in the just and loving actions that follow from such attitudes. All forms of living by the flesh leave people with unworkable forms of life. Being separated from worshipping Yahweh in the name of Jesus Christ, they suffer the disastrous consequences to which God has turned them over. They suffer what such non-worshippers of the Christian's loving and saving God feel as the "wrath of God."

To those in the Christian community in Rome who think that Christians must still participate in Jewish practices such as circumcision or obeying dietary or sabbath regulations, Paul offered as a counterexample Abraham. Abraham faithfully worshipped God more than even his son whom he loved as much as any father could. Abraham's faithfulness made him righteous in the eyes of the God he worshipped and trusted. This righteousness existed long before the rules and requirements of Mosaic law and David temple worship existed. Using the example of Abraham, Paul tried to show that the point and purpose of Hebrew laws and regulations were to bind the communities of Moses and Ezra/Nehemiah together as worshipping communities, but now that is accomplished by people living as parts of the unified, messianic body of Christ.

There are several metaphors that Paul uses that need special explication since they have often been misinterpreted with unfortunate consequences. Paul always portrayed God as a loving and merciful God. In this letter, however, he uses a legal metaphor and an old temple metaphor to account for Christian salvation. For Paul it was his conversion experience of hearing the voice of Jesus Christ that triggers his transformation from being Saul in a world of flesh into being Paul in the Christian world of spirit. Paul said almost nothing in his letters about the life, teachings, or actions of Jesus of Nazareth. The only thing he mentions is the crucifixion of Jesus. In this letter to the Romans he offered his claim about the relation existing between the crucified Jesus and the resurrected Jesus Christ whose presence the followers of Jesus felt and whose voice Paul heard on the road to Damascus. Although he rejects the idea that the resurrected Jesus Christ is a resuscitation of the corpse of the crucified Jesus of Nazareth, he also wants to claim that without the crucifixion there would not have been any Jesus Christ to be encountered and worshipped by those saved out of a life of flesh into life in the Kingdom of God. He uses two metaphors to make this claim. Using the legal metaphor, people living in the flesh are characterized as criminals whose crime of unfaithfulness to God deserves the punishment of death. Using the temple metaphor, the crucifixion of Jesus is interpreted by Paul as an act of sacrificial love paying the legal requirement of death that all people deserve because of their criminal unfaithfulness. Hearing the good news of Jesus's loving sacrifice of himself provides the motivation for people to convert from living according to the flesh into living according to the spirit of Jesus Christ.

Although many readers of the book of Romans have done so, there is no need to interpret this metaphorical talk as a description of a resentful god threatening to punish people with death for failing to acknowledge him as god, a god whose thirst for bloody punishment is so great that he can't just let it go in forgiveness, and a god who is willing to crucify his own son because that is the only way his thirst for punishment can be met. Often Paul points out that the God he worships does not have to punish people. They do that to themselves by being separated from worshipful life with God. Also, his God is Hosea's God who welcomes back into the Kingdom of God everyone who wishes to do so, no matter how they were living in the world of the flesh. The point and purpose of his metaphors is to point out that it was Jesus's sacrificial love, of the sort described in Corinthians, that made it possible for him, Saul of Tarsus, to hear the voice of Jesus Christ. It is Jesus's sacrificial love, emulated by Stephen, and testified to by Paul, that has enabled thousands of Christians to have faith in Jesus Christ, Jesus their messiah, Jesus their savior. It is this faith that allows Christians to recognize in the crucifixion of Jesus of Nazareth the truth that neither the power of Rome nor the inevitability of physical death can prevent the messianic Kingdom of God from coming to be.

There is another figure of speech that Paul used to make a point that can easily lead to misunderstanding. Paul never pretended to be a wise Greek philosopher giving explanations for the cosmological character of the world. He did want to make the point, however, that the problem with the worlds of flesh is not just that individual persons do ungodly sorts of actions. There is something basically wrong with the social institutions and practices in these worlds such that people are nurtured to do unjust and ungodly sorts of things. It is not enough that individual persons living in worlds of the flesh get converted to live in the Christian world of the spirit. The messianic project aims at replacing all worlds of the flesh, especially the Roman way of life, with the Christian way of living grounded in love. In making this point Paul wrote in Romans as if sin were a cosmic force that a cosmic Jesus Christ had to war against and defeat. This is the language of Iranian Zoroastrianism in which there is talk about a good cosmic being warring with an evil cosmic being in the souls of people to gain dominance. Paul made it clear, however, that he is a monotheist. His God of worship cannot have a competing second being or force. I suggest that the best way to interpret his talk about a battle between Jesus Christ and Sin is to read him as claiming that when Christians worship God in the name of Jesus Christ they are involved in the creation of new righteous practices and institutions that will suck life from world of Flesh practices and institutions. The processes leading to the death of the world of Flesh is now under way and Christians may live with the faith that the new Kingdom of God will continue to live even though they all will die. As we shall see, forty years later, when the Roman way of life continues to live on, Christian writers like the author of the Gospel of John provided a different interpretation of the relation of the Kingdom of God to the Roman world. John will proclaim that the end of the world has already come.

There are two clarifications that Paul offered in his letter, anticipating Roman Christian objections to his understanding of Christianity. First, celebrating freedom from certain kinds of Jewish laws does not mean celebrating moral lawlessness. Paul pointed out that the Christian God is the God of universal justice, just as the prophets Amos, Hosea, Micah, Isaiah, Jeremiah and Second Isaiah had written. Second, declaring that Christians already have gained blessed lives in the Kingdom of God does not mean that ruthless Roman power has disappeared or that it won't be used against Christians. Not only are we now living in an in-between period in which the Christian way of life has been born but the Roman way of life remains still in existence, but the kind of blessed happiness that Christians have already acquired is not one that rules out suffering and death. Enjoying blessed happiness does not mean enjoying eating and the absence of toothaches. Christian blessed happiness is a timeless kind of happiness. That is what it means to say it is eternal. It doesn't come and go. It consists of a positive, unchanging attitude toward life no matter what happens. No matter what the Romans do to them, Christians do not despair or curse life. No matter how unfair life may seem to non-Christians, Christians continue to worship their good and loving God, just as Job ended up doing. Greek wisdom cannot justify such worship of God and celebration of life, but that is the gracious gift that the crucifixion of Jesus and the resurrection of Jesus Christ offer to those who permit themselves entry into the Kingdom of God.

The letters of Paul were the first Christian texts written. They make up more than half of the New Testament. They were circulated among the early Christian churches and often were read as part of the religious services conducted in these churches, especially his narrative of the Last Supper. Luther identified his claim that Christians are to be freed of practices existing in the church governed from Rome with Paul's claim that Christians have been freed of irrelevant practices required by the Pharisees in Jerusalem. The disagreement between Paul and the Jerusalem Apostles lead by James ended when James was killed during the Roman suppression of the Jerusalem revolts, but it was reborn when James's authority was transferred to Peter who had gone to Rome. Although both Paul and Peter were killed in Rome, the Roman destruction of Jerusalem meant that the mother Christian church had moved to Rome. Paul's critique of practices accenting ritual performance over faithful attitudes and actions never died even after the Roman emperor made Christianity the official religion of the empire and thereby strengthened the power and legitimacy of the bishop of Rome. It was to Paul that Augustine and Luther turned to support their understanding of Christianity. Although it is outside the scope of my presentation today, it would be very interesting to study today's ritual practices in Christian churches to see from which rituals Paul would claim Christians need to be freed.

Professor Kiely, that concludes my presentation.

Thank you, Mr. Eckerle. You have left us with so much to think about. Romans is so difficult a book to interpret and so important.

As was pointed out, Paul never met the man Jesus. He does not really write about what Jesus of Nazareth said or did. He doesn't write about how people viewed Jesus before his crucifixion or about how Jesus viewed himself. There are texts, however, that do this, and it is to these texts that we will now turn. I have asked Mr. Dan Zeltner to present his take on the two Biblical writers who wrote about Jesus before Jerusalem was destroyed: Q and Mark.

Mr. Zeltner.

Thank you, Professor Kiely.

Let me begin with Q. As Professor Kiely pointed out, the book of Q needs to be reconstructed out of the books of Matthew and Luke. The passages making up what scholars call the Book of Q are the passages in both Luke and Matthew that are not passages in Mark. By analyzing its contents, scholars conclude that Q probably was written around 50 CE, twenty years after Jesus' crucifixion and 20 years before the Romans destroy Jerusalem.

Q is focused on what Jesus taught about a new kind of Kingdom of God that people are encouraged to enter. In Q there is no mention of the birth or death of Jesus and no talk about a resurrected Jesus Christ being seen by Jerusalem apostles or heard by Paul. The writer of Q does not mention the formation of a Jerusalem Christian community under the leadership of James and Peter. The text is totally focused on the new way of living that Jesus was inviting people to adopt. The text begins with Jesus joining the movement of John the Baptist, who had been preaching that a new kind of Kingdom of God was going to come and who had been baptizing people wanting to wash away an old way of living and to begin living clean and fresh in a new way of life. According to Q, Jesus chose to be baptized, joined John's movement, and then began to spell out what life in this new kingdom was all about.

The Kingdom that Jesus invited people to join is very different from the kingdom of wealthy, ritualistic Jerusalem priests or the kingdom of militarily powerful Rome. In the new kingdom, the people who are prized, welcomed, and blessed are the poor, the hungry, the sad, the gentle, the merciful, the pure in heart, the peacemakers, those hated by the priests and the Romans. It is a kingdom based on a kind of love that is different from the love people have towards their family members or friends and different from the kind familiar to Jews and Romans. The people who love in this new way of life love their enemies, turn the other cheek when struck, treat others the way they themselves want to be treated, don't judge or condemn others, don't hypocritically focus on a speck in other people's eyes while one has a plank in one's own eye.

People in this new kingdom of God will not just talk the talk but they will walk the walk. They will do what John the Baptist says they should do, what their Jesus, called by Q "the teacher," tells them to do. Q also calls Jesus the "son of man," the title the prophets of old were called. Q writes that one need not be some high priest, Greek philosopher, or Roman Caesar to know what to do. Any child can understand this instruction to love and be kind. Be as lambs hurting no one and be willing to be shepherded by one's teachers. Love even the Romans. According to Q, Jesus taught that we in this new Kingdom of God, this kingdom of love, know something that the old Hebrew Kings and prophets did not know. We know the

God of this kind of love and we know that the God we worship is a God who loves us no matter who we are.

Therefore, with your feet confirm your baptism. Q has Jesus say, drop everything you have been doing in the old way of life and begin to live the life of love, begin to do what John was doing and what I am doing, which is spreading the good news of this new way of living. By being imitators of me, you gain the authority to do what I am doing. If people reject you, they are rejecting me and the opportunity of a lifetime. Even if they reject you, love them. Love the Romans. Be as lambs, and not as rebellious zealots.

Q says to his readers, I know that some of you may question whether this is a workable way of life. After all, you are surrounded by violence, bandits and rebels terrorizing priests and the rich and calling for revolution against the Romans. The Romans mercilessly are crushing these rebels and crucifying them. The writer of Q responds to these concerns. He writes that all we need to lead this new way of life is love, and if we keep worshiping the God of love we will have what we need. Q is saying something very similar to what Paul said in his letter to the Corinthians. By living in a loving way in the Kingdom of God, that exists here and now because of such love, and by worshipping the God of love with all our hearts, minds, and actions, we enjoy the blessings present in this new way of living.

Through our love of everyone, including those who threaten us, we show that we are not a violent threat to anyone. By loving each other and by worshipping our God of Love, we show that we have no intention of violently ending temple abuse or economic injustice or Roman domination. We are not striving to restore some David to power. We understand that the Kingdom of God, in which we live with the kind of love we are talking about, cannot be created through violence or coercion. Violently trying to destroy the economic injustice of temple abuse will only produce a new form of violence backed injustice and abuse. Isaiah and Jeremiah knew how misguided it was to try to militarily defeat Assyrian and Babylonian power. Rome has so much more power, and nothing is achieved by violently trying to defeat her. Q writes to his fellow Christians that by living lovingly and joyfully, Christians show to warring and unjust powers that there is an alternative way to live, and to live well.

Q acknowledges that this is a very new way of living for people used to living in a different kind of kingdom. He warns that all Christians need to be careful about falling back into old ways of doing things. He tells them not to look for some supernatural sign that the old worlds of power and violence are coming to an end. The only sign, he writes, that exists for those in the Kingdom of Love is the sign that Noah received, the rainbow that guarantees that there is nothing powerful enough, neither Rome nor death, to defeat the God of love who is worshipped by those living in the new Kingdom of God. If you keep looking for supernatural solutions to the problem of living in a world of violence, you will lose sight of what our kind of love calls for us to do. By loving we will live faithful to Amos's twofold call to us. We will be acting justly, and we will not substitute participating in rituals for acting out of love. Knowing that every hair on every head is precious, even hairs on Roman head's, we will love and forgive even those who renounce the son of man. We will forgive without limit even when those who have caused harm don't repent and ask for forgiveness. By not responding to the spirit of love and by attacking the spirit of love, people prevent themselves from experiencing forgiveness. That is the one unforgiveable sin, not because we find such people unlovable but because they make themselves immune to the power of love.

The kingdom of God is partially here already, Q proclaims. This kingdom of love is like a magnet that will attract more and more people into it. It is like a tiny mustard seed that will grow into a large tree in which beautiful birds can rest. It is like the yeast that causes the bread to swell and feed spiritually hungry people. Love and faithful service to the God of Love has the power to move mountains. Priests, rebels, Roman governors and emperors are outnumbered by the poor, crippled, blind, lame, and those who appear in the eyes of others as the least significant humans existing. They are the many who will find a world of acceptance and love in the Kingdom of God. Yes, this is a new kind of Kingdom. It shouldn't surprise anyone that some who are attracted to life in the Kingdom of God might backslide. However, when such prodigal sons realize that the old ways of life don't work, and they return home to the Kingdom of God, their family will welcome them with open arms and rejoice over their return. Q reminds his readers that Hosea taught them this truth long ago.

Q may have been a lost gospel, but it is now available for us to consider. I personally see it as presenting a powerful and challenging kind of good news. Many non-Christians find that Q says important things to them, even if they choose not to join Christian churches as they exist today. With that, let me turn things back to Professor Kiely.

Thank you, Don.

Now Mr. William Weinkauf will take us through the book of Mark, the other book that scholars think was written before the destruction of Jerusalem.

Thank you, Professor Kiely.

There are three features of the book of Mark which strongly suggest that, for its author, Q was expressing a wish for there to be a nonviolent kingdom of love rather than presenting a picture of something already existing. First, Mark includes a passion narrative that it is totally absent in Q. In that narrative Mark writes about throngs of Jews welcoming Jesus into Jerusalem on what we call "Palm Sunday," only to totally abandon him in disappointment when the Romans arrest Jesus and crucify him for inciting a revolution against Rome. Q never mentions any such welcoming mob and never says anything which would lead those cheering people to be disappointed when he does not destroy Rome but instead is killed by the Romans. To the mob, his crucifixion proved that he was not the messiah they expected. Q never mentions any crucifixion.

Second, Mark writes that no one, including the closest assistants of Jesus, understood what Jesus was teaching, and that is why they expected that Jesus would be the kind of messiah who would liberate them from Roman rule. What the author of Mark understood, over thirty years after the crucifixion of Jesus, is what Q understood and wished for ten or fifteen years earlier. No one, however, at the time of Jesus had that understanding. There is no historical evidence that Q's kingdom of love came into existence in Judea, even as a mustard seed, prior to the death of Jesus. By the time Q wrote, perhaps a mustard seed had begun to grow, but the Christian form of nonviolent pacifism that did appear after the destruction of Jerusalem seems to have been grounded more in a pragmatic recognition that violence against Rome was counterproductive than in a general principle of the Christian way of life. Certainly, once the power of Rome was backing the bishop of Rome, non-violent pacifism became at best an idea pushed to the margins of Christian life.

Third, Mark writes knowing what Rome is doing to revolutionary Jews in Jerusalem. Q shows no knowledge of that slaughter. The author of the book of Mark wrote in Greek to Christians in Rome while the Jewish revolt was being brutally crushed In Galilee and Judea. Probably, when Mark wrote his book, Jerusalem had not yet been burned down or he would have mentioned it. There is a decidedly Greek influence on the writer of Mark that is not apparent in the writings of Q. Even quotes in Mark from the Hebrew Bible are taken from the Greek version of the Hebrew Bible, the Septuagint, written in Greek in Egypt two centuries earlier. The text we now possess has a very complicated history. The Christian leader, Clement of Alexander in Egypt (150-215 CE), wrote that there were two versions of the book of Mark, one written in large rounded letters and one written in small cursive letters, one written for Romans and the other written for Christians in Egypt. During the 6th Century CE, the Latin Vulgate version of Mark was written, and it was this that Erasmus translated into Greek in 1516. The King James English version was a translation of Erasmus's Greek translation of the Latin Vulgate translation. An Alexandrian Greek version was sent to King James' translators, but it arrived too late to be used. The 1950's Revised Standard English translation of Mark was based on all the available versions.

The point and purpose of the book of Mark is twofold. First, he wrote in Rome to Roman Christians at a time when Rome was slaughtering rebels in Galilee and Judea. At the same time, Christians in Rome, such as Peter and Paul, were being put to death because the Romans did not differentiate Christians from Jews. Mark argues that Jesus never was the leader of an armed uprising against Rome and that his followers in Rome are not supporters of the Jewish uprising in Jerusalem. His intended audience consists of Christians who need encouragement in a very threatening time and Roman leaders who mistakenly see Christians as a threat to

Roman rule. Mark's second purpose was to portray Jesus as the son of the God of love, as the perfect offspring of such a God, as the perfect embodiment of Godly love.

The author of Mark pointed out that Jesus never was talking about establishing an earthly, political kingdom. His followers, however, Mark claimed, misunderstood what he was saying. When they were arguing among themselves about who was to be Jesus' second in command in his new kingdom, Jesus chastised them and told them that greatness in his kingdom consisted in being a servant, not a powerful chief minister. It consisted of providing loving care to needy children. Mark went on and wrote that, although a misguided mob celebrated his entrance into Jerusalem, they all abandoned him because his acceptance of arrest by the Jews in the Garden of Gethsemane showed that he was not the warring messiah for whom they were looking. The many bandit-warriors in Galilee and Judea had been claiming that they were such a messiah, but, when the Roman's put them to death, the people recognized that they were false messiahs. The mob hoped that this time with Jesus they had found a messiah who could draw upon supernatural powers to liberate them from the Romans. When he peacefully accepted arrest, they concluded that he too was a false messiah. Tragically, according to Mark, priests in the Jerusalem temple persuaded the Romans that Jesus's opposition to their corrupt temple practices meant that he also was a violent threat to Rome. The author of Mark desperately wanted Rome to believe that Jesus was not a dangerous rebel.

The author goes on to point out that many times Jesus supported Roman rule against the wishes of the scribes or the Pharisees. He did not condemn the Jewish agents of Rome who were tax collectors for what they were doing. He only wanted to work with them as a loving physician introducing to them the medicine of life in the loving Kingdom of God as a cure for the sickness people are suffering apart from such love. The author also points out that when the Pharisees tried to trap him into showing disloyalty to Rome, he did not condemn paying taxes to Rome. He was not calling for people to engage in a tax revolt, but he was inviting them to worship a God of love by loving all people whether they are Jews or Romans. Mark's message to Rome was that Jesus was no military threat to Roman rule and neither are the Christians now living in Rome.

Mark presumes that the authorities in Rome had no knowledge of the specifics of the crucifixion of Jesus. So many Jew were being crucified. Therefore, he takes pains to point out to the Rome's authorities that Romans in Jerusalem never considered Jesus a threat to their power to rule. Yes, Jesus did join the movement begun by John the Baptist, and, yes, John was perceived as a dangerous threat to current practices, but John was not put to death by the Romans but by the appointed Jewish leader, Herod, for petty personal reasons. John had condemned the Herod for marrying his brother's wife. Mark wrote that early in Jesus' short career of teaching and helping people, the Pharisees and Herod's police, the Herodians, worked together trying to find a way to destroy Jesus. It was they who saw Jesus as a threat to their power, not Pilate.

In the Passion Narrative in Mark, a major effort is made to point out that it was Herod and the Chief Temple Priests, Ananus and Caiaphas, who ordered the crucifixion of Jesus, while Pilate judged that he found Jesus to pose no threat to Roman rule. In this case, the author of Mark probably was publishing fake news in Rome to protect the Roman Christians from being lumped with the Jews being slaughtered. Neither Herod not the temple priests had any power to crucify anyone. Only the Romans could do that, and they only did it to those perceived to be threats to Roman rule. The Romans might have perceived Jesus as such a threat. They understood what Jesus was saying and doing even less than the crowd welcoming him into Jerusalem. The author of Mark constructs an elaborate narrative of Pilate taking an interest in Jesus's case and them washing his hands of the whole business. From all we know about Pilate, however, he never showed the kind of sympathy for Jews that the author of Mark has him show toward Jesus. The Romans were crucifying so many Jewish rebels claiming to be messiah or King of the Jews that it is quite possible that Pilate did not have anything to do with Jesus's trial. It served the interest of the author of Mark, however, to whitewash the Romans and to attribute the death of Jesus to the very Jews the Romans were trying to destroy. The historical tragedy is that the effort by the author of Mark did not work in the short run (the Romans kept killing Christians; Roman authorities never read anything Mark wrote) and it caused immeasurable harm in the long run as Christians persecuted Jews for centuries for being killers of Jesus whom by then was called God.

The Romans may have crucified Jesus, but it was the Pharisees and temple priests that were his primary enemies during his teaching mission, and for good reason. According to the book of Mark, Jesus condemned hard-hearted scribes who criticized his attempt on a sabbath to help a paralytic man who was brought to him by friends who believed that Jesus would care about him and care for him. He told the Pharisees that the sabbath was made for man and not man for the sabbath, and that it is not going through the motions of obeying sabbath rules that matters. Mark has Jesus say that it is the loving spirit of the son of man that gives the sabbath significance. According to Mark, Jesus said the same thing about the old traditions of cleansing one's hands before eating, pointing out that Isaiah also had criticized people who honor God only with their lips and not by worshipping God in their hearts and actions. Just before he was arrested by Herod's police, Jesus entered the temple in Jerusalem and knocked down the tables the priests used to sell the materials and animals used in sacrifices, thereby making themselves rich. He echoed Second Isaiah by claiming that it is a temple for all nations and not a den for priestly robbers who profit from Jewish tribal feelings. He warned his listeners about scribes who try to keep enforcing the hundreds of traditional rules governing Jewish worship in the temple and at home. Mark writes that Jesus declared that there are only two commandments that worshippers of the God of love must obey. "...you shall love Yahweh your God with all your heart and with all your soul, and with all your mind, and with all your strength" and "you shall love your neighbor as yourself."

As Q had proclaimed, the author of Mark was reminding Roman Christians, and any Roman officials listening in, that the new kingdom Jesus was talking about is a kingdom of love, a kingdom in which a certain sort of spirit animates life, not a political kingdom that could be a competitor to Rome's kingdom. The author made this point by claiming the Jesus is the son of man, prophetically judging the faults of the those running the current Jewish way of life – the Pharisees, Sadducees, Scribes and Temple priests. Mark also claimed that Jesus is the son of God bringing in God's messianic kingdom of love. In the very first verse in his text, the author proclaims that Jesus is the son of God whom Isaiah said would prepare the way for people to genuinely worship Yahweh and whom John the Baptist said would fill people with the spirit of the God of Love. The author has Jesus accept Peter's claim that Jesus is the Christ, the saving Messiah, while also pointing out that even Peter didn't understand what kind of Messiah Jesus would be. He has Jesus do the same thing when the priests charge that Jesus had said he was the messiah and the "Son of the Blessed" and when he replied in the affirmative to Pilate's question, "Are you the king of the Jews?" According to the author of Mark, what the priests believed about the messiah and the Son of Blessed God, and what Pilate means by "King of the Jews," is not what Jesus believed or meant. This illustrates what scholars call the "irony of Mark." Mark is telling his readers something about the life and teachings of Jesus that is quite different from what people thought about his teachings and his conception of himself while he was alive. The author probably is writing ironically when the centurion at the foot of the cross, impressed by the courage of Jesus, said. "Truly this man was a son of God." The author of Mark quite probably saw Jesus as a very different kind of "Son of God" from what the centurion saw.

Like Q, the author of Mark has nothing to say about Jesus's birth or life prior to his joining the following of John the Baptist. Talk about that would add nothing to what Jesus is doing to bring about a true messianic age in which a kingdom of love would exist within and between people who whole heartedly love the God of Love in the manner and name of Jesus the messiah. In the book of Mark, many times Jesus points out that his kind of messianic mission would require him to be the suffering servant about which Second Isaiah wrote. He would be misunderstood, and that meant that he would be crucified. The author of Mark, seeking to encourage Roman Christians to remain loyal even if they were attacked as dangerous Jews, has Jesus say that even if he is crucified, the messianic project that he has begun will not die with him. Jesus knew that anyone talking about establishing a new kingdom faced the threat of crucifixion by Rome. A Christian community that understands what kind of messiah and kingdom of God Jesus was talking about will live after Jesus is dead. It will live as a community filled with

Jesus's spirit of love and as the messianic spiritual body that will be an enlightening light to the nations. The writer of the book of Mark does not talk about any resurrection visions or voices, but he does say that three women went to the cave where Jesus had been buried and found it empty and heard a young man there tell them that Jesus, the messiah, the Son of God, really was not dead and that the disciples should return to Galilee to learn what they now should do.

Let me turn things back over to Professor Kiely. I have tried, through me presentations of the writings of Q and Mark to give you two perceptions of Jesus and his teachings that existed prior to the Roman destruction of Jerusalem and the Jewish Temple. Much of what they wrote gets incorporated into the texts of Matthew and Luke written 15 to 20 years after the destruction.

Thank you, Bill.

Reverend Kennedy, I believe that it is at this point that you have scheduled a break.

That is right, Professor Kiely. Let's take a break and stretch our legs. Let's reassemble here in fifteen minutes. There is coffee, tea and cookies just outside the Lecture Hall doors.

Everyone back in their seats? Let me turn things back over to Professor Kiely and her students.

Mr. Weinkauf was right when he said that all of Q and much of Mark are to be found in the books of Matthew and Luke. Ninety percent of Matthew's narratives about the actions of the adult Jesus come from Mark. Although the passages in Q and Mark are found in Matthew and Luke, the use that each of them made of these passages is very different. They were writing to audiences different from those of Q and Mark and different from each other. The point and purpose of writing what they wrote are very different. The readers of Matthew and Luke knew that Roman power still ruled the Mediterranean world. Their readers resided outside of Galilee and Judea. Many of them knew some of Paul's letters which were being used as sermon materials in Christian churches. They knew what Q and the author of Mark had to say. After all, Matthew and Luke were copying passages from both texts.

I have asked Joyce Lawson to present to us Matthew's message.

Thank you, Professor Kiely.

Scholars know that the book of Matthew was written in Antioch, Syria around 85 CE, fifty years after the death of Jesus and fifteen years after the destruction of Jerusalem. It carries the name 'Matthew', but no one knows the actual name of its author. Like many writers at that time, the author of the book chose a name well known to his readers. We know that this writer is not the Jewish tax collector Jesus met because this book is written in fluent Greek, something a Jewish tax collector in Jerusalem in 30 CE would not have known. To minimize confusion, however, I will just use the name the author chose, Matthew.

Its literary form makes it clear what the author's purpose was in writing it. It is a teaching manual addressed to Christians in Antioch who had been holding worship services in the Jewish synagogue in that city until they were denied permission to continue doing that. The Jewish leaders of the Antioch synagogue were simply obeying the Birkat-Haminim directive, issued by Jewish leaders at the Council of Jamnie five years earlier. These Jewish leaders operated on their conviction that a crucified man cannot be the messiah. Matthew wrote his manual to educate the Antioch Christians about the similarities and differences between them and the Jews. They are similar in that they also worship the God of Abraham, Moses, and the prophets. They also cherish the Torah. They are different from the Jews, who were following the leaders at the Council of Jamnie, because these Christians believed that the very Jesus who was crucified is the fulfillment of all the expectations of Abraham, Moses, and the prophets. Crucified Jesus, resurrected as Jesus Christ, is the embodiment of the Torah. Worshipping God in the name of Jesus Christ is worshipping in the true spirit of the Torah, a spirit that had been driven out by legalistic Jewish interpreters of the Torah.

Sprinkled throughout his book are quotations from the Hebrew Bible that Mathew had included to show that Jesus Christ is the fulfillment of messianic expectations and the embodiment of the Torah. Isaiah 7 had said that Judea would be saved from the threat of Assyria by the time a child, born of a young woman and named Immanuel (God is with us) reaches maturity. Micah 5 said that from the little, insignificant tribe of Bethlehem there will come a person embodying the faith of Abraham and Moses who will be a spiritual ruler of Israel. Jeremiah 31 proclaimed that after the destruction of Jerusalem a new set of worshippers of Yahweh will covenant with Him in their hearts and not just by obeying the letter of Mosaic laws. Isaiah 40 said that in the wilderness outside of Jerusalem the glory of Yahweh will be seen when institutional mountains are leveled and Yahweh's spirit lives among people who are justly treating other people as equal children of Yahweh. Deuteronomy 8 reminded Jews that they must not crave tribal power and wealth, but they must live justly and lovingly with each other. Psalm 91 sang that, if one but listens, the messengers speaking Yahweh's words (the Angels) will help people avoid dashing their feet. This is something that would happen if they tried to walk through fields of legalistic hard rocks. Deuteronomy 6 reminded them that worshipping God means loving Yahweh, their Elohim, with all their heart, and all their soul, and all their might. Malachi 3 warned that Yahweh's messiah is coming to the temple to burn off its distorting practices, to wash clean its unclean priests, and to refine people so that they can offer the right kind of spiritual sacrifices to Yahweh. Isaiah 6 said in poetry what was applicable then and is so relevant in Matthew's time, something that many children of Israel heard but did not understand. The poem said that there will be a small stump of the mighty oak of Judea, one filled with the true spiritual seed of Yahweh, that will live on no matter how many times Judea, Jerusalem, and the temple are burned to the ground. Finally, Jeremiah proclaimed that although the house of David is smashed like a potter's clay vessel, still a new kingdom will be molded as a new vessel in the lives of those who listen in their hearts and actions to the call of Yahweh. Mathew located these quotes in his narratives and in the discourses of Jesus, thus giving them a Christian meaning.

In writing his teaching manual, Matthew took passages from Q and Mark and packaged them together into five discourses that he then attributed to Jesus. In none of the other New Testament writings do we have any claims made that Jesus gave such lengthy lectures. They are Matthew's discourses to his readers in Antioch using materials in Q and Mark, adding some other material that helps him achieve his literary purpose. He constructed a narrative of Jesus' life, 90% of which was taken from Mark, dividing his life into five segments and separating each segment with one of the discourses attributed to Jesus, using primarily material borrowed from Q and Mark. Matthew constructed two narratives of his own to support his primary claim, and he placed them as bookends strengthening the narratives and discourses placed between them. At the beginning of his text, he placed his narratives about the birth and childhood of Jesus. At the end, he placed his take on the experiences of the early Christians in Judea and Galilee with the resurrected Jesus Christ. The book of Luke, written around five years later, also contains birth and resurrection narratives but they are significantly different from Matthew's, something to be expected given the differences in the point and purpose of Mathew's and Luke's writings.

In the dialogue that he constructed between quotes from the Hebrew texts and Q and Mark, Matthew instructed his readers about what is the new Christian spiritual meaning of old Jewish laws. He wrote that Jesus is not calling for the abolishment of the old laws but the fulfillment of them. In that fulfillment Christians will exceed in righteousness that of the scribes and Pharisees. They said you should not kill, but Jesus said you should not be angry with your brother or insult him. They said you should not commit adultery, but Jesus said you should not look at a woman with lust in your heart. They said that if you divorce your wife you should give her a certificate of divorce, but Jesus said that you may divorce your wife only if she, through adultery, in fact divorces you. They said you should not swear falsely before officials, you should not falsely declare formally that you promise to do something, but Jesus said that one should not say, "I swear by God or by Jerusalem to tell the truth." Instead, one should just answer questions asked of one with a simple "yes" or "no." They said, "An eye for an eye and a tooth for a tooth," but Jesus said, "Don't resist, turn the other cheek, give to beggars and lend to those who request." They said that one should love one's neighbors and hate one's enemies, but Jesus said love your enemies because in this way you show how different life is in the Christian community, where people love the God of Love, from the way the Romans and corrupt Pharisees live.

Mathew wrote to his Antioch Christians that they are different from the legalistic Jews driving them out of the synagogue. They live by the spirit of Hebrew and Jewish law and not be a spiritually dead reading of the law. To make the point that Jesus Christ is a descendent of Abraham, Moses, and David, physically as well as spiritually, Matthew opened his book with a genealogy, one that probably was already in circulation, but it immediately causes him a problem in constructing his narrative. In the genealogy Jesus's linkage to David and Abraham goes back through Joseph, but, in his narrative of the birth of Jesus Christ, Joseph is not the father of Jesus.

The narrative of Jesus' birth and childhood is written by Matthew to make as strongly as possible the case that Christians in Antioch, who worship Yahweh in the name of Jesus Christ, are not abandoning the worship of Yahweh or obedience to Hebrew law. They believe that the messiah through whom they worship Yahweh (Jesus Christ) is the true descendent of David, Moses and Abraham. In making his case Matthew utilized common beliefs that may not fit into his use of Q's characterization of the spiritual character of the new Kingdom of God. A common belief held by many Jews at the time of Matthew was that the human desire to control things began with Adam's rebellion in the Garden of Eden. It couldn't be a part of God's original creation because God saw that everything he had made was good. Furthermore, this rebellious feature of human nature was passed on generation after generation through sexual reproduction, something that exists in the kingdom of the flesh and not in God's spiritual kingdom. Matthew. therefore, told a story of Jesus' birth that guarantees that he has not physically inherited this rebellious tendency from Joseph and thus from Adam. Matthew claimed that the spirit of Yahweh placed in Mary the seed that would grow and be born as Jesus. Jesus has no contaminated physical origin and thus he and he alone can live as a sinless messiah. Matthew quoted Isaiah to substantiate the claim that the messiah will be given birth by a young woman and the boy will be called Emmanuel (one who is with God) and thus free of the rebellious spirit of those not with God. He quoted Micah to show that this Emmanuel will be a true spiritual descendent of David, and thus a legitimate occupier of the spiritual, messianic throne of David, because he will be born in Bethlehem, materially the weakest of the twelve tribes but spiritually the originator of the messianic lord of the kingdom of God.

Having been crucified does not make Jesus ineligible to be the messiah because, as Second Isaiah said, it is through suffering that the messiah will be a light to the nations. Matthew was claiming that it is the unique spiritual nature of the birth of the sinless messiah, Jesus, that legitimates his status. Since many people believed that Joseph was the father of Jesus, Matthew included a story about Joseph discovering that Mary was pregnant, although he never had sex with her, deciding to cancel their wedding, but then changing his mind when he dreams that God is informing him that Jesus is God's son destined to be the messianic savior of all people.

To his readers in Antioch who were familiar with tales that had come from Persia, of a group of Zoroastrian religious leaders famous for their astrological readings and predictions, Matthew added a story about some such magi coming to honor the birth of this future messiah. Christians in Antioch should ignore their rejection and expulsion by legalistic Jews, just as these Persian spiritual leaders did on the day of Jesus' birth. Mathew's story about the Persian Magi also provided him with a literary bridge to his effort to show parallels between the life of God's chosen savior out of Egypt, Moses, and God's chosen messiah and savior in the age of Rome, Jesus. Matthew wrote that the Magi, when looking for the Jewish messiah, went to Herod to ask where he might be found. Herod used Micah's text and said that the messiah would be born in Bethlehem. The Magi left Herod, but he was worried. He had spent his whole carrier killing off rebels and self-appointed messiahs who threatened Roman rule. In Matthew's story, Herod believes the astrological prediction of the Magi and therefor takes preventive measures to guarantee that another messiah did not show up. Just as the Egyptian Pharaoh did when Moses was going to liberate Hebrew slaves, so Herod orders the killing of all Jewish boys in Bethlehem under two years of age. Just as the baby Moses was saved from Pharaoh's murderous plan, Matthew wrote of baby Jesus being saved from

Herod by his family fleeing to Egypt, just as Joseph's family had fled to Egypt to avoid starvation. Matthew also wrote that, just as Moses liberated the Hebrew slaves by leaving Egypt, so Jesus and his family came out of Egypt so that Jesus could grow up in Galilee and carry out his messianic mission of saving people from spiritual death under legalistic interpretations of Moses' law. According to Matthew's story, Jesus' family originally went back to Judea because Herod the Great had died. From the writings of Q and Mark, however, all of Matthew's readers knew that Jesus lived in Nazareth until he went to be baptized by John. Matthew, therefore, said in his story that Jesus' family was concerned that Archelaus, who had replaced his father, Herod the Great, as Jewish king of Judea, might be a threat to Jesus and therefore they went north to live in Nazareth in Galilee.

The narrative of Jesus' adult life that Matthew wrote basically is the same as Mark's. Jesus leaves Galilee and comes to the Jordon River to be baptized by John the Baptist. Beginning with his treatment of John, Matthew made a major change in Mark's characterization of people's reactions to Jesus and his teachings. Mark's irony was that people at the time that Jesus was with them did not understand what Mark and his Christian readers, thirty years after Jesus' death, understood about what Jesus was saying and that Jesus was the messiah. Matthew changed that story line to fit his purpose. It was the Jewish scribes and Pharisees who did not understand. According to Mark, John simply baptizes Jesus into his community. According to Matthew, John recognizes Jesus as the messiah who will baptize people into the Kingdom of God and tells Jesus he should not baptize him. Matthew had Jesus insist that he baptized to fulfill all the requirements for righteousness. What is that requirement? It is the requirement of purification through baptism that all humans need because they all have received from Adam the contaminated inclination to seek to be God in control of things. Here again, Mathew's narrative conflicts with his story about Mary being impregnated by the holy spirit, thus leaving Jesus undirtied by any male's seed. Matthew's birth story says that Jesus does not need purification or baptism.

Matthew added detail to Mark's cryptic statement that after baptism Jesus was in the desert for forty days tempted by false conceptions of the role of the messiah.

Matthew spells out three forms of Adam's temptation to be God in control of everything, and he has Jesus reject all three. He rejects the idea of the messiah as someone who can turn people into subjects totally dependent on him by exercising some unearthly power to meet their material needs. He rejects the idea that the messiah is someone who gains followers by performing incredulous, mind-boggling tricks like jumping off the pinnacle of the temple and avoiding being harmed. He rejects the idea that the messiah will be a powerful, political king ruling all the kingdoms of the world. Matthew had Jesus realize that these are Adam-type temptations to be God controlling everything, temptations to be rejected. Matthew had Jesus accept his calling to be the son of the God of Love worshipping and serving only this God.

Before having Jesus give his first discourse, the Sermon on the Mount, Matthew wrote about Jesus moving through Galilee, selecting two sets of brothers to be his special assistants, and drawing to him huge crowds of followers from all over Galilee and Judea. They were attracted by his teachings and by a reputation that he, like most itinerant preachers of his time, had as a healer. The unified sermon that Matthew puts in Jesus' mouth consists of many passages spread throughout the texts of Q and Mark. The sermon written in Greek is addressed to the kinds of people attracted to Jesus's Q-like teachings, Christians who made up the Christian community in Antioch: the poor in spirit, the mourners, the meek, the people hungering and thirsting for righteous, the pure in heart, the peacemakers, those reviled and persecuted for faithfulness to God, the salt of the earth, and the light of the world. Matthew would have his readers compare Jesus' Sermon on the Mount to Moses' sermon on Mt. Sinai.

After contrasting old legalistic Jewish ways with new Christian ways, Matthew had Jesus remind these Christians that they must be genuine in their worship of God and not pretentiously trying to show others how righteous they are, or hypocritically talking religiously while acting unjustly or unkindly. They are to help the poor because they need help and not to make a public display of how charitable they are, doing this to gain public approval. They are to pray in secret to the God they worship in their hearts, liturgically using only the simple words contained in the prayer they have learned as Christians (what we now call the "Lord's Prayer").

Matthew also had Jesus remind them how different living in Jesus Christ's Kingdom of God s is from living outside it. Seeking worldly treasures is not the Christian's primary goal. Justly and lovingly treating others as you want to be treated is the goal. Doing that may diminish your wealth, but don't let that make you anxious or tempt you to abandon the messianic community to go back and make money. Matthew had Jesus remind these Christians, who have been chased out of the Jewish synagogue, to make the right choice about how to live. The Christian way of life is a form of life that is very demanding and not popular outside the Christian community. It is a form of life, however, that bears good and not unjust fruit and that is a workable way of life in the long run. It is not one attractive for a moment only to lose its foundation because of the shifting sands of history.

In the narrative between Matthew's first discourse and his second discourse, he wrote about all sorts of people who had faith in Jesus and received his compassionate help. There is a leper, a Roman centurion, Peter's mother-in-law, people possessed of "demons", paralytics, tax collectors, rulers, and a woman who had been hemorrhaging for years. Writing fifty-five years after Jesus died, Matthew included in his narrative many of the claims that had accumulated over the decades since Jesus death, about Jesus healing people's medical conditions. The point that Matthew seems to be making to his readers is that living faithfully in Jesus Christ's Kingdom of God is a good and workable way to live.

The second discourse that Matthew writes in Jesus' name to the Christians in Antioch aims at doing two things. First, it supports his claim that Jesus Christ is the embodiment of genuine Hebrew worship of God. Referring to the twelve tribes that existed before the temple was built in Jerusalem and before Jewish legalism became so strong, Matthew has Jesus appoint his twelve apostles as leaders of the twelve tribes and instructs them to go to the Jews in Galilee and Judea and proclaim in word and deed the same thing that he is proclaiming, that they should put to death their old legalistic and empty ritualistic ways and should let themselves be reborn in the Christian way of life. What Matthew is saying trough Jesus to the apostles is what he was saying to the Antioch Christians who had been forced out of the Jewish synagogue. Go to the Jews. Speak the truth. If any of them welcome you into their homes and lives, stay for a while and celebrate their entrance into your family. If they won't listen to you, don't aggressively argue with them, but be innocent of violence, even as doves are, and be pragmatically as wise as a garden snake about to be stepped on by a human, just move on. Matthew was telling his readers that many Jews will be furious with you because some members of their own families might join your new community of love. Don't let their threats stop you. The scribes and Pharisees never understood Jesus and they turned against him. You might have to suffer as Jesus did. It is worth it. You will receive the spiritual rewards of living in God's Kingdom where all members celebrate God's presence and love each other in all manners of simple ways like giving cold water to thirsty child.

Mark began his narrative with Jesus being baptized into John's community. In Chapter Three of his book. Matthew gives to John an awareness that Jesus is on a messianic mission. Then, in the narrative between discourse two and discourse three, Matthew gives John a Hebrew legitimation for setting the stage for Jesus by identifying John with what Isaiah wrote about someone preparing the way for the messiah to come. He has Jesus say that people like the Antioch Christians, who are newly born babies in the Kingdom of God, understand what the supposedly wise Jewish legalists don't get at all. Mathew's tired and heavy-laden readers understand God because He is the God of Love that Jesus Christ reveals through his life and death. The scribes, Pharisees, and legalistic leaders of the Antioch Synagogue have no living knowledge of God's messianic spirit, something that is shown by their focusing more on obeying old rules governing Sabbath behavior than on feeding the hungry and healing the sick and those who cannot see or speak. Those who hear the words of Jesus and do not understand what is being said are people who do not have the messianic spirit that makes all Christians members of one family, a family determined not by biological ties but by shared attitudes and actions.

In his third discourse, Matthew has Jesus tell the sower, good seed, mustard seed, leaven, hidden treasure, good pearl, and fisherman's net parables, Mark wrote that no one before Jesus' crucifixion understood these parables. Matthew said that no one, not even his disciples initially understand them, but these disciples at least had the capacity to come to understand them when their meanings are properly explained. He points out that it is useless to try to explain them to the scribes, Pharisees (and legalistic Antioch Jews) because they do not want to understand them, being filled with a spirit that totally rejects the spirit of faithful members of the messianic Kingdom of the God of Love. Those disciples filled with the spirit of Jesus Christ, however, can receive and understand his teaching about the meaning of the parables. In the same way, the Christian readers of Matthew's teaching manual can understand what Matthew is teaching them.

In his fourth narrative, Matthew wrote to comfort Christians who now have a new status in Antioch. He wrote telling them that they live in a new Kingdom of God based on their faith in Jesus Christ, the messianic son of the living God they worship. He told them that because of their faith they are different from the hypocritical Pharisees who focus on rules about washing hands before eating but who preach that it is O.K. to dishonor one's parents if you give offerings to the priests. Mathew wrote that If they faithfully lived in the new Kingdom of love, then, not only will their basic needs for loaves of bread and fish be met, but they will be able to do truly marvelous things. In doing these marvelous things, he said, they will feel as if they were walking on water. Matthew told his readers that they should not let the Pharisees try to persuade them that the messianic age has not arrived through Jesus Christ, simply because John the Baptist was murdered by Herod or because Jesus was crucified. Matthew wrote that Jesus understood what legalist Jews do not understand and that is that being a suffering servant is a necessary condition for inaugurating the messianic Kingdom of God. Peter was wrong to try to save Jesus from what was to be his fate. Still, Matthew made Peter's faith, and thus any Christian's faith, that Jesus Christ is the son of the living God, the rock on which the Christian community is built.

In his fourth discourse, Matthew has Jesus explain two of the key features of life in the new Christian community of faith and love. First, no one is to think that he or she is better than anyone else in the community. Humble yourself and see yourself as a little child dependent without resentment on others for everything; love everyone the way a child loves it parents and the way you as a parent love your child. Second, Christians in their new community understand that a necessary feature of worshipping God is acting justly and kindly toward others. Talking about

God forgiving you is empty talk, if you do not forgive others for what they have done to you. Forgive them again and again if necessary, 70 times 7 if necessary. Wherever there are two or three Christians with such humility, justice, love, and mercy, there is the messianic Kingdom of God.

On the surface, Matthew's fifth narrative is about Jesus's journey from Galilee to Judea and Jerusalem. Matthew, however, focused not on the journey but on what Jesus said to blunt the attacks that had been made against him and his teaching while he was alive. Matthew selected them to undercut the many attacks made against Christianity during the decades since Jesus died. Cheering crowds welcomed him into Jerusalem, some thinking that he is the son of David who will restore a prosperous earthly kingdom and some claiming that he is a prophet. Matthew showed how different Jesus is to people's expectations, how differently the Christians in Antioch should view themselves in contrast to those outside their kingdom. Yes, he wrote, you are to obey the ten commandments that the Pharisees preach but do not follow. You, however, are to do so much more. You need to be willing to sell everything you have and give your wealth to the poor. Economic life in the Kingdom of God, therefore, will be very different from what exists outside it. Equal blessings, Mathew claimed, come to all members no matter when they came into the community, but these are not monetary blessings. It is easier for a camel to go through the eye of a needle than for someone worshipping money to be a part of the messianic kingdom. The Christian Kingdom of God is not a material competitor to the kingdom of Rome. Christians will pay their taxes to Rome but they will lovingly serve their God of love. Although the apostles will lead all 12 of the old Hebrew tribes into the kingdom, no one in the kingdom will have more authority than anyone else; no one will have a special seat sitting on the right-hand side of the messiah.

Matthew, as a writer, took advantage of Jesus' visit to the Jerusalem Temple to criticize the culture of hypocritical priests, scribes, and Pharisees. Jesus overturned the tables of priests who changed ordinary money into the temple money needed to buy sacrificial animals, a scheme that made priests rich. The scribes and the Pharisees dress up in fancy clothes, but they are like whitewashed tombs full of dead bones. They give petty offerings but neglect justice, mercy and faith. These pretentious religious fakes are just like the one's condemned by Amos, Isaiah and Jeremiah, just like the ones who tried to kill those prophets. Matthew has Jesus tell a parable to show to his readers that they, and not the legalistic leaders in the Antioch synagogue, are the faithful guests at the messiah's table. Abraham, Moses, and the prophets are like a king, Matthew wrote, who gave a feast but his chosen ones whom he had invited never showed up and so he had his servants go out and bring in ordinary people to enjoy his blessed feast.

Matthew had Jesus present himself as a messiah, living with the spirit of the prophets leveling special accusations on those who have distorted the call for righteousness issued by Moses and the prophets. Matthew charged that the scribes and Pharisees pretend to be worshippers of Yahweh, but they are now acting like the ones condemned by the prophets whom they tried to kill. Worse than that, they are corrupting the temple itself. Matthew presents Jesus Christ as the new Moses, endorsing the ten commandments given by Moses and then adding the greatest commandment of all, "You shall love the Lord your God with all your heart, and with all of your soul, and with all your mind. You shall love your neighbor as yourself."

It is in this narrative that Matthew addressed a question on the minds of many of his readers. It is the same question Paul tried to answer. What is the resurrection of the dead going to be like? He told them of the time when Jesus carried on a conversation with the Sadducees who rejected the claim of the Pharisees that there would be a resurrection of the dead. Matthew's readers in Antioch most likely knew about Paul's claim to have heard the voice of the resurrected Jesus Christ and to have heard about resurrection appearances to Jesus' disciples. The Sadducees sarcastically asked Jesus about who would be the wife of a resurrected man who had seven wives before he died. Jesus gives a very interesting reply. First, he declared that people living in the resurrected Kingdom of God were not going to be there as occupants of any social roles like being a wife or a husband. Second, he charged that the God of the fathers (Abraham, Isaac, and Jacob) is not a God of the dead but a God of the living. As Jeremiah and Ezekiel wrote, it is in the hearts of worshippers that God covenants with his faithful worshippers. Matthew had already told his readers that wherever two of three of them gather together in the resurrection community, there God is in their midst. His narrative closes by preparing his readers for Jesus' last discourse by having Jesus mention, what he and all his readers already know in 85 CE, and that is that Jerusalem will be destroyed.

Matthew' final discourse is a reminder to his readers that the Jerusalem temple had been destroyed and that they now worshipfully encounter God in a new way. Whenever they render help to the hungry, the thirsty, the naked, the stranger, they are encountering God. When the messianic gospel has been preached throughout the world and people everywhere are encountering God in attitudes and actions, then God's spiritual kingdom will be fully present. Don't be misled, Matthew wrote, when false messiahs come along and proclaim that present wars and calamities are signs that the full kingdom is at hand. No one now knows when that will occur, but Christians will know that when that glorious day comes there will be people in all corners of the world encountering God by serving humans in need. For now, he wrote, carry on the messianic mission.

The final narrative in Matthew' book consists of his edited version of Mark's narrative of the Jesus' last days in Jerusalem. Matthew made two significant additions to Mark's story. First, Matthew wrote that when Jesus died the curtain in the temple, hiding the holy of holies and through which only the high priest could go, was torn in half. Priestly mediators, he is claiming, no longer are needed. Christians encounter God directly whenever they are caring for the needy. Second, after Jesus's death, the women who go to the cave where they put his corpse meet not just a young man but an angel telling them that Jesus Christ has risen from the dead and that he would meet the disciples in Galilee. Joyfully receiving this message, according to Matthew, they experienced the presence of the resurrected messiah. Matthew, using the formula that had become traditional by 85 CE, wrote that the disciples went to Galilee and heard Jesus Christ tell them to go to all nations and baptize in the name of the Father, the Son, and the Holy Ghost. To his Antioch readers, he also explained away the efforts of some Jews since the birth of Christianity to say that there was no resurrection and thus that Jesus was not the Messiah. Matthew dismissed their efforts to discredit the Christian's resurrection faith. He pointed out that after Jesus's death, the Jewish leadership in Jerusalem, to prevent his disciples from stealing Jesus's body, had placed guards at the sepulcher. Matthew repeated the charge Christians had been making for four decades, that after the sepulcher had been found by the guards to be empty, the guards were bribed by Jerusalem priests and Pharisees to say that the disciples of Jesus came at night and stole away the body.

This, therefore, was the teaching manual that Matthew wrote for his readers in Antioch, making the case that Christians are the true preservers of the faith and spirit of Abraham, Moses and the prophets. The living body of Jesus Christ, the Christian Community, is the first fruits of the old and new Kingdom of God.

Thank you, Joyce, for showing us how Matthew used Q and Mark in writing his teaching manual. Q presented the teachings of Jesus about a Kingdom of God based on love and the worship of a God of Love. Its focus was on the teachings and not on the teacher. There is no mention of the birth or death of the teacher. It is written by someone in this new Kingdom of Love to other members of the Kingdom. Mark does present a narrative of the life and death of Jesus. He is not interested in Jesus' birth, but he is very much interested in his death because he wants the Romans to know that neither Jesus nor the Christian community are the kind of threat to Rome that the Roman emperor thinks the Jews are. Mark keeps making the point that Christians are not Jews and Jesus was not crucified by Rome for advocating violent overthrow of Roman rule. Matthew wrote at a different time, in a different historical setting, for a different purpose. Jerusalem and its temple had been destroyed. Christians in Antioch had been chased out of the synagogue. Matthew wrote to these Christians to establish their religious credentials. They are the proper inheritors of the religious legacy of Abraham, Moses, and the prophets. Their new kingdom of love is the worshipping community that Abraham, Moses, and the prophets sought to establish. To achieve this purpose, Matthew added to the book of Mark a birth narrative and a short extension of Mark's story about finding Jesus's tomb empty. He also collected together into five discourses the teachings of Jesus that are spread throughout Q and Mark. These discourses tell the Christians who read them what it means to be a Christian.

Now let's look at what the writer named Luke did with the materials he borrowed from Q and Mark. He writes in a very different historical setting and for a very different purpose. Delores Thom will try to help us understand better the book Luke/Acts which now appears in our Bibles as two separate books.

Ms. Thom.

Thank you, Professor Kiely.

Even though early Christian leaders divided the book Luke/Acts into two distinct books, originally it was a single text, the longest book in the New Testament. Its writer, who takes for himself the name of Luke, dedicates the text to Theophilus, an honored title among educated Greeks and Jews meaning "lover of God" and "loved by God." It was written several years after Matthew, around 90 CE, sixty years after Jesus' died and 30 years after Paul died and Jerusalem was destroyed. Luke writes in "high Greek" that was used by the intellectual elite in the Greek/Roman world. It was written to Gentile Christians in the communities that Paul had established. It shows no knowledge of Matthew's Antioch Christian community or of the discourses that Matthew had written collecting Jesus' teachings in Q into five sermons. The materials shared by Luke and Matthew are those taken from Q and Mark. Luke's point and purpose in writing his text is quite different from Matthew's effort to portray Jesus as the new Torah.

To Christians in Paul's churches, and to potential Christians throughout the Gentile world, Luke presents a single, developing narrative of the life of the spirit of God from Adam to Noah to Abraham to Moses to David to the Prophets to John the Baptist to Jesus to the Jerusalem Apostles to Stephen to the Samaritans to Paul and thus finally to Rome. Luke's story line is that God created a good universe, that humans worshipping finite false gods make a mess of things, that new worshipping communities were born filled with the spirit of God, and that the present community is one such community filled with the spirit of God. Luke uses this narrative of the historical life of God's spirit to explain why the Jewish community of Pharisees and temple priests has been crushed by Roman power, but the Christian community is flourishing among the gentiles. Luke claims that these Jews drove out the spirit of God, but it is now present among Christians because John the Baptist, Jesus, the Jerusalem Apostles, Stephen and Paul were filled with the spirit of God and spread it throughout the world. The power making this rapid spread possible was the crucifixion of Jesus and the resurrection of Jesus Christ in his new body, the Christian community filled with God's spirit. Neither Roman Power nor physical death are strong enough to stop the forward movement of God's spirit.

What Luke wrote shows the point and purpose of writing this two-part narrative of the life of God's spirit from the time of the conception of Jesus to the death of Paul in Rome. This, however, is not what Luke says is his reason for writing. He says that he knows that his Christian readers are aware of various accounts of the life of Jesus that are in circulation and that he feels a need to construct out of these accounts an orderly narrative that would teach his readers the truth about what they have learned from these accounts, from reports of what happened to the early apostles in Jerusalem before its destruction, and from the letters of Paul. He uses texts in Q, Mark, Paul's letters, and in other unnamed sources, and writes his narrative of the life of God's spirit, the big Truth he wants his readers to understand.

Luke constructs a very different narrative from Matthew about the life of Jesus before he joins the movement of John the Baptist. Matthew wrote a birth narrative aimed at reinforcing his claim that Jesus' birth mirrored events at the time when Moses helped Hebrews exit from Egypt. Luke lays the groundwork for his claim that, in the baptism of Jesus by John, the holy spirit of God animated Jesus and his messianic movement. Luke takes a story contained in the book of Genesis, about the conception of Isaac, to show how the spirit of God was operating in the cases of John and Jesus just as it had been with Isaac. Isaac's mother, Sarai, was too old to have the son Abram needed to be the spiritual father of the Hebrew people, but the spirit of God would not be stopped by this, and Isaac was born. John's mother, Elizabeth, was both barren and too old to have a child, but the spirit of God again would not be stopped, and John was born. Mary, the mother of Jesus, was a young woman who had not had sex with any man, but the spirit of God lived on in her child in such a way that he was not contaminated by Adam's sin infecting all future generations through sex. Matthew, in contrast, never mentions anything unusual about John's birth.

Luke in turn does not ever mention anything about Magi coming to pay honor to the baby Jesus. Instead, Luke has lowly shepherds, not Persian astrologers or Jerusalem scribes or temple priests, come and honor the baby Jesus. He used the image to an angel of God to indicate that this baby was special. He wrote that thirty years later Jesus would be filled with the spirit of God. Matthew never tells any such story. For Luke, the story about the life of God's spirit is the story. Luke, to tie the spirit of God in King David to the spirit of God that will envelop the mature Jesus, drew upon a common story circulating in Christian circles. Luke explains why Mary and Joseph left Nazareth and came to Bethlehem, the city of King David, where Jesus was born. Luke wrote that Caesar had ordered a world-wide census and that Joseph had to go back to his home city of Bethlehem. Rome, however, which left behind meticulous records of every census conducted, shows no record of the census about which Luke wrote. Writing ninety years after the birth of Jesus, Luke had no reason or means to check out the story he had borrowed. As further indication of what would happen later at his baptism, Luke writes of Jesus traveling from Galilee to Jerusalem and dumbfounding the scribes in the temple by his knowledge of the history of the spiritual life of the Hebrews. Matthew never tells any such story. He, like Mark, says nothing about Jesus's years as teenager. The differences between Luke and Mathew should not surprise us. They are writing to different audiences, and, although both use Q and Mark, they as writers are trying to do very different things. They both feel completely free to cut and paste the material found in Q and Mark to achieve their literary purposes.

In Biblical wisdom literature, the writers of Ecclesiastes and the poem of Job personified wisdom. She (Sophia) was with God when he created the world. Luke personifies the spirit of God which inspires Abraham, Moses, David, the Prophets, John the Baptist, Jesus, the Jerusalem resurrection community, and finally Paul. The critical reader of Luke/Acts needs to figure out how to make sense of this talk about a holy spirit of God inspiring Biblical figures. Luke is writing to a religious community whose members see themselves as the living body of Jesus Christ (Jesus the Messiah). The feel bound together by a certain kind of messianic and evangelical spirit, by a set of shared practices, attitudes, feelings, commitments, intentions and actions. What kind of spirit is he writing about. I suggest that, in a similar but much more mundane way, we talk about school spirit, the American spirit, the modern spirit of our times. We talk about a spiritual wasteland. We talk about the dangerous spirit animating fascism, monetary materialism, racism, and sexism. Luke, in his narrative of the history of God's spirit, presupposes that the spirit of Abraham's worshipping community of nomads is historically linked to the spirit of the worshipping communities of Moses, David, the prophets, John the Baptist, Jesus, Jerusalem apostles, and Paul. The practices, attitudes, commitments, and actions giving later communities their identities are tied to the spirit animating the worshipping lives of earlier communities. Rather than talking about how John, Jesus, James, Peter, and Paul were manifesting and developing a personal and communal spiritual inheritance, Luke wrote about a personalized spirit coming upon them, sustaining them, inspiring them.

Luke writes as the great champion of Paul and the communities founded by Paul's preaching, communities filled with a spirit tied to the past and looking forward to a future. Luke endorses Paul's claim that in his conversion experience on the road to Damascus he heard the messianic call of Jesus Christ and was filled with God's holy spirit. For Luke, as for Paul, Paul's conversion experience became the paradigm of all experiences in which the holy spirit of God and his messiah comes upon individuals and communities. For Luke, writing 55 years after the birth of the first Christian community, it is in the ritual celebration of the Lord's supper that Christians experience what Jesus and Paul experienced, spiritual union with their God seen as the creator of a good world and the loving redeemer of people now yet filled with the spirit of God.

In the book now called Luke, the texts of Q and Mark play major roles. It is in Luke, as in Mathew, that are found Q's teachings about the Christian Way of life. It is the spirit of Theophilus' lovers of God who are loved by God, as expressed by Q in the teachings of Jesus, that envelops the treatment of Jesus in the book of Luke. The writer of Luke follows the narrative first set forth thirty years earlier by Mark. After being baptized by John, Jesus teaches and heals in and around his home in Galilee and then travels to Jerusalem where he is crucified. Luke adds a postlude to the statement of the greatest commandment that Mark has Jesus enunciate (Love God with all one's mind and heart, and one's neighbor as oneself). The postlude gives an example of what such love would like if an actual person, filled with that spirit, encountered someone in need of help. Luke, validating Gentile Christians who were not members of the Hebrew/Jewish tribe, tells the "Good Samaritan" story to make clear who is to love one's neighbor and what such loving is. The temple priest and the Levi priest do nothing to help the man robbed and beaten, but a Samaritan, like those killed by Jews just before their foolish decision to rebel against Rome, showed mercy and went beyond the call of duty to help the man. For Luke, all his readers, all Paul's Gentile converts, can be and are to be such Samaritans. Every human in need is to be treated by Christians as the robbed man was treated.

Let me repeat my primary interpretive thesis. The book Luke/Acts is primarily a narrative of the life of the holy spirit that defines the Christian community to which Luke is writing. To achieve his literary goal, Luke, therefore, adds in his text materials not present in Mark's narrative. He writes that John the Baptist predicted that Jesus would baptize people with the Holy Spirit, the very spirit now present in the Christian community to whom Luke is writing. He writes that when Jesus is baptized this very Holy Spirit descended on him like a dove, like the dove of peace that enabled Noah to create a new worshipping community. He writes that it is Jesus's newly acquired Holy Spirit that enables him in the wilderness to distinguish popular but false conceptions of the messiah from Second Isaiah's conception of the suffering servant messiah. He writes that the apostles, Peter, John, and James, went with Jesus to a mountain, and that there, when Jesus was praying, they came to understand that the spirit of Jesus is one with the spirit of Moses and Elijah. That spirit is the spirit of Yahweh to whom Jesus was praying. Luke, writing after sixty years of Christian communal living, writes that there is a kinship between the spirit of Yahweh and the spirit of Jesus such that Jesus can call Yahweh "Father" and Peter, John, and James can think of Jesus as the Son of God.

Given Luke's conception of the Holy Spirit, there is no possibility that it can die when Jesus dies. Rome, and the Roman way of life filled with the spirit of Rome, cannot destroy the Kingdom of God filled with the spirit of God and it cannot destroy the true messiah of God. The holy spirit In Jesus will be resurrected. Luke writes that Jesus' last words on the cross were his committing of his spirit to his godly Father, trusting that later, in others worshipping God, this spirit will be resurrected in a new body of Jesus Christ, in the Christian community worshipping God in spirit, mind, and action. Writing sixty years after Jesus' death, Luke communicates to his readers his understanding of the resurrection of Jesus Christ. It has nothing to do with the resuscitation of a dead corpse. Unlike Mark and Matthew who wrote about Jesus Christ being resurrected in Galilee, Luke has people experience a resurrected Jesus Christ in and around Jerusalem. Luke's narrative of the life of the holy spirit has its movement go from Galilee to Jerusalem to Samaria and then to Rome.

Luke put his own ending to Mark's narrative of women finding the cave empty where Jesus' body had been placed. He writes that the women find two men in dazzling apparel who remind the women that Jesus, when in Galilee, said that the "Son of Man" would be resurrected in Jerusalem. The women tell this to the disciples in Jerusalem, but they are not believed. In Matthew, the women had an experience with the resurrected Jesus Christ, but in Luke they do not. Words even from men in dazzling apparel are not enough for Jesus' disciples to be filled with the spirit of a resurrected Jesus Christ. Matthew wrote about attempts by temple priests to discredit reports of a resurrected Jesus Christ, but Luke did not. Such talk was irrelevant to his narrative about the Spirit of God.

According to Luke, what did prepare the disciples to be filled with the same spirit of God that filled Jesus were their personal experiences in celebrating the Lord's Supper, their experiences of becoming the body of Jesus Christ filled with his Holy Spirit. By the time Luke wrote, the celebration of the Last Supper, the eucharist, had become the central ritual of worship in the Christian community. Luke writes of two disciples walking to the village of Emmaus and meeting a man whom they did not recognize and talking with each other about their experiences with Jesus, his crucifixion, and what the women had reported after going to the empty cave. After this man interpreted the Biblical writings about Moses, the prophets, and the messiah, and after celebrating together the Last Supper, Luke says that the disciples recognized that the resurrected messiah was there with them and, once they experienced the presence of the Jesus Christ, the man vanished out of sight. The two disciples returned to Jerusalem and told the other disciples what had happened. Luke wrote that it was not until they had understood what Jesus had taught them about Moses, the Prophets, and the Psalms and they had eaten together that they experienced the presence of the resurrected Jesus Christ. Luke writes that even this experience, comparable to Paul's experience on the road to Damascus, left them with doubts. Perhaps they were just experiencing some ghostly spirit and not the Spirit of God, fully present in Jesus when he was alive, and now present in the resurrect Jesus Christ in their midst. Luke has the disciples hear of the need to wait in Jerusalem for the Spirit of God to descend upon them.

That next step in the life of God's Spirit is what Luke writes about at the beginning of the book now called "The Acts of the Apostles." In this text, Luke writes a historical narrative of Christianity from its origin in Jerusalem around thirty CE to the death of Paul in Rome in 67 CE. Luke is writing sixty years after Christianity's birth and twenty-five years after Paul's death. Looking backward, as a Gentile Christian filled with the spirit of God, the writer of Luke/Acts writes a narrative of a string of people being filled with a God-centered spirit and then passing it on. In the first half of his book, Luke writes that Jesus is transformed at his baptism by that spirit that will define Christian life. Then, Jesus transmits enough of that spiritual way of life to his disciples that they stay in Jerusalem, where he had taken them, ritually re-enacting their last supper with him and feeling his presence. Feeling his presence and remembering that Jesus had told them they are now to be his resurrection body, they become convinced that neither Rome not death can kill off the messianic spirit that now is beginning to dominate their minds, and actions. They lived, Luke wrote, with the expectation that the spirit of their new community would be the spirit of a people dedicated to the messianic mission of spreading this spirit throughout the world.

The book of Acts begins by writing of the apostles experiencing the presence of Jesus as Christ, expecting to be consumed by his spirit, and choosing Matthias to replace Judas as the twelfth apostle. Luke, the spokesperson for Gentile Christians, then writes of the spirit of God so filling the lives of the apostles that it was like tongues of fire burning away their old way of life and leaving them with a burning passion to be Jesus Christ's living body preaching the good news to people throughout the world. As Paul had pointed out, one did not have to be a Jew or a Greek or a Roman or an Egyptian to understand this communication. Drawing upon the Tower of Babel image of people trying on their own to build a tower to reach God but ending up in tribal lives unable to understand each other, Luke reverses the image and says that people from many different lands with different languages could hear and understand what the apostles were preaching as if they were speaking in their own language. United by this common spirit, Luke wrote that these first Christians shared their material possessions so that no one failed to have their needs met. A community of people loving others and feeling loved by God was born and it grew and grew and grew. In Luke's eyes, the Spirit of God was on the march and mobilizing the hearts of Christians.

Luke writes a narrative demonstrating the power that is possessed by a community with this kind of spirit. It is far more powerful that the spirit of Red Sox fans, the American Legion, the NACP, or Beatles' fans. The old enemies of Jesus (the temple priests, Pharisees, and Sadducees) recognized that his spirit lives on in his disciples and therefore also threatens them. The Jewish leadership also recognized that these Christians will not back down or run away. Stephen, a Hellenist convert to Christianity, inspired by the new Christian spirit, proclaims without reservation that the crucified Jesus and the resurrected Jesus Christ is the true Messiah. He courageously dies rather than renounce his faith.

The spirit of God marched on. Phillip preaches to the Samaritans and the Christian spirit powerfully spreads among old enemies of Jerusalem Jews. Saul hears Stephen preaching and watches him courageously die. Saul becomes Paul experiencing the presence of the resurrected Jesus Christ and, being filled with this new Christian spirit, preaches the good news throughout the Greek world. The spirit of God marched on. Community after community are changed by the power of the spirit that is communicated to them by Paul. Luke finally writes that like Stephen, the Christian spirit, making Peter and Paul the men they are, gives them the power to withstand their imprisonments and deaths.

Emphasizing the sameness of the spirit of God that defined the lives of Moses, the Prophets, Jesus, the Jerusalem Christian community and Paul, Luke de-emphasizes the conflict between Paul and the Jerusalem leaders, James and Peter. He tries to side with Paul and with James and Peter. He does not diminish Paul's claim that his authority to found Christian Churches comes from his conversion experience and not from the Jerusalem Apostles of Jesus. He also writes, however, that Jerusalem always blessed Paul's work. Luke writes that Paul was filled with the Christian spirit when a Christian in Damascus, Ananias, cured him of his conversion blindness and placed his conversion experience in a Christian historical context. He also writes that, persuaded by Barnabas, the Jerusalem Christians endorsed Paul's preaching to the Gentiles. This endorsement, wrote Luke, was further validated when Peter also was successful at instilling a Christian spirit in Gentile communities to which he had preached the good news. Luke further testifies to the power of the Christian spirit by writing about Paul besting philosophers in Athens who, recognizing the inadequacies of worshipping the twelve gods in the Greek pantheon, had postulated that there was another unknown god. Luke, while endorsing the Mosaic claim that no graven image can be made of God, that no verbal description can be given of God, also claimed that those possessed by the spirit of Jesus Christ and living as the body of Jesus Christ can be certain that they are worshipping the God of creation, the God of justice, mercy, and forgiveness, the God living in their hearts and animating their lives with a spirit that has the power to create a Kingdom of God on earth. Living by a spirit that results from surrendering themselves to the God they worship in the name of Jesus Christ gives them a kind of wisdom that cannot be gained by philosophers worshipping their own intellectual and rational power.

For the writer of the book Luke/Acts, the story he is telling is not really a story about men (John the Baptist, Jesus, Peter, James, Stephen, Paul) but rather a story about the spirit of God that lives in the lives of these men. He is writing to tell his Gentile lovers of God who are loved by God that they are who they are because they possess true Christian spirit. People filled with this spirit can do marvelous, powerful, loving things in the world. Luke is writing that this has been happening for the past sixty years and that now they are engaged in the marvelous adventure of spreading the Christian spirit throughout the world.

Professor Kiely.

Thank you, Ms. Thom. With Matthew and now with Luke we have two Christian writers borrowing the texts of Q and Mark to achieve two different literary purposes. Written in different locales and addressing different needs and interests of different readers, they organized their borrowed materials in different ways and added different preludes and postludes. Despite these differences, there is no doubt that they are written by Christians for Christians. They are not, however, proceeding the way some modern historians or biographers would proceed, checking out the "objective" accuracy of claims about what Jesus, Peter, or Paul did or said. Matthew and Luke just take the texts and oral traditions of which they are aware and creatively write a text aimed at achieving their specific point and purpose. I think that they would be very disappointed if we did anything different in reading them, if we turned their texts, or modern translations of them, into idols that we worshipped. Roman and Greek stone and gold idols are not to be replaced by paper idols. Living with the spirit of Jesus Christ in the Kingdom of God as the messianic body of Jesus Christ does not consist of worshipping a book. Mathew and Luke would claim that it consists of joyously living grateful for the goodness of the natural world, despite its floods, droughts, cancers, deaths, and randomness. It consists in living justly and lovingly with all one's neighbors. It consists in preserving and passing on the good news. It consists in trusting in the power of the spirit of Jesus Christ, in trusting that living and acting with that spirit will have consequences that live far beyond the death of one's body. It consists of living on the belief that it is not unreasonable to seek to enlarge the kingdom in which the spirit of Jesus Christ rules, trusting that, wherever two or three faithful worshippers are gathered together, there God the Father, the Son, and the Holy Spirit are present.

Let me now introduce Mr. Scott Schneck, who will present his analysis of the Gospel of John, the most quoted book in the Christian New Testament. The writer of the book of John is creating a text not bound by the structure of Mark's narrative of the life and death of Jesus. It is so different from Mark, Matthew, and Luke that it seems to many scholars to be presenting a gospel radically different from the good news written about in the three synoptic gospels.

Mr. Schneck.

Thank you, Professor Kiely.

The book of John was written around 100 CE, seventy years after the crucifixion and thirty years after the destruction of Jerusalem. As Professor Kiely said, it is very different from what is written in Paul, Q, Mark, Matthew, and Luke. There is no birth story. There is no talk about Jesus' genealogy. Jesus is not baptized by John. He is not tempted in the wilderness. There are no quotes from Q. He does not engage in arguments with Pharisees and Sadducees about their legalistic interpretations of Moses' law. He does not speak in parables which Mark said his disciples misunderstood and which Matthew said the temple priests and Pharisees misunderstood. For John, all mankind does not understand God and Jesus Christ's relationship to God. What the writers of Mark, Matthew, and Luke say about who Jesus Christ is John has Jesus say about himself. For John, there are no false spirits to be exorcized. John writes in his book that Jesus' ministry lasted three years and not just one, as Mark, Matthew and Luke wrote. Most of what is written in John is not to be found in Mark, Matthew or Luke, and vice versa. Whoever the author of the book of John was, he was writing with very different concerns than Q or the writers of the Synoptic Gospels.

The book of John probably was written in Alexandria, Egypt to two groups of converted Christians, Jews very familiar with the writings of the Jewish Neo-Platonic philosopher, Philo, and Gentiles living in Egypt and immersed in Greek philosophy. The first thirteen verses in the book of John give a clear indication of the point and purpose of its writer. He is giving a philosophical characterization of God and of God's messianic mission of saving people in the world by becoming flesh and thereby enabling people to recognize who they really are and how they can be reunited spiritually with God. The writer of Ecclesiastes personified wisdom, Luke personified the spirit of Christians, and John personifies Logos, the Word.

In Greek philosophy, the word 'Logos' is used to talk about the ultimate principle in terms of which one can give an account of everything that exists and everything that happens.

Aristotle (384 – 322 BCE), the tutor of Alexander the Great, had claimed that all people wonder why things are as they are when it seems that they could have been different. He created a metaphysical explanatory theory to answer that question. Using a biological model of things, he claimed that the world we observe is a dynamic changing world in which all change is growth from what something is potentially to what something is actually. Acorns become oak trees dropping acorns. Babies mature into adults who act in reasonable or unreasonable ways, form virtuous character traits or vices, and give birth to babies. The dynamics of the whole biological world is governed by an ultimate, unchanging law which Aristotle called "The Unmoved Mover", the Logos. 1500 years after Aristotle, after his metaphysical writings were discovered by Europeans during the crusades, his ideas were given a Christian interpretation by Aquinas in Paris. During the early Christian years, however, for many historical reasons, these writings were not influential. It was the writings of Aristotle's teacher, Plato, that dominated thinking in Alexandria, and heavily influenced what John wrote.

Plato (427-347 BCE) saw all observational objects and events as understandable only if they were viewed as appearances of unchanging ideal forms, structures, or laws that themselves were organized in the only possible way that they could be organized, in a good and ideal way, in a way mandated by the form of the Good. The form of the Good is the Logos, the ultimate answer to the questions, "Why does everything appear as it does? Why are all things as they are? Why do all things happen as they do?" Being the ultimate answer to all questions, one cannot ask why the form of the Good is as it is. One even cannot say anything else about this form except that it is good. To gain any understanding or knowledge of anything, one simply must come to see, after working out penultimate explanations of appearances and the organization of the forms, that the Form of the Good is and must be the ultimate Logos. Through such an intellectual effort it is possible to see everything from the point of view of the Form of the Good. Then, one can live with an understanding of the goodness of everything despite appearances.

Philo (25 BCE – 50 CE) was a Jewish philosopher who lived in Alexandria, was heavily influenced by Plato, and heavily influenced the writer of the book of John. For Philo, Plato's form of the Good must be so ultimate that it is impossible for there to be anything other than it, any countable second or third being. The ultimate, the Logos, is One without the possibility of a second. Philo replaces the Greek pantheon of Gods by the One, the Greek Logos, in terms of which the manifold of things in the observable world gain their status. For Philo, this Greek Logos is the Jewish Yahweh. For Philo, what is written in the Hebrew Bible is a metaphorical expression of his Neo-Platonic philosophy.

In Greek metaphysical theorizing there is a principle that must be obeyed. One must save the appearances. If the ultimate, the Logos, is different from the observable things and events of which it is their explanation, then the metaphysician must explain why there are any appearances at all to be explained and how the Logos, which is one without differentiation and is different from all appearances, is the reality responsible for the existence of the appearances. As appearances, as observable things and events, they are something. If, however, the Logos, the ultimate One, is without any kind of internal or external second, then why and how does it appear to people as many finite objects and events. Philo appeals to the goodness of the Form of the Good and the love of Yahweh, to supply the answer which "saves the appearances." Pure Goodness and Love overflows the oneness of the Logos, and the world of observables emanates from it. Emanation is the way that Philo the philosopher says what Philo the Jew says when talking about God creating the world and declaring it good.

As the myth of Adam and Eve points out, however, emanating and creating observable things and people carries with it a great risk. People might start thinking of themselves as independent creatures. In their forgetting that they are creatures of God, mere emanations from and appearances of the Logos, they will be ignorant of who they are and what successful living requires of them. They ignorantly and foolishly will think they are more than appearances of divine emanations, more than mere shadows on a wall of observable appearances. They will think, feel, and act as if they were independent gods rather than dependent creatures of God. They will always live miserable and dissatisfying ways of living because they will not know that they can be satisfied only by being lovingly reunited with the source of goodness and love that originated them. Most people don't know it, but they yearn to be reunited to the loving Logos which gave them birth. In ignorance they yearn to be God but what they really yearn for is reunion with God as emanations from God, the Logos.

It is while he is swimming in Philo's world of Platonic philosophy that John writes his book, giving his Christian interpretation of Philo's Neo-Platonic Jewishness and Philo's Platonic interpretation of Yahweh's creative and saving activity. John is a Christian giving Christian content to a philosophical theory that he and his readers found themselves using. It is not Neo-Platonism that leads the author of John to worship God in the name of his savior, Jesus Christ. John is not a Gnostic who claims that philosophical, theoretical ignorance is the problem of human existence, a problem to be solved by gaining theoretical, metaphysical wisdom. The Hebrew Wisdom Literature had rejected that move. Even Philo is too much of a Jew to claim that. Paul had sought to give Christian content to the "Unknown God" of Greek religion. Philo gave Jewish content to the Neo-Platonic ideas of the Logos and emanation. John gives Christian content to Philo's Jewish Platonism. John gives to Christians, already worshipping God in the name of Jesus Christ, a philosophical account that can help them understand and thereby strengthen their faith.

The author of the book of John takes every title that is used in the Hebrew Bible to designate the messiah and has Jesus apply them to himself: Bread of Life, Light of the world, Door for the sheep, Good Shepherd, Source of Life, True Vine, Resurrection and Life, Son of Man, Son of David, Son of God. John is not satisfied in writing that others believe that this is who Jesus Christ is. He has Jesus himself say that this is who he is. For John, Jesus Christ is the appearance and reality of the Logos itself, the One who is the ultimate source of all things and all knowledge of things. John's whole narrative about the life and teachings of Jesus prior to his crucifixion is written from the perspective of one who in his resurrection faith is in a living relationship with Jesus Christ, Jesus Messiah, Jesus Christ Incarnate God, Jesus Christ Revelation of God, Jesus Christ Savior, Jesus Christ Redeemer. Starting from the position of his Christian way of living with Jesus Christ, John gives a Neo-

Platonic way of understanding Jesus Christ and of Christians worshipping, in their minds and hearts, God in the name of Jesus Christ.

The author of the book of John agrees with Philo's identification of the Hebrew God of creation with the Logos, who out of love creates people and their world, people who are essentially good and capable of being in a loving relationship with the God of Love, but who like Adam revolt and thus live in the darkness of an ignorance that results in human tragedy. The author then adds his Christian perspective. In Jesus Christ, whom Christians accept as their savior, there is one created person, one emanation of Logos' love, who did not rebel like Adam, who understood who he was and who was his creator, and thus was able to reveal to others who they are and how they can be related to their loving creator, how they are to live in a kingdom in which they knowingly and willingly let their loving God rule. All people are sons of the loving God who created them, but their rebellion prevents them from knowing this. They don't know who people really are or from whence they originate and to whence they yearn in their hearts to go. Only a totally non-rebellious person can reveal the God who created people and their world. Only a person remaining completely faithful to himself as a flesh and blood lover of the God of Love who loves all God's children, faithful even through an unwarranted and cruel crucifixion, could awaken people to a living knowledge of their rebellion and the possibility of the fulfillment of their deepest yearnings, to live as people created out of love and to live with love of their creator and of all the rest of God's children. Such a non-rebellious and faithful person would be and would appear to be a Son of God and only a Son of God. Encountering him would be encountering God. He would be completely flesh and blood and completely God, the incarnate Logos itself.

The book of John begins, "In the beginning was the Logos, and the Logos was with God, and the Logos was God." Through and from this Logos everything was made. Jesus Christ, the Logos, is, first a flesh and blood instance of the life given through creation to all people, and second, the rebellion free life that can enlighten all people now lost in the tragic darkness of ignorance. In the goodness of every living person there is a light, an ability to be enlightened, that is not overcome by the ignorant darkness produced by rebellion. In the life of Jesus Christ, the Logos, the one person who has not rebelled and has faithfully lived and died, there is a light shining in the darkness, a darkness that cannot overcome this light's ability to enlighten and save rebellious and ignorant people. Looking back, a Christian like John now can understand that John the Baptist was enlightened enough to tell the world that an enlightening light was coming that could redeem people from the horrors of rebellious sin and dark ignorance and could redeem them into being what they were created to be, children of God loving the God of love who lovingly created them and loving all the rest of God's children.

The beginning of which John writes is the philosophers ultimate primordial beginning not describable in terms of spatial relations between things or temporal relations between changing things. As John writes, the only way to know the Logos is through a Christian's living faith in the non-rebellious, totally faithful Jesus Christ seen as the Son of God, the incarnate perfect revelation of the Logos which is the loving father to whom everything owes its origin, of the loving Logos willing to do anything to enable created children to escape from the horror of ignorance and to live in the glorious kingdom of God, loving God and each other as all people were created to do.

Perhaps the one Biblical passage that is quoted by Christians more than any other is John 3: 16. "For God so loved the world that he gave his only Son, that whoever believes in him should not perish but have eternal life." The meaning of the passage seems so simple when it is taken out of its literary and historical context. Tragically, however, tearing it out of its context has resulted in some very unfortunate interpretations. Some people have interpreted the words "believe in" as meaning "believe that." Believing in something involves much more that saying one believes that something is true, more even than sincerely believing that it is true. Many people say that they believe this but do not show in their lives a Christian way of loving God and all his children. When one believes in democracy, constitutional rights, and the rule of law, one does not just mouth platitudes and wave a flag. One trusts this way of life and one puts the demands of democracy and the rule of law above personal interests or party or tribal interests.

To understand what John means, in writing about God giving his son to enable people to avoid perishing and to have eternal life, it is crucial to look at what he writes in John 3: 17-21. Here John presents his Christian judgement that Jesus Christ, who reveals God and God's will, is not in the world to judge people but to save people. Jesus Christ is not a sacrificial lamb that must be crucified to satisfy some vengeful God seeking to punish people for rebellion. Jesus Christ only reveals a loving Logos and God. Jesus Christ does not reveal God as legalistically craving some balancing of scales, with the crucified Christ paying the penalty that rebellious people ought to pay. The Logos does not consist of such a legalistic principle of retributive justice. The loving God that Jesus Christ reveals does not have to compromise who God is by engaging in the petty human practice of getting even. John writes that rebellious people get punished by their very rebellion and their craving to be God, their craving to be the ultimate lord over the lives of themselves and others. Because people do not believe in a loving God or in the loving Jesus Christ who reveals this loving God, they condemn themselves. God is not in the judging business but the saving business.

The eternal life that John claims Jesus Christ makes possible for rebellious people who believe in Jesus Christ as the revelation of the Logos, God the Father, Son, and Holy Spirit, is not a matter of continuous life as an embodied person in time. For John, all people have at the core of who they are a yearning to worshipfully live with God who lovingly created them with such a yearning. Believing in Jesus Christ, John writes, yields people living with a Christian spirit in the Kingdom of God, people who worship God the Father as revealed by God the Son, a God of Love, an ultimate spirit of love, a Logos which is One without a second, One radically other than all the good observable beings created by God, emanating from the Logos. To have satisfied this inborn yearning to be lovingly united with God is to have eternal life. No matter what happens in time (the tragic horrors of rebellious life, the crucifixion of Jesus Christ) nothing can separate one from the love of God and from finding joyous satisfaction in loving God. That will remain timelessly present.

For the author of John, writing seventy years after the birth of Christian communities, there is no need to wait for the Kingdom of God. It is already present in Christian communities in which people, believing in Jesus Christ, are worshipping the God he reveals in an enlightened spirit of truth about the significance of everything, living in ceremonious practices and loving actions as the body of Jesus Christ bringing saving light to all people living in tragic darkness.

Back to you, Professor Kiely.

Thank you, Scott. Before we break for lunch, let me just say something about some texts written by people who called themselves Christian that were not included in the canonized version of the Bible. There were four such texts. *The Secret Book of James* claims that it is not Peter but James, the brother of Jesus, who is to be the leader of the new community of Christians. *The Gospel of Thomas* claims that Judas Thomas, known for experiences of mystical ecstasy, was to be the head of the Christian Church. *The Secret Book of John* fuses together the Neo-Platonist story about emanations from the One and the Biblical creation myths. The reason I point this out is to accent what you have already heard. Different people in different historical and cultural contexts wrote about Jesus Christ and the Christian Kingdom of God in very different ways.

Reverend Kennedy, any instructions before we go for lunch.

Not really, Professor Kiely.

O.K. Everybody. Eat up. Share your ideas with each other while eating. Let's come back in an hour.

Chapter Nine

Jacksonville's Final Response

Welcome back. Take your seats. We have a Herculean task ahead of us. Staying awake after eating that impressive lunch. In order not to make that even more difficult, I will keep to a minimum what I am going to say to you. I want to know what you want to say to each other. I walked around during lunch break and I heard all of you involved in animated conversations with others at your tables. Now you can share with all of us what these series of lectures have meant to you. Meaning is a funny thing. You can't pin it down to a single thing. What these presentations meant to you could be quite different from what they meant to the person next to you. What each of us already is, in terms of our background beliefs and linguistic skills and practices, frames what we hear and how we understand it. Similarly, what speakers here in the auditorium and the writers of the New Testament took for granted colors what they intended to say or write. Besides, the speakers or writers may not have succeeded in saying or writing what they wanted to communicate. Finally, there may be potential meaning in what was said or written that is different from what a speaker or author meant or what listeners or readers so far have gotten out of listening to or reading what was said. People with backgrounds very different from ours may now or in the future find different meaning in what was said. We all heard the same lectures but the meaning of what each of us heard might be quite different. That is why it is so valuable to each of us to hear from each other what these lectures meant to have meant to us.

We also want to hear your evaluations of what you heard. Which of the statements made do you think are true? Are there some "Truths" you heard that you want to believe in and live by? Like meaning, truth is a funny thing. Unless something is true to someone, it doesn't seem as though it can be true to anyone. Of course, I may believe that some statement is true and be mistaken. We often find reasons for changing our minds about what we think is true. I might think something is true and you think it is false, but I might change my mind and come to agree with you. That is why dialogue among us is so valuable. We all need to be ready to be surprised by discovering that we want to change our minds or that, even more surprising, someone else we were talking with changed her or his mind and came to agree with us. When we claim that our opinion is true we mean more than just that it is our opinion.

Having said that, truth still a funny thing. The word 'true' seems to be a double negative. Normally we just express our beliefs and we do not say that they are true. Only when someone or something throws doubt on one of our beliefs, and we still want to hold the belief, do we reply by saying "My belief is true." Of course, saying that the belief is true is more than just asserting it again with a louder voice. We can say of one of our own pasts beliefs that we found out that it is false. When we claim truth for one of our beliefs we are both re-asserting the belief and we are implying that if ever in the future we find reason to say it is false, then we will say that I was wrong about my earlier belief. I should have said "It is false." The point I am trying to make is that whenever something is true or false, it is true to someone or it is false to someone, and that it is more than that.

It doesn't help to say that opinions are true if they tell us how things really are. The word 'real' also is a double negative. A diamond is real if it is not a fake or glass. His teeth are real is they are not false teeth. All talk about truth and reality is talk about people believing something about something. When it comes to truth with a capital 'T', it is talking about believing in something, about faithfully holding certain attitudes, having certain habits, engaging in certain practices, and doing certain sorts of things.

Having said that, assuming you are still awake, let's open the floor to whomever has something to say in response to the lectures you have heard.

Lydia, you have your hand up. You begin.

Yes. Thank you, Reverend Kennedy. I guess I should have expected it when I enrolled in this lecture series. I never guessed, however, that there would be so many words. Words! Words! Words! Despite being almost drowned in words, I did learn something I didn't know before. There were many different people writing about Jesus and they said many different things. Before, everybody I know only talked about what the Bible said. I found it interesting that these writers said different things. It doesn't really matter to me very much, however. It's what Jesus taught and what how he treated people that always has interested me. All the different things these writers were saying to different people in different places doesn't seem to change that. Jesus taught us that everyone is important and counts for something. That means a lot to me. I have never been a big-shot. To most people I am a nobody. I don't think that anybody was a nobody to Jesus. If Jesus were here now, I don't think that he would think I am a nobody. That's not what he taught. That is not how he treated other people. I realize we can't prove that Jesus said this or did that. To me it doesn't matter. He must have said and done lots of things like what the Bible says he did or all these people who wrote about him would not have wasted their time writing what they did. Besides, I don't think it makes any difference. The Jesus whom I love and try to be like is the one I find in the words of these writers of the Bible.

There is one other thing I want to say. Sure, there were a lot of folks in my home church who looked down on me but there also were a lot of folks who treated me as one of the family. They seemed to be filled with that sense of Christian spirit that was talked about in the Bible. I felt a strong connection with them. We sang together. We prayed together. I liked what was said just now about our communion service. We ate the bread and drank the grape juice together and it was like being a part of the same body. I couldn't give much money to people in need, but some of the richer people in the church gave a lot. We did work together, however, in running the soup kitchen for the homeless. I couldn't help very often. Sometimes on Tuesdays, however, I cooked and they served and washed dishes. I felt a spiritual kinship with them. We all believed what Jesus said about kindness and we often talked about what Jesus would do if he were there with us.

When I leave here I probably will go back doing pretty much the same things I was doing. I guess I will be talking more now. Whether that is good or bad is something we all will have to wait and see.

Thank you, Lydia. I hope you got to feel at home here too. Your life is the evidence that proves the Truth of much of what has been said here.

Who's next?

Mark. I think you had your hand up.

Yes. Let me first say how much I agree with Lydia. The Christian teachings about humility and kindness are very inspiring. As are the things these Christian writers are saying about what Jesus did. At lunch I was telling Ms. Binyan how familiar the teachings in Q sounded to me. I hadn't thought about him for a long time but, as the student was presenting Q, my mind went back to what I had been told about Master Hillel and his teachings.

Hillel was born several decades before Jesus and he was teaching during all the years when Jesus was alive. He was originally from Babylonia and like Saul came to Jerusalem to study under the Pharisee scholars. His teachings have had a great impact on Jewish thought for centuries because it was through his study of the Torah that he formulated his teachings, and, when Jerusalem and the temple were destroyed in 70 C.E., Jews in the diaspora formed the Talmudic tradition of focusing on the study of the Torah in the synagogues. Hillel is taken by Jews as the founder of this tradition. His teachings and what is contained in Q are remarkably similar.

Hillel taught a negative version of the Christian "Golden Rule." He wrote, "What is hateful to you, do not do to others." Ms. Binyan pointed out to me that this is exactly what Confucius had written. Scholars have called it the "Silver Rule." It doesn't tell us to do to others what we want them to do to us. Rather, it tells us to avoid doing to others what we don't want them to do to us. It tells us what not to. Don't harm others. Don't humiliate others. Don't steal their dignity or freedom. Of course, there is a positive aspect to this commandment. We don't want others to ignore us or those we love when in need of help. Therefore, we not only should avoid doing evil, but we also should do good. Sometimes doing nothing and letting harm occur is almost the same as causing harm.

There were many other things that Hillel taught that are very similar to things Q wrote. Humble yourself and do not think you are better than others. Do not judge others without putting yourself in their place. See yourself as part of a larger community in which all are concerned about the well-being of all others.

I see myself as a cultural Jew. I believe in all these teachings of Hillel and Q.

I also can identify with Lydia's desire to participate in her church's rituals. As I said, I and my family do that with many traditional Jewish rituals. We are not members of any organized Jewish temple or synagogue, but we don't feel that this is necessary to see ourselves as part of a larger community. I worry about people getting too attached to a religious institution. Often, doing that has led to an exaggerated tribalism that prevents us from seeing ourselves as part of the whole human community. Along with Hillel I agree with Second Isaiah's criticism of extreme tribalism. When the writers of the Christian texts wrote about removing all legalistic barriers to membership in the Christian community, I heard them echoing the words of Second Isaiah, Jonah, and Ruth.

I am not suggesting that Christians should stop believing in what these Christian writers wrote or that they should stop participating in the practices that for hundreds of years defined what it is to be a Christian. People reared in Christian teachings and practices don't need to try to shed their historical, cultural skin any more than I need to do so. I don't think there is any need to say that Christians should be Jews or Jews should be Christians. I think we should say that we are just different, neither better nor worse than each other.

Mark, let me jump in here, if that is O.K., Reverent Kennedy.

Of course, Hannah. What do you have to say.

I just want to agree with Mark, and then take his comments one step further. As I listened to what these Christian writers were saying about Jesus's teachings, I heard so many echoes of what my teachers taught me about Hindu and Buddhist teachings. It is an old Hindu teaching that disaster occurs if one treats oneself as the most important thing in the world. If one focuses one's life on gaining pleasure and avoiding pain, then not only will one show disrespect for others by using them, sometimes in terrible ways, as means for serving one's own pleasurable interests, but one will show disrespect for oneself by denying to oneself the joys of being friends with others or loving others (one's parents, siblings, children, or neighbors). Friendship and love often demand giving up pleasures of one's own, in order to care for someone else. Similarly, if one focuses on gaining personal power over other people or even over nature, one never can gain a satisfying way of life and one will cause horrendous harm to others. Not only do economic, political, and military tyrants make the lives of others hell on earth, but these tyrants never can gain enough wealth, political power, or armaments not to have to worry about someone else trying to pull them down and replace them as king of the hill. Hindu philosophers also point out that it is not enough to transfer one's passion from one's own pleasure or power to a passion to obey and enforce the laws and conventions of one's community. Social customs and legal rules may have been established by people with economic and military power to serve their passion for power. Conventional law-abiding citizens too often show no respect for other people or for nature, both of whom they see as merely raw materials or human resources to be used to satisfy their individual or tribal passions. For the Hindu, self-respect requires living by universal respect. When Christians talk about worshipping one God, and not any graven image, and lovingly respecting all people and natural phenomena as creations of his one good God, I hear Hindus talking about living as one inescapably linked to everything else. This is how I interpret their talk about one's real self (Atman) being inseparable from everything (Braham)

Similarly, as I listened to the students talking about Christian writers saying people should not crave to be better than others and or to judge others as beneath them, it reminded me of the Buddhist claim that the chief cause of suffering is people craving to be better than others: smarter, stronger, wealthier, prettier, more popular. Buddhists claim that when people crave such comparative superiority, they will do anything to get it: lie, cheat, dominate, humiliate, bully, threaten, and even kill. Their craving to dominate the past and the future leaves them suffering the kind of despair and anguish that make people suicidal. No matter how much they try, they can't rid themselves of anger and resentment over what people have done to them or of the feelings of guilt and shame because of what they have done to others. As the Buddhist sees it, it is this same craving to be the master of everything that leads them into cursing life when they think that nature is warring against them. When Christians say, "Cherish God's good created world no matter what happens" and when they say, "Have faith in God's justice and love no matter what happens", I hear Buddhists say, "Let things be in their suchness apart from any human evaluations of them."

Mark just said that we should see Judaism and Christianity as different but not superior or inferior to each other. I used to think that I had to find some sort of spirituality that was better than Christianity. Now I think I want to say that when we consider Judaism, Christianity, Hinduism, and Buddhism at their best, then we should say they are different but not better or worse. One of the Buddhist monks who had been my teacher was from Thailand. He once asked me why I was trying so hard to be a Buddhist like him. Did I really think that I had to shed by whole Western cultural and social skin to be spiritually enlightened? Why didn't I learn how to live as a Western Buddhist? Perhaps even a Western Christian Buddhist or a Western Buddhist Christian. I think I can answer those questions now. As important as the differences are, their importance does not compare to the significance of what is common. Different, but not better or worse. Right now, I think that this is what is most important.

There is one other thing that struct me when listening to these lectures about Christianity, especially the presentation of the ideas of Philo and John. They claimed that the goodness of the Logos lies within each of us but that our rebellion hides from us our own inner nature. They claim that in our rebellious ignorance we think we want to be king of every hill but what we really want is to release ourselves from out self-made prisons, so we can be reunited with the Logos, God. As I understand it, that is exactly what mystics are trying to achieve. I have read that mysticism always has been a part of Christianity, but it was never allowed to be on center stage. The Christian mystic wants to move beyond the dark ignorance that comes when one worships something finite, something conceptual, something one mistakenly thinks one is and wants. Moving into the light of spiritual enlightenment means leaving behind attachments to one's ego seeking superiority, to words and descriptions and observations and feelings serving the forces of darkness. It means uniting experientially with God or the Logos and living as one loved by the ultimate and as one loving every creature containing the mark of the ultimate within it. My teachers have told me that in every major religion there is a mystical aspect. That doesn't mean that all mystical experiences are the same, but they do share important family resemblances. The experiences cannot escape the cultural and social context in which the mystic lives, or the different disciplinary practices followed to gain enlightenment and harmonious bonding with the best there is, but those differences don't matter. To me what does matter is that all mystics end up not worshipping anything finite.

As my Buddhist teacher told me, the popular metaphor of talking about many paths leading to the same top of the mountain may not be the best metaphor to use. Jews, Christians, Muslims, Hindus, and Buddhists are climbing different mountains, and the impossibility of saying anything positive about the top of any of the mountains probably means that things will look different to the climbers when they look back from the peak to the world from which they came and to which they will return as changed people. The world they look back at will be the one that their concepts permit them to experience. Still, none of them will worship what they see, even though each of them will live with different icons pointing to the top of the mountain and calling them not to worship anything finite. All of them will be able to shout in Joy, "I've been to the mountain top and everything I see is fundamentally wonderful and good, like something a loving God would create or something that would emanate from a loving Logos or something that in its suchness is simply good." Each climber will love the point of the mountain, even though it is an indescribable point. Each climber will seek to be like what each climber loves, the indescribable point from which one sees everything with a loving and grateful spirit. My point is Mark's point. Different? Yes! Better or Worse? No!

Woh! Mark and Hannah, you have given us so much to think about. I am so happy that these lectures have stimulated you to share your profound responses with us.

Who would like to be the next person to share your ideas with us. Scott, I guess it is you.

Thank you, Reverend Kennedy.

When Mark and Hannah were talking about their reactions, I kept thinking about what Second Isaiah said about taking the light to the nations. I think that maybe that light also can illuminate the powerful ideas and spirits of the people being enlightened and this in turn can enlighten the ones taking the light. Christians like Paul always want to do missionary work by preaching the Good News to those in other places. I think Christians also need to learn how to listen. When I was in Japan I heard about this one Christian University that had established a center for Buddhist-Christian dialogue. I thought that that was a good idea back then. It seems needed even more now. I know that in some places in America there are groups engaged in Jewish-Christian dialogue, but I don't think there are many involved in Christian-Islamic dialogue. It seems to me that each of the world's great religions have light to offer each other that would deepen and strengthen the spirit of each. Seeking to convert seems so unnecessary and pretentious. We need no see differences as better or worse They also need to be seen as less than perfect, as something that can be improved.

Different Christian Churches, it seems to me, need to learn this same lesson about differences. There are so many different branches to Christianity and so many denominations within Protestantism. I remember the many different churches represented by chaplains when I was in the military. These chaplains were required to respect each other and the different religious affiliations of the service personnel who came to the chapel to worship. I don't know whether all of them did respect these differences, but they were under orders to do so. As I see it, churches in the U.S. today are not doing a very good job in respecting denominational differences.

Ministers and members in some churches won't even consider people in other churches as Christians. Mormons, Christian scientists, Quakers, and Jehovah Witnesses aren't Christian. Churches with gay pastors aren't Christian. Churches welcoming same sex marriages aren't Christian. Churches celebrating infant baptism aren't Christian. Some churches claim to have moved beyond denominational differences by being interdenominational, but they seem simply to have added to the multiplicity of denominations. Besides, most of them seem to reject as Christian anyone who questions their Biblical "literalism" or legalistic interpretations of what they think God demands of all people. If Christians can engage in dialogue with Buddhists and Jews, they should be able to have dialogue with Christians different from them. Dialogue, however, means listening to what others are saying and being open to the possibility that one can gain additional enlightenment.

In my experience, I have seen very little dialogue, not just because people have different interpretations of the Bible or different worshipping practices, but because very unchristian attitudes and practices have found a home in Christian Houses of God. Racism, nationalism, tribalism, selfishness, and fear often play a much more dominant role in the lives of Church people than does the spirit of Christianity. All sorts of talk are used to legitimate these enemies of the Christian spirit and to blind people to their true motivations, but they create a house divided against itself that saps Christianity of its powerful potential for building a Kingdom of God on earth.

Racism was a problem when I was a child. My church only had black members. Racism in Christian churches was almost impossible to hide after many "Christian" schools opened after "separate but equal" nonsense was struck down as unconstitutional by the Supreme Court. As I see it, most of these "Christian" schools were just hiding places for white parents who did want their kids to go to school with black children. The men responsible for killing civil rights workers attended "Christian" churches. In the last year, people openly have defended racism. I hear all these arguments about how we must protect our borders from bad immigrants and about how we must kill Muslim terrorists in Afghanistan or they will kill us here. So many American church goers buy in to this talk. To me, it all seems to be just more racism, greed for Middle Eastern oil, and exclusion of potential Democratic Party voters. In these cases, the people being treated as inferior are not Black Americans but brown skinned Mexicans and Muslims. Back when I was in the air force, this chaplain's assistant I used to talk things over with mentioned this Christian philosopher who attacked what he called "Christendom." These were congregations of people who called themselves "Christian" but who did not act in a Christlike way. I think that there is a lot of Christendom around today.

I said my piece earlier about Christians supporting American war efforts in Vietnam and Iraq, of supporting the gigantic "industrial-Military industry" as President Eisenhower called it. I just don't understand how anyone can read what Q writes that Jesus taught, and claim to be a Christian who wants to be like Jesus, and still with a straight face support our use of military force around the world. The spirit of Christendom seems far more like the spirit of Rome than the spirit of the Christian kingdom of God that Jesus and the early Christian writers died to establish. I am a Christian and a veteran and I don't want to judge or show disrespect for anyone, much less the men and women who died and were crippled when serving in the military. I am criticizing policies and practices, not veterans. Jesus criticized practices and this is what he would do if he were here today. I want to criticize Christendom in the strongest voice possible, but I still want to worship as a Christian. I believe in the power of the Christian gospel and the Christian spirit. I believe that the best way, probably the only way, to lessen the power of Christendom and to support the Christian Kingdom of God is to keep speaking and acting as a Christian. Christian Churches contain a lot of un-Christian dirty clothes, but this is dirt in my church and that is where I must try to wash things clean.

I could keep on talking but I think I have said enough. Who wants to hold forth next? Dorothy?

Yes, thanks Scott.

I also am an insider every critical of much that I find my fellow church members believing, feeling and doing. I still am not sure how I want to interpret God talk but I know what kind of God does not exist. As I said earlier, I don't believe that any of the classical philosophical arguments for the existence of God are sound. I also don't believe that one can simply back off and admit that the proofs are no good but still claim that one believes without proof that such a god exists. The whole idea of a perfect, eternal being outside space and time, knowable only as the ultimate reason why everything exists, is incoherent and it certainly does not make religious sense. If it is eternal, it cannot change, but creating things is an action in time. If it is outside space and time, then it cannot be the personal God whom Christians think hears their prayers. To me, all talk about a first cause or an ultimate personal being or dead humans living on in heaven is just superstitious talk.

As a Christian I don't need such a God in the sky, or above the sky, or in a fourth or fifth or sixth dimension. I like what Luke had to say about living with the spirit of a Christian way of life. I like what several of the gospel writers said about worshipping liturgically and being part of the living body of Christ. It is how we worship in word and deed that makes us Christians, not what claims or dogmas we believe are true. I am reminded of a short story that the Spanish writer, Unamuno, wrote about a village priest, seen as a true believer by a mother and daughter. The mother's son came back to the village a convinced atheist. Because the man's mother and sister very badly wanted him to worship with them, the priest told the son, who was an atheist, that he also didn't believe in God, but he performed his priestly duties because they meant so much to people like his mother and sister. The priest urged the atheist son to do the same. He did, and his mother and sister were delighted. His sister told him how happy she was that the priest had persuaded him that God exists. The brother told his sister that he had not dropped his atheistic beliefs and that the priest also was an atheist and that they pretended to believe only because so many people needed them to participate in their religious rituals. The sister said to herself, "Oh, what a smart priest he is. He pretended not to believe to get her brother to worship again." To me, that story said that it is what one does, and the love in which it is done, that matters; not what beliefs one says are true. I am not sure which one of you said it, but I think it is true. What matters is what one believes in and not what one believes that. Christian faith is faithfulness to the Christian spirit and not belief in creeds or dogmas.

Scott mention a philosopher who called for Christian faith but condemned Christendom. I think that was Kierkegaard, the nineteenth century founder of existentialism. He wrote as a poet imagining what it would be like to live various sorts of life. A lot of them, he wrote, are at war with themselves, but living faithfully as a Christian works. No one can prove to an outsider that it works. The proof is in the pudding, in the living of the life. Trying to live only by scientific beliefs, about how things in the world happen to be, does not work because such beliefs cannot tell one what attitudes one should have towards that world. Just being a conformist, going along with whatever one's parents, teachers, and heroes have led you to believe, does not work because there are so many conflicts among beliefs that just are taken-for-granted. One must put one's own individual stamp on one's way of life. One must live faithfully in the pursuit of some goal that one prizes above all others. When one does that, then it will determine what one considers reasonable to do and believe. That is why beliefs as reasons can't tell one what one is to make ultimate in one's life. A leap of faith in pursuit a personal goal and way of living is required.

Leaping in faith is necessary to attain a workable way of life, but Kierkegaard did not think it is sufficient. One can end up worshipping false gods and thus end up with unworkable ways of life. Some people try to live by the principle "I am only going to do what I am interested in doing, what interests me at any particular time." Imaginatively putting himself into someone living that kind of life, Kierkegaard concludes that one loses too much when living that way to make life worthwhile. One denes oneself having any friends or anyone to love because maintaining such relationships sometime requires one to do things one doesn't find interesting. Babies often need diapers changed at 2 AM, but few people find it interesting to wake up and do what is required for the child one loves. Some people try to live by the principle of being morally responsible to others as these responsibilities are spelled out in one's own social and cultural norms and roles. There are two factors that guarantee that this also is an unworkable way of life. Kierkegaard reminds us that people, limited in knowledge or control of social norms, create social norms and thus these norms often contain conflicts within them. He also points out that we can't free ourselves in such a way of life from feelings of guilt for having failed to do what we believe we ought to do. Sometimes a person must choose the least evil option available. A husband lies to his wife to keep her out of harm's way. Even when the lie is justified, however, the husband knows he has done something that is the wrong sort of thing to do. He needs forgiveness. Social norms cannot provide such forgiveness.

There is one other unworkable way of life that Kierkegaard poetically imagines. People try all on their own to draw up a blueprint for a good way of living. They then test it out to see if it works. If one plan fails to work, they will try another, never giving up hope that eventually they will find one that works. After many, many trials and errors, they resign themselves to the fact that they are always failing but they can't give up trying. The problem here, Kierkegaard suggests, is that such people are still trying to stay in control, to be the maser of their fate, to be the God they worship. They can't accept anyone else's plan, even God's. The solution to the problem, Kierkegaard suggests, is to quit trying to be God and to let God be God. By all the standards of reasonableness operating in other ways of life, it is absurd to make the leap of faith necessary to trust the goodness of the gift of life and one's world. It is doubly absurd, he writes, to live faithfully in the Christian Kingdom of God as the body of Jesus Christ. Kierkegaard writes that there is no way to prove that believing in God is reasonable. Likewise, there is no way to prove that encountering Jesus Christ in one's heart and in the Christian community filled with his spirit will enable one to feel that one is forgiven, enable one to let the past be remembered but remembered as forgiven.

Kierkegaard is my hero. I try to live as a faithful Christian without depending upon any beliefs about supernatural beings or actions: No divine being out there, no super bell-hop boy, no healing miracles, no God blessing America in its wars or its unchristian economic, immigration, or gun polices, no resuscitation of dead bodies, no heavenly encounters with my parents or with Jesus or with Kierkegaard, or with you. I am delighted to have had a chance to meet you and listen to these lectures, but, quite probably, I will never meet any of you again, here in this life in Jacksonville, and certainly not in some next life. That's O.K. with me. Now is enough.

Dorothy, I am not so sure about not seeing us again around Jacksonville. Previous students in my Life Long Learning seminars have contacted me from time to time and have told me that they still are carrying on conversations begun here.

We'll see, Reverend Kennedy.

Yes, we will.

Yoshiko, I saw your hand up earlier. Do you want to share your thoughts with us?

Yes. I do. I wish I could say that this class has answered the question I had before this class began. It hasn't. It hasn't done that, but it has helped me look at the question in a new way. I hear what Scott is saying about there being so much Christendom masquerading under the name Christianity. After listening to the presentation of Q, I just don't believe that Jesus would have done what the American military did during World War II. I don't know if I am a pacifist or not. I don't know whether Jesus or the early Christians were pacifists. I think that Scott was right in questioning whether any of America's twentieth century wars were morally justified. It seems to me that if the world leaders and their supporters who claimed to be Christians had been Christians trying to follow the teachings of Jesus, these wars could have been avoided. I am convinced that America's leaders were not thinking as Christians when they engaged in strategic bombing and the use of Atomic bombs.

The strategic bombing of cities and the killing of non-military people was begun by the Japanese in China and the Germans throughout Europe. These bombs made no distinction between privates and generals, on the one hand, and grandfathers and children, on the other. The opponents of the Japanese and the Germans did not turn the other cheek; they began strategic bombing on their own of German and Japanese cities with the same tragic results. President Truman and his generals said that they were justified in dropping the atomic bombs on Japan. They argued that had they not done so millions of Japanese and American soldiers would have died in the American invasion of Kyushu that would have occurred. I just don't buy that argument. There were so many other things they could have done. They could have shown the devastating impact of an atomic bomb by doing a demonstration bombing of an uninhabited Pacific Island. I understand that they had only two bombs and they did not want to waste one. So what? What was the big hurry? America soon would make more bombs. The Japanese navy and air force had been destroyed. The Japanese army was stalled everywhere. Factions within the military already were sending out peace feelers. Japanese diplomats in Europe were reporting back home about the charitable treatment being given to Germans by the Americans and British. Christian love seemed to play no part in the thinking of the responsible American leaders who went to church regularly. Their Christianity did not protect the tens of thousands burnt to death at Hiroshima and Nagasaki or the mutated children, grandchildren, and great-grandchildren of those who have continued to suffer from radiation poisoning.

As I think back, and I as I look around American today, I see so much Christendom and so little of the Christian spirit. I know that there are some people who try to live with a Christian spirit. This course has led me to think of Christianity only as an ideal goal at which people can aim. I know that Christianity says that people always remain sinners needing forgiveness and help to do better. I only wish that more people who said this really felt a need for forgiveness for all the injustices from which they had benefitted. Black slavery, Native American genocide, exploitation of Chinese builders of the transnational railroad, exploitation of industrial workers, destroyers of clean air and water, petty tribal nationalists in a global world. The Christian teachings in Q sound so beautiful, but they seem to be too good to be true. Very few Christian church members follow them or even treat them as ideal goals at which to aim. I am glad to have heard about what Q wrote because the words he has Jesus speak have given me a great ideal against which I can measure human behavior, that of others and that of myself.

I came into this class asking myself many questions. "Why did my grandparents suffer as they did?" "Why wasn't I at ground zero when a sun burst blotted out the sun?" I think that now I have a better way to look at those questions. Many of the things said in these lectures and by you have convinced me that there are no big answers to these kinds of questions. There are just the little answers. A bomber pilot did not want to carry a bomb back to Guam and so he dropped it without worry about what it hit. The home of my grandparents just happened to be at the end of the bomb's path. Why wasn't I at Hiroshima? Because I was living in the States when the atomic bombs hit. Millions of people aren't where bombs explode, terrorists or angry gunmen slaughter people. There is no big reason Why. There is just life.

Of the many things I have heard about in these lectures, the one that has impressed me the most is the way some Biblical figures responded in positive ways to the tragic events that had happened to them. The Hebrews came out of slavery in Egypt and under the leadership of Moses built a community filled with a holy spirit that gave birth to three of the major religions of the world. Jerusalem was destroyed by the Babylonians but the Priestly writers in exile gave birth to a universalistic respect for people in all places and walks of life. Jesus gets crucified and a messianic spirit comes to life in Christian communities. Jerusalem gets destroyed again, this time by the Romans, and writers get inspired to write inspiring words to people in many different, very difficult situations.

I am beginning to believe that what those people did people today can do again, in our post Hiroshima and post holocaust era. So many forget. Some of us remember. I have recorded the memories of many of the victims of the atomic blasts. Others have recorded the stories of people trapped in the holocaust. We need to keep these memories alive. I think I have passed beyond feeling bitterness over what happened, even though I don't ever want to stop feeling indignant. Horror and injustice must always remain vividly in our minds and feelings as horror and injustice. Just as Jews remembered their exile in Egypt and Babylonia, and Christians remembered their crucified Jesus, so we must remember the unimaginable horrors that happened not so long ago. Forgiveness? Yes! But, as several of you have said, remembered as forgiven.

I was so happy to hear Hannah remind me about things that Buddhists say, things similar in many ways to things Christians say. I don't think I will ever go back to singing Christian Sunday school songs. I think I want to move more toward a Buddhist way of life. It doesn't seem that different from what my parents tried to tell be about Shinto. I don't think it matters. The differences don't make any one of them better or worse than the other.

That's all I want to say.

Thank you, Yoshiko.

As I said the first day, the purpose of this course is not to convert anyone in to or out of their stance towards any specific religion or towards religion itself. Our goal has always been one of setting forth information and arguments so that each of you will be a helped a little in critically thinking through your old positions and any new ideas that have arisen in your minds.

Does anyone else have any comments or questions? Since this is the last day for this class, we would like to hear from all of you.

Yes, Reverend Kennedy. I have a few things I would like to say to Scott and Yoshiko. Both of you have pointed out the suffering and injustice caused by people claiming to be Christian. I understand that. As I said earlier, I have felt some very unchristian looks given to me by members of my husband's church because I am not like them. I am aware of the discrimination Chinese and Japanese people suffered in the past. I know that new forms of discrimination against Asians are going on now. Quotas are being set up in some universities because Asians high school students are studying harder than their classmates, getting better grades, and appear to admission committees to be better prepared for college.

Pointing out that people who call themselves Christians are doing these sorts of things, however, is only telling half the story. Take the case of quotas. When we cry "discrimination" we are operating on an old Asian assumption that success in grades and examinations is sufficient for gaining admission into college. Those who utter this cry forget the old Confucian mandate to consider what is best for the community as well as the individual. Perhaps we are not yet thinking about ourselves as members of this whole American community. To achieve harmonious living in a national community it is necessary to think about the way that Mark suggested. Differences in the distribution of benefits and burdens in a community should be made in a way that serves the best interests of the least advantaged in the community. Often many Asians are the least advantaged. Sometimes, however, we have been lucky enough to have been raised in a community that accented the importance of education and motivated parents to work extra hard to educate their kids, and perhaps their children were motivated in the same way to spend extra hours studying. If we, the lucky Asians with outstanding test scores, were to put ourselves in the shoes of applicants who were raised by a single mother working two or three jobs, then we could see that the good of the whole requires focusing in two directions at the same time. Reward those who have worked hard so they can increase the size of the pie and help those who are the least advantaged in our community. Yes! Have grades count a great deal in determining admission to college, but do not have them trump all other considerations. Diversity in a student population most likely will aid in lessening discrimination and in nurturing non-Asian families to increase their appreciation of the value of education. Keep improving the well-being of the least advantaged in our nation.

Sorry. I got side-tracked. This issue of college quotas is not what I really wanted to talk about. I'm concerned about focusing too much on the failures of Christians to live up to their own ideals. True, people calling themselves Christians have done a lot of bad things. Through my studies of Western history, however, I have come to appreciate the Good things that Christianity has done. Scott told us about a lot of the dirty clothes to be found in the history of his fellow Christians. I suggest that we think about the fact that he can stand up here and criticize his community for having so much deadly, dirty clothes. I grew up in China during the years of Mao when exposing clothes, as dirty as anything in the history of Christianity, would have resulted in a bullet in the back of one's head and a bill being sent to the critic's parents for the price of the bullet.

I may not be a Christian, but I am convinced that much of what is good in Western culture and political life is due to Christian influence. The Protestant Reformation called for people to act as individuals thinking for themselves and not just as social robots doing what the Church and Royal authorities said one should do. This Protestant position played a major role in motivating the Seventeenth Century scientific revolution, in which scientists charged that all beliefs about how things are in nature need to be justified to every scientist by appealing to observational evidence. As I see it, it also played a major role in the establishment of the Western democratic principle that political authority to use violence to enforce a rule of law governing individual actions must be derived from the consent of the individuals being governed. The West's whole accent on civil rights also seems to be derived from Jewish and Christian principles. When one talks about the civil rights of individuals, whether embodied in the American Bill of Rights or the British unwritten constitutional traditions or the United Nation's Declaration of Human Rights, one is saying that one has obligations that go beyond the legal obligations and social customs of a national state. Appeals to human rights can be used to criticize state actions as being inhumane. I know that historians point out that there were forces other than Judaism and Christianity that influenced this historical development, but that doesn't cancel out my claim that this Western religious tradition played an important role. That's a plus that must be added to the story about Christianity's minuses.

Let me share a little bit more of my personal experiences in China so that we can understand what it is like to live in a world in which democracy and civil rights did not exist. For most of the Twentieth Century the Chinese people had suffered in ways and numbers that most Westerners cannot comprehend. I am not talking just about the horrendous suffering caused by the Japanese invasion into China. I don't mean to demean that suffering. The Chinese cannot forget the Japanese massacre of thousands of women and children butchered and raped in Nanking. There is another kind of suffering that I don't want us to forget. I am talking about the suffering of the Chinese people caused by Chinese officials. It is a tale about what happens when political and economic power resides in the same hands and democracy and civil rights are non-existent. After the fall of the Manchu dynasty, economic and military power was centralized in the hands of warlords and the Kuomintang. The peasants were just fodder for their bank accounts and armies. After the People's Republic of China was established in 1949, all economic, political, and military power was placed in the hands of the Central Committee of the Chinese Communist Party and its chairman, Mao.

One State caused disaster after another resulted. Immediately after the end of the civil war, thousands and thousands of earlier supporters of the Kuomintang and their families were slaughtered. In 1951, hundreds of thousands of Chinese "volunteers" were compelled to fight and die in the Korean war. In 1956, thousands of intellectuals were fooled by the "Let a Hundred Flowers Bloom" propaganda of the Communist Party that claimed to support intellectuals and journalists to express all their ideas, no matter how critical of the party and the Chinese government. Once identified, these writers were killed or imprisoned. From 1958-1991, during the "Great Leap Forward," millions of Chinese starved to death when Mao called for industrializing China by having the Chinese melt down their farming tools and cooking utensils. From 1965-1969 the Great Proletarian Cultural Revolution swept through China with the whole country lost in social chaos as high school "red guards" backed by Mao and the military attacked anyone who even seemed to have ties to the West or pre-revolutionary China. Schools were closed. Commerce was disrupted. Thousands were killed or imprisoned. Red guard factions fought each other. Eventually, the military stopped the chaos and thereby increased its power over the Communist party and the government.

In the 1970s, the Chinese government under the leadership of Deng Shao Ping recognized that China needed to use its greatest resource, manpower, to gain from capitalist countries through trade what it needed most, capital. Opening China to Western trade also opened it up to Western ideas that challenged the monopoly of economic and political power held by the Communist Party. In 1989, students, intellectuals, and journalists failed to appreciate the immensity of the power of the government, and the commitment by those in power to retain that power. The 1989 uprising in Tiananmen was brutally crushed and thousands again were killed or imprisoned. The behavior of the Chinese government today shows that, while it is trying to improve the economic well-being of its people, it will not tolerate threats to the power of the Communist Party and the Chinese government. Today's Chinese form of "democracy" does not recognize that sovereignty lies with individual Chinese citizens or that the best interests of the Chinese people, even its least advantaged, lies in granting and protecting an individual's human right to criticize the actions of the Party and the Government.

The lectures I have heard here have been very helpful to me. I am not a Christian, but I greatly appreciate its contribution to creating democratic countries that have entrenched individual civil rights in their way of life. I wish that Western nations were more democratic and protective of civil rights. That I and other critics can say this and work for this shows that there is more good than evil in these democracies. I think the same is true of Christianity. There is so much of what Dorothy called "Christendom" in Christian communities, but this is something many Christians are pointing out. One of Christianity's great virtues is that it authorizes and even demands self-criticism. I am not a Christian, but I am tempted to be one. I think that more of the great potential lying in Christianity can be brought forth only by internal critics. That's a temptation I am just going to have to let sit for now.

Reverend Kennedy, back to you.

Thank you, Ms. Binyan. A little later I want to say something about what tempts you. For now, however, I want to let everyone else have a chance to share their thoughts. Christopher, you have the right name to go next.

Thank you. I want to say something about what I think is hampering Christians from doing more of the self-criticism Ms. Binyan is talking about. I think that the lectures we heard today provide conclusive reasons for saying that one cannot understand the Christian New Testament if one does not locate these texts in their historical contexts. Dogmatic preachers trying to talk about the literal meaning of Christian writings are doing a major disserve to Christians. The only way to get to the literal meaning of these texts is to remember that they are English translations of things written by specific people located in a specific situation trying to achieve a specific purpose in writing to a specific group of potential readers. Mark wrote to Christians facing the possibility of the same punishment that Romans were unleashing on Jews because of the violent revolutionary efforts taking place in Jerusalem. Matthew was writing to instruct Christians in Antioch who had been forced to quit worshipping in Jewish synagogues and he did not hesitate to group Q's writings into long discourses because he thought this would give these Christians the "Teaching Manual" they needed. He repeatedly compared Jesus Christ to the Torah. He added narratives about Jesus's birth to show that Christians should not have been chased out of the synagogue because their claim to be worshipping Jesus as messiah was proper; their messiah in fact was doing exactly what Moses did in giving the Torah to the Hebrews. Luke wrote to Paul's converts to accent the Christian message the Christians anywhere and at any time can live by the spirit of Jesus Christ which is the same spirit possessed by all past worshippers of Yahweh. John wrote to Egyptian Christians who were wrestling with the problem of relating their Christian faith to the Greek philosophical ideas taken very seriously by many intellectuals in Alexandria where they were living.

The first Christian readers of these texts were familiar with and living in the cultural circles in which they were written. Most of the readers of one specific Christian text probably didn't even know that other texts had been written by other Christians. As we look back now, we can understand why these texts say different things. Our task is to inquire critically into what they can say to us today. It seems that they are saying many different things to us here right now. One thing is common to all the texts, however. They are written after the crucifixion of Jesus and the birth of Christian communities who proclaimed that they were now worshipping God in the name of Jesus Christ, Jesus Messiah, Jesus Savior, who lives in the lives of Christians even though the power of Rome had ended the life of Jesus. It was their faith in a resurrected Christ that was common to all the early Christian writers. It was by living with the spirit of a resurrected messiah that they were inspired to write what they did.

I worry not only about all the Christendom existing in Christian churches today. I worry about churches in which God as creator is hardly worshipped at all. I worry about churches in which people are not worshipping God in the name of Jesus Christ, in the spirit of Jesus Christ, as the living body of Jesus Christ. I choose to be a Christian and not a Jesus addict. I go to so many churches here in Jacksonville and they sound like my daddy's church back in Arkansas. They totally ignore the great scholarship that has been done locating Christian texts in their contexts and thus making intelligible their meaning. I hardly hear the word "God" mentioned. All I hear is: "Jesus did this or Jesus did that," "Take Jesus as your savior," "Sister Jones is now with Jesus in heaven." By now Christians should know that we will never be able to construct a picture of Jesus' life that could have been captured by TV cameras and broadcast to the world. The historical Jesus of Nazareth might have been the revolutionary that the Romans crucified because that's who they thought he was. The wonderful teachings in Q might have been a Christian borrowing of Hillel's teachings put in the mouth of Jesus to convince the Romans that Jesus was not a revolutionary and that his Kingdom of God was a spiritual kingdom and not a threat to Roman rule. As we have heard here, all the many different narratives of Jesus' life are written by people looking through the lens of their resurrection faith. When evangelical literalists preach that Jesus did this or that, they imaginatively are constructing their own narrative of the life of Jesus. This might be unobjectionable if it were not for the fact that their imagination is restricted by nationalistic, economic, and social biases and supernatural superstitions. The God worshipped in the name of Jesus Christ is not a tribal god of America exceptionalism, nor an obvious supporter of capitalism and the iron law of markets, not a racist or homophobic.

What I am trying to say is that the first step Christians today need to take to increase their ability to critique Christendom is to critically study the Christian New Testament to get beyond dogmatic and biased "literalism." I also believe that the way to get the inspired power to do this is to celebrate with fellow Christians the

Lord's Supper, the Eucharist, and to serve together in soup kitchens or their counterparts on Wall Street or in the corridors of government or in war rooms.

That's what I believe. I think I have said enough. Let me give the floor to Anita. I think you're the only one who hasn't had a chance yet to share your thoughts about today's presentations.

Thank you, Chris. I don't really have anything more to say. I agree with most of what you have said about how to read the New Testament. I appreciate the many different things that its writers had to say. I also appreciate the profound things that the writers of the Hebrew Bible had to say. I just wish there were some way to tie the different pieces together.

Reverend Kennedy, I am hoping that you can help us here. You haven't really told us what you believe. I realize that this is not the role you think you should play in this course. You have done a great job in bringing in all these professors and students to talk to us, but now, as we wrap up this series, I think all of us would like to hear from you. Maybe you can help a little in tying pieces together.

Thank you, Anita. I was planning on making some closing remarks. Please remember, however, that I am just one more interpreter. Don't let what I say do anything more than help you in your own critical reflections. Buddhist writers have often claimed that a Buddhist Bodhisattva said, "If you see the Buddha, kill the Buddha." This fully enlightened Buddhist was urging his fellow Buddhists not to make the Buddha an authoritative figure whom they could use as their authority on truth. The reason I mention this is that I don't want you to believe what I say simply because I say it. I don't think I have anything to worry about this with you in this class. You already have shown your commitment to critical thinking.

I do want to offer some preparatory remarks about truth and certainty. Authorities never are the final voice of truth. This is a hard lesson for young college students to learn today. Many times, when issues of justice or injustice are debated, some skeptical student will end up saying, "Who's to say?" Ending the debate that way, however, presupposes that there must be some expert authority upon whom one can rely when evaluating the truth of a belief. The assumption is that one can be certain about the truth of some claim only if one is certain that there is an expert who can certify that claim as true. That is not the claim the Buddhists are making. They are claiming that one can be certain about the four noble truths and that this cannot be known, in the living way required, by taking the Buddha as an authority to be blindly followed.

Who's to say? The answer is, "Anyone who wants to do the hard work of uncovering evidence and constructing sound arguments." Experts are experts only because they can back up their claims with evidence and sound arguments. When skeptics says, "Who's to say?" they are assuming an expert is needed and they don't believe that the needed expert exists. This is the lazy student's way out. This often is the kind of talk that is introduced by students who think that there is no truth to be discovered. It is crucial to teach students that their kind of relativism is self-contradictory and necessarily false. They are basically saying that sincerely believing something is sufficient for the belief to be true. If this general statement were true, then the statement of the person rejecting relativism would also be true, if sincerely made. The relativist student then is saying that truth is relative (that is what I sincerely believe) and that truth is not relative (that is what the person rejecting my claim of relativism sincerely believes.)

Often relativists use a confused argument about rights to back up their relativism. They claim that people have a right to believe anything they want to believe. That may be a legal right in a democracy guaranteeing civil rights. No one should be coerced into believing something they don't believe. Having a legal right, however, is very different from having an epistemological right, a right to claim that one's belief is true and justified. In addition, one's legal right to believe something does not grant one a legal right to act on that belief if it harms someone in an unjustifiable way. I believe that what I am about to say is true, but I am willing to change my mind if someone can give me a good reason to think it is false. Dorothy, I think that is what you said claims to truth are like. That people are willing to say that some of the things they believe might be false does not mean that they are so uncertain that they won't live and even die trusting their beliefs. One of the most difficult things that many people need to learn about life is that that many of their beliefs must remain open to challenge and that nevertheless they have no choice but to act on the beliefs they now hold. My doctor told me yesterday that I am in excellent health, and I am going to go on doing my work today and tomorrow. Still, I know that I might have a stroke tonight.

Having said all that, let me say what I think is true.

Let me begin by talking about God the way the Hebrew Bible does once it gets beyond locating God in an assembly of gods. Two claims about God are the crucial linchpin for everything else said about God. The first is that one must worship no god other than God. The second is that one is to make no graven image of God. Start with the second claim. God is such that nothing can be an image of God: no statute, no painting, no verbal picture, description, or representation. We can only picture or describe things, people, institutions, and events that are locatable somewhere at some point in time. No such thing can be done with God. Treating God as any such describable being would be to worship a false god. This is the reason why the first and second claims imply each other. To worship only God is not to worship anything finite and describable: not an animal, not a king, not a nation, not a building, not a book or set of books, not a set of social norms and laws, not a political or economic system, not ourselves. To make this point. Hannah used the metaphor of the point at the top of mystical mountains. I like that, but I would put it differently. I suggest that we begin thinking about talk about God as talk that is expressing a double negative. The Biblical injunction to worship God and only God is the injunction not to worship anything finite, not to make anything finite into one's god.

You might ask, "Why then worship at all?" Why not just tell oneself not to make a god out of anything? If everyone could let that intellectual understanding determine their whole way of living, their feelings and attitudes, their commitments and actions, then perhaps that would be enough. As the Hindus point out, however, very few people can gain such spiritual enlightenment through intellectual effort alone. Hebrews and Christians point out that such an intellectual approach can easily slide into worshipping one's intellect and thus oneself. As Ecclesiastes, Job, and Kierkegaard's Knight of Infinite Resignation point out, trying to live only on an intellectual understanding often leaves one living in despair. For many people today in the Western world, the most effective way to avoid worshipping anything finite is to worship God who cannot be likened to anything finite. For the person worshipping God, God simply is God and nothing else and not like anything else.

I do believe nevertheless that people can have a close personal relationship to this God who is the One unlike all others. For a theist, one's deepest, life defining attitudes are so focused on God that nothing in the finite world can become one's God. Who one is and what one feels and does is determined by this attitude focused on the absence of any finite God. In worship and prayer this absence becomes the presence of one's infinite God. As we well know, the presence of absences can have a powerful effect on our lives. One sits at the dinner table and looks at the chair that had been occupied for decades by one's deceased spouse and one is overcome by the presence of this absence. So likewise, for people who begin worshipping the infinite God, after having lived lives in which they deified finite things, the conversion experience or the enlightenment experience is earth shattering. In one sense, nothing has changed. In another sense, everything has changed. The presence of the absence of all finite gods becomes a presence to which one surrenders oneself. For the converted person there is no other God to worship. Using the most superlative words in our vocabulary we give praise to the infinite God we worship, knowing full well that no words will ever be adequate.

Coming to understand that there are no finite gods to worship is not the same thing as worshipping the infinite God. Recognizing the absence of gods in the world can drive one into cursing the world and wishing one never had been born. After having lived for years thinking that there is something finite that one can devote oneself to, something finite that can make one's life meaningful, coming to realize that there are no such finite gods upon which one can depend often drives people into suicidal despair. People worshipping God react with very different attitudes. They live with positive attitudes towards their world and their lives. They celebrate being alive and they live by the conviction that it is better to be than not to be, no matter what suffering occurs in life. Worshippers of the infinite God give expression to this attitude towards the whole finite world by saying that it was created by God and that all created things are good. To our praise of God is added our expressions of gratitude and thanksgiving for the gift of life itself and for the natural world in which we live. No one can intellectually prove that such a positive attitude towards life is the correct attitude to have. A leap of faith is required here. Worshippers of the good God of creation can point out, however, that they are happy with their leap of faith, whereas, it seems to them, that the nay-sayers are far from being satisfied with their lives cursing existence itself. They also can point out that many thinkers who do not worship God have made the same leap of faith: the Greek philosophers, Existentialists such as Kierkegaard and Nietzsche, and Hindus and Buddhists. All these thinkers also say that one will not thoroughly endorse the wonderfulness of life until one is living with the positive attitudes expressed in such endorsements.

Having identified their God as the Good God of Creation, it is only natural that worshippers of the infinite God would also express gratitude to God for being the loving Lord of History. Worshippers of God as the Lord of History express their trust and hope that the life of humans is not getting worse and worse but is always showing that the goodness in the hearts of humans can never be totally snuffed out. This is not the trust and hope that led people before World war I to believe in material, political, cultural, and spiritual progress. The horrors of the twentieth century should have cured all of us of that simple version of progress. Hebrews and Christians provide a much more sophisticated version of progress. They live by faith in the goodness of the people God created and by faith that this goodness cannot be killed no matter what people do to themselves.

The same worshippers who sang praises to the imageless God and gave thanks to the creator of a good world also told the story of Adam's rebellion in the garden of Eden and the disastrous consequences of his hubris of making himself the God determining all truth and justice. The Hebrew worshippers, however, included in their creation story the claim that people were created in the image of the imageless God. This claim carries with it two powerful implications. First, as good created images of the imageless God, no graven image of any individual person should be made. People are not just instances of biological or social characterizations. They are singularly unique and transcend all such classifications. They should be treated as singularly unique. That obligation is the basis for all principles of justice. Worshipping God as a God of justice is just an extension of worshipping God as the good creator of people in God's imageless image. This means that for the worshipper of God the demands of justice transcend the laws of nation states. Justice demands the respect of human rights and in terms of these demands the action of nation states can be judged. Each person is singularly unique, and all people should treat themselves and every other person as singularly unique and good creations of God.

Second, the worshipper of God as the Lord of History treats the flow of history as determined by the dynamic interaction of two factors: the goodness of people as images of their good creator and as rebellious people craving to be God in control of everything. This, it seems to me, is the truth that lies in Zoroastrianism. There is a war going on in the soul of people between who they are and who they crave to be. It is the truth I find in all the religions of the world. Given this dynamic, trusting in God as the Lord of History does not mean being confident that things historically are getting better materially for people. Percentage wise, fewer people may now be in poverty but the number living in refugee camps, shanty towns and slums seems larger than ever. We seem to be living in a constant state of war, with more and more terrible weapons being used and collateral damage being taken for granted. To me, worshipping God as a Lord of History means living confident that the worst that people can do to each other cannot destroy the goodness that lives in every human life. This conviction lets me believe in the possibility that any person can be saved from self-destruction and can gain enlightenment. There is much in life to be pessimistic about, but I always remain a realistic optimist.

Time and again, Hebrews and Christians have resurrected worshipping communities out of the living hells created by people. The great Hebrew epic tells the story of people being delivered from slavery and for life in a community of joy. The prophets condemn human hubris but remain confident that God's people will survive. The Hebrew priests in Babylon began the process of creating a worshipping people who share their faith and life with all people everywhere. Christians develop resurrection communities worshiping God in the name of Jesus Christ. Jews move beyond the destruction of Jerusalem and their temple and establish throughout the world communities worshipping in synagogues and new temples. Time after time, worshipping Jews and Christians are persecuted but their spirit continues to be reignited in new communities. Not even the holocaust has been able to kill off the Jewish love of life. It is true that often worshippers of God are their own worst enemy using God talk to legitimate their worship of false Gods. Even these traitors to the cause cannot destroy the power of the spirit in the hearts of God's worshippers. Amos, Isaiah, Jeremiah, Job, Hillel, Jesus, Augustine, Luther, Kierkegaard, Martin Luther King appear. Thanking God, the creator of all good things, means thanking God whose worshippers always keep alive the spirit of God.

Let me now say a few things about why I believe in Jesus Christ. I am not particularly interested in trying to do the impossible, figure out what the historical Jesus of Nazareth was like or what he said. The Jesus who becomes my Jesus Christ in whose name I worship God is the one we meet in reading Q, Mark, Matthew, Luke and John. Here I agree with Lydia. There may have been many good reasons these writers had for picturing Jesus and his teachings as they do, but that is important only for reminding us that that we cannot go back behind their pictures to find the real Jesus of Nazareth. It is not necessary to do so to be saved by the Jesus Christ given life by the writers of the New Testament. The only Jesus we can know is the one pictured as Jesus Christ by these Christians living years after what we surmise was the time when the historical Jesus lived. These writers present to us what they took to be their messianic savior, Jesus Christ, writing about his actions, teachings, crucifixion and resurrection as seen through their worshipping eyes. They saw a teacher explaining to people what it is like to live in a kingdom in which an imageless, good, just and loving creator God and Lord of history ruled in the hearts of people worshipping this God. They constructed a picture of a man who was so worshipful, wise, kind, just, and self-sacrificing that no stains of Adam's rebellion scarred his life, and thus he could reveal to them the God they worshipped. Mark, Luke, Matthew and John drew a picture not only of Jesus as he lived from the time of his baptism by John the Baptist until his death upon the cross, but they also provided written pictures of Christians experiencing the presence of God's messiah who could not be destroyed by Roman power or physical death. Out of their resurrection faith they wrote their gospels about God being present among them in human form.

Above all else, the writers of the New Testament wrote about Christians who had been spiritually changed as they took the crucified and resurrected Jesus Christ as their savior. Saul had a saving conversion experience on the road to Damascus. These writers confessed that they also had their conversion experiences and so did the people to whom they wrote their texts. From living one way of life they were converted to living another way of life. They were saved from worshipping false gods and from refusing to face their faithlessness in God. They were saved from the destructive results of feeling guilty about their faithlessness. In feeling the presence of the crucified and resurrected Jesus Christ, they experienced the liberating power of being forgiven, of being able to let the past be a remembered but forgiven past that was not an anchor drowning out any chance for a joyous future. They were converted from an unworkable way of life into a new workable way of life.

Part and parcel of that new way of living in the Kingdom of God, they wrote, was preaching with words and deeds the goodness that salvation was possible. The Christians pictured in Paul's letters or in the texts of the gospel writers were never presented as people in control of their conversions. It was not what they did that saved them; it was what they let happen to them. What happened to most Christians was to encounter Christians like Stephen who revealed to the world their Christian spirit. What about the first Christians, those who lived before Stephen was converted.? The New Testament writers tell us that the first Christians were converted by sensing the presence of a resurrected Jesus Christ and by being filled with the spirit of Jesus Christ. They tell us that this is what one should have expected to happen. Given the way in which God as creator has so created people, it follows that, in spite of human rebellions, God can be Lord of history. The details of the first conversions never will be known. It doesn't matter. Christianity was born and by word and example Christians have motivated others to let themselves be converted and saved.

Whatever were the details that motivated these writers to make the needed leap of faith, they were now writing as Christians living in God's kingdom, as Christians in whose hearts their existed a covenantal relation with God, as Christians who proclaimed that they had been saved and now believed in Jesus Christ as the Son of God. They and their readers, then and now, are Christians who experience the presence of Jesus Christ every time they participated in the Eucharist. They are Christians who see themselves as the living body of Jesus Christ. All genuine Christians also understand that, as close a personal relationship as they now have with God and God's Son, as transformative as their salvation from worshipping themselves has been, they always will face the problem of personal hubris and the lack of faithfulness and trust. As some of you have pointed out, surrender to the temptations that transform Christian faith into Christendom behavior have been with Christianity for two thousand years.

I try to be a Christian. It is no easy task in this world and with Christendom being present in so many Christian communities. I believe that I can be a Christian without believing in any supernatural beings or any superstitious practices. I believe that I must believe in God and Jesus Christ. I do not believe that everyone else must believe in God or Jesus Christ. I know that Jews, Muslims, Hindus and Buddhists believe in other ways of life. I see them as different but not better or worse than my Christian way of life. Believing in God is for me the best way to avoid worshipping some false, finite god. Seeking to do the will of my God means doing what a good creator of people who are made in the image of this imageless creator does, cherishing each one of them in their singularity. Worshipping God in the name of Jesus Christ is for me the best way to relate myself to my good and loving creator and to experience a forgiveness that frees me from guilt and shame and for priceless life with my fellow Christians. Worshipping as best I can my God in the spirit of Jesus Christ and as the Living body of Jesus Christ protects me, at least to some extent, from the power of my constant temptation to worship myself or something in my finite world. I believe that in the lives of Christians there is to be found a workable and joyous way of life. I don't think that Christians or anyone else can produce heaven on earth, but I do believe that the Christian way of life can make the lives of everyone a little less hellish.

O.K. That concludes our sessions together. After a prelude to Biblical writings, we focused on the role that Jerusalem played in the writing of the Bible. The Hebrew National Epic, the earliest Biblical text, was written in Jerusalem when it was at the height of its glory. The destruction of Jerusalem by the Babylonians was the centerpiece of Prophetic and Historical writing leading up to its destruction, and the Priestly writings were composed in Babylon by people looking back at the destruction. The point and purpose to New Testament Christian texts turn on them having been written just before and after the destruction of Jerusalem by the Romans. Our sessions began in Jerusalem, but they ended up here in Jacksonville with you and your take on these writings.

I want to thank all of professors and students who presented their research to us. I want to thank all of you for opening yourselves up and sharing your responses with us. I know we all have benefitted greatly from your reflections.

If you haven't done so already, I suggest that you exchange your e-mail addresses with each other. I am sure that some you will want to continue the dialogues you started here.

Made in the USA
Columbia, SC
08 August 2018